Republic of Ireland
Gifted in green

by Adam Ward

hamlyn

Republic of

Ireland
Gifted in green

by Adam Ward

hamlyn

Contents

The history of Association football in Ireland has not been an easy one. It is a game which has its origins in England and, for this reason as much as any other, 'soccer' was long-regarded as inferior to native sports, such as Gaelic football. The Republic of Ireland international team was born in 1926, and made its international debut in a 3-0 defeat against Italy in Turin. But in those early days there were few idols for the country's young players to aspire to and, with the standard of

Introduction

domestic soccer far from impressive, the game struggled for popularity. Further hindrance was given by the often questionable decisions of the international selection committee, who were frequently blamed for the team's lack of success on the field.

It was not until 1988 that the Republic of Ireland made it to the finals of a major tournament. And by then, of course, the much-celebrated Jack Charlton had arrived as Ireland manager. A trip to the World Cup finals in Italy followed two years later and, for his efforts, Big Jack was hastily ascribed the status of demigod by the people of Ireland. It would, however, be wrong to runaway with the

notion that Charlton was the sole-saviour of Irish soccer. The boys in green had been making steady, if unspectacular, progress since the 1960s and much of the foundation for the success that followed was laid by those managers and players who came before.

In 1965, the year I have chosen as the starting point for *Republic of Ireland – Gifted in Green*, the Irish team made it to a play-off match against Spain to determine qualification for the World Cup finals in England. The match was somewhat controversially played in Paris and Ireland lost 1-0. In the years that proceeded the match against Spain, however, discontent with the selection committee grew and in 1971 the players led a successful revolt which precipitated a switch to a manager/sole-selector system. The modernisation process continued under the management of Mick Meagan and Liam Tuohy, while during the tenures of both John Giles and Eoin Hand, Ireland came agonisingly close to reaching the grail of qualification for the finals of a of a major competition.

The Republic of Ireland's rise to the status of international contenders is a tale of both drama and intrigue. From the days when Noel Cantwell and Charlie Hurley policed Dalymount Park to the current team of the two Keanos – Roy and Robbie – more than 175 players have pulled on the famous green jersey. Some like Packie Bonner and Paul McGrath have enjoyed long and successful international careers, while many more have had

To the memory of my grandfather Patrick Enright. A sporting Irishman who died too young.

ACKNOWLEDGEMENTS

The author would like to thank the following: Lindsay Johnson and Joe Ward; Julian Brown and Tarda Davison-Aitkins at Hamlyn; Ivan Ponting for advice, encouragement and his thoughts about the many Irish internationals who have worn the red jersey of Manchester United; Kevin Connolly for his views on Arsenal's Irish contingent; Stephen F. Kelly for sharing his thoughts about Liverpool's Irish; Graham McColl for his thorough editing work and for taking the time to discuss Celtic's Irishmen; Peter Arnold for advice throughout; Tom Tyrrell for pointing me in the right direction; Tim Tuomey who showed me great hospitality and who gave me access to a treasure trove of reference materials; Dave Kelly for access to his extensive programme collection; Eamon Dunphy, Mick Meagan and Liam Tuohy who took the time to share memories, good and bad, of their time with the boys in green; John O'Sullivan at the Irish Library in Dublin; Marj and Pete Johnson and Harry and Moira Ward for their encouragement and support; and finally to Damien Richardson for giving his time so generously and for sharing his extensive knowledge of Irish football.

less illustrious stints in Ireland colours. But whether one cap wonders or international stalwarts, all are here.

I have provided written profiles of every player who has played for the Republic of Ireland since January 1965 and, in all but a few cases, there are pictures too. Numerical information has been kept to a minimum since there are already several excellent statistical works on the Irish national team. I have restricted myself to basic facts and figures, focusing only on the player's international career. The clubs listed are those at which the subject was registered when he was capped and the number of caps referred to is the sum of appearances made from the start and as a substitute.

Republic of Ireland – Gifted in Green focuses on the players who have represented Ireland during the last 35 years, and career details are correct to the end of May 1999. Much space is, of course, devoted to the men who achieved so much during the reign of Jack Charlton. But as the new millennium approaches, the hope is that the gallery of stars featured within these pages will soon by joined by many of the bright young things who have been so expertly groomed in Brian Kerr's junior teams. And after Ireland's success in the UEFA under-18 Championships in 1998, the signs are that the triumphs of Charlton may yet be eclipsed.

Executive Editor: Julian Brown
Editor: Tarda Davison-Aitkins
Executive Art Editor: Keith Martin
Design: Darren Kirk
Picture Research: Daffydd Bynon
Production Controller: Lisa Moore

First published in Great Britain in 1999
by Hamlyn, an imprint of
Octopus Publishing Group Limited
2-4 Heron Quays, London E14 2JP

A catalogue record for this book is available from the British Library

Printed by Graphos SA

World Cup play-off

REPUBLIC OF IRELAND 0 SPAIN 1

Spain's Ufarte scores the goal that denies Ireland a place at the 1966 World Cup finals in England. Goalkeeper Pat Dunne can do nothing to avert the course of the Spanish midfielder's goalbound shot, which had arrived with the Irish defence flat-footed by an incisive attack from their opponents. But after the game it was the FAI rather than the vanquished team's defence that was most vilified. Ireland's football administrators were alleged to have co-operated too freely with Spanish demands that the game be played in Paris rather than London. There was even talk that financial incentives had been offered to get the match switched to the French capital, where the continental European's would enjoy greater support.

The fall out from the Spain defeat would bring the FAI under close scrutiny from both media and supporters, and would also help bring forth a modernising era in Irish soccer. The proceeding years have seen more than 170 different players wear the famous green jersey, and the careers of all are profiled within the following pages.

Colombes Stadium, Paris, 10 November 1965

Noel and team-mate John Bond brought a new dimension to full-back play.

1953–1967

36 CAPS   **14** GOALS

BORN ● Cork, 28.12.32
DEBUT ● v Luxembourg 28.10.53
CLUBS ● West Ham United, Manchester United

When Noel Cantwell took the field for the Republic of Ireland, a red cape would have been more befitting of his superhuman efforts than the standard green shirt. In a 14-year international career, the Cork man proved to be a versatile and skilful performer. Most significantly, he captained the team throughout a difficult era for the boys in green.

Noel Cantwell

Noel's rise to international-stalwart status began with his home-town club Cork Athletic. In 1952 he moved to England to work in the Midlands where he received a visit from West Ham United manager Ted Fenton. The Hammers boss had heard great things about the 19-year-old Irishman from former player Johnny McGowan and had rushed up from London determined to get his man. It took some time for the charismatic Cockney to convince his target to join the Upton Park club – apparently Noel did not believe he was good enough to play in the Football League. Fenton proved the better judge: by the end of the 1952–53 season Noel had made four appearances in the number three shirt for West Ham.

The 1953–54 season began well for Cantwell but not for the Republic of Ireland. A disastrous World Cup qualifier defeat against France in October led the selection committee to make changes for the next match, against Luxembourg. Three new caps were handed out, with Liam Munroe and George Cummins making their debuts alongside Noel, who had been impressing at left-back for the Hammers. For his first match for Ireland, Noel played at centre-half and performed commendably in a 4-0 victory. However, this was his only contribution to the 1954 World Cup qualifying campaign and it was more than two years before he won his second cap. This early international sabbatical came to an end for the Cork man when he took the place of Joe Lawlor at left-back for a friendly against Spain at Dalymount Park in 1955. Thereafter the powerful defender became a fixture in the team.

At West Ham, Noel and team-mate John Bond brought a new dimension to full-back play. By the mid-1950s the pair had become an integral part of the Hammers attack with their overlapping runs and powerful shooting. But it

was off the pitch, as members of the Hammers' famous 'Academy', that the Cantwell/Bond partnership had gelled. Throughout the 1950s, senior West Ham players would assemble in a cafe near Upton Park after training to discuss tactics and all-things football. Much to the dismay of Ted Fenton, and the approval of the Hammers faithful, new patterns of play became commonplace in the East End of London as Cantwell and co. put their thoughts into practice. The reward for this extra-curricular activity came in 1958 when the Hammers won promotion to the First Division.

West Ham took their place in English football's top-flight knowing that their number three was both an international penalty taker and captain. Noel had been chosen to replace Peter Farrell as skipper and led the Ireland team out for the first time against England in a World Cup game at Dalymount Park in May 1957. Alas, there was to be no dream start. After Alf Ringstead had given Ireland the lead, Noel stretched to clear and in so doing presented a simple chance to John Atyeo. A 1–1 draw ended the Republic's hopes of reaching the 1958 World Cup finals.

For the rest of the 1950s, Noel and Charlie Hurley were the cornerstones of the Ireland defence, providing stern resistance against all-comers. However, when the selectors decided that they needed to add a physical presence to a lacklustre forward line it was Noel who was asked to step forward. From an unfamiliar position in the centre of attack, he responded in typical fashion – cracking home a memorable 40-yarder against Austria in April 1962. By this time the Hammers had decided to cash in on their prize asset, selling Noel on to Matt Busby's Manchester United in November 1960. Three years later, Ireland's charismatic captain skippered the Reds to an FA Cup final triumph over Leicester City. The same year saw Noel pick up his bronze statuette for reaching 25 caps, a landmark he celebrated with a goalscoring performance against Scotland.

There followed a one-game spell as Republic of Ireland manager, but the most memorable of many Cantwell highlights came in 1963 during a European Nations Cup game against Austria in Dublin. With the scores level at 2–2, Ireland won a penalty in the 89th minute. The Dalymount crowd erupted, confident that a spot kick was as good as a goal. And Noel did not disappoint them, keeping his cool to slot home his second goal of the game to earn Ireland a quarter-final tie against Spain.

The sight of this 5'3" forward dancing his way down the wing was too much to bear for many burly stoppers.

1956–1966

32 **3**

CAPS GOALS

BORN ● Dublin, 17.2.36
DEBUT ● v Holland (H) 10.5.56
CLUBS ● Arsenal, Blackburn Rovers, Millwall, Celtic, Bristol Rovers, Shelbourne

Joe Haverty was an adroit and sprightly winger with an impish quality that marked him down for special attention from fans and opposing defenders alike. When Joe ran at his marker it seemed he was as much gratified by the torment he administered to his victim than with the attacking advantage he gained.

Joe Haverty

But the sight of this 5'3" forward dancing his way down the wing was too much to bear for many burly stoppers and in an age when men were men and wingers rightly nervous, Joe's trickery earned him several spells on the sidelines. The most famous occasion came during a match against England at Dalymount in 1964. The visitors' full-back, George Cohen, decided he had seen enough of Haverty's heels after a humiliating opening five minutes and administered a tackle that brought a premature end to Joe's match and left the forward nursing a broken ankle.

'Little Joe's' teasing wing play may have irritated his opponents but for those watching it was a joy to behold and he was always a popular figure with fans wherever he played. That is not to say that he was without his doubters. Joe was rightly criticised on several occasions for over-elaboration and for failing to make the most of a powerful shot. His goalscoring potency was never more clearly shown than on his debut for the Republic of Ireland when, after an hour, he struck with a perfect volley against the Dutch in Rotterdam.

It was a breathtaking start for the former youth International at a time when the Irish team was in transition. Joe had made his debut alongside fellow new boys Liam Whelan and Tommy Dunne in a match that saw Con Martin make his final appearance for his country. The other two debutants struggled to establish themselves in the Republic team but Joe wasted little time in adjusting to the demands of international football. With the powerful figure of captain Noel Cantwell behind him at left-back, he proceeded to make the number 11 shirt his own. A second goal followed in Joe's third international, a friendly match against West Germany, but two in three

was a misleading strike-rate and the next 29 internationals, spread over ten years, brought just one more score.

Despite this unimpressive goalscoring record, Joe played in all of the Republic's qualifying matches for the 1958, 1962 and 1966 World Cups. He had come to prominence as a St Patrick's Athletic player and moved to Arsenal as an 18-year-old. In 1956 Joe had won a place in the Gunners' first XI and, with his confidence augmented by a growing international reputation, he began to produce his best form. The World Cup group matches against England brought disappointing results but much acclaim for Joe Haverty who ensured that Billy Wright and co. did not have things entirely their own way.

Injuries took their toll on Joe's career during the late 1950s and early 1960s, and though he was able to win back his place in the Ireland team from Liam Tuohy, his domestic career took a step backwards when he left Arsenal for Blackburn Rovers in 1961. Ewood Park was not the happiest of homes for Joe and after a year he returned to London to join Third Division Millwall where he enjoyed two productive seasons. Thereafter, Joe's League career waned and after a short spell at Bristol Rovers and a single match for Celtic he headed home to play for Shelbourne.

When Joe's international career came to an end in December 1966 he had won few medals but many friends. However, more significantly, he remains the benchmark by which many Irish football fans judge the merits of the green shirt bearing the number 11. Expectations are high for Kennedy, O'Neill and Duff.

Alan was an agile goalkeeper... both quick and decisve when leaving the safety of his line.

1956–1973

47 CAPS **0** GOALS

BORN ● Dublin, 5.7.36
DEBUT ● v West Germany (H) 25.11.56
CLUBS ● Drumcondra, Preston North End

It is a football truism that goalkeepers are judged on their mistakes rather than on the saves they make. The most acrobatic, finger-tip stop will bring fleeting applause, but a dropped cross or misjudged leap can bring a chorus of derision that stains the custodian's reputation for many seasons. Fortunately Alan Kelly made few howlers in a 17-year international career with the Republic of Ireland. He did not receive the adulation of outfield team-mates such as John Giles and Noel Cantwell but he was no less valued by selectors and supporters alike.

Alan Kelly

Alan was an agile goalkeeper and was both quick and decisive when leaving the safety of his line. At his best, he could be a commanding figure in the penalty area and – unlike several of his challengers for the number one jersey – he was unflappable when claiming crosses.

In 1957 Alan won an FAI Cup winners' medal with Drumcondra. A year later he left Dublin to join First Division Preston North End. Alan arrived at Deepdale as a full international, having won his first cap against West Germany in a friendly at Dalymount in 1956. A clean sheet on his debut saw Alan retain his place for the next fixture – a World Cup match at Wembley against England in May 1957. Alas, it was to be a rare off day for the young keeper and Alan conceded five goals. Manchester United's Tommy Taylor grabbed a hat-trick that included one goal headed from the hands of Ireland's youthful custodian. A five-year absence from international football followed as the selectors chose to overlook Alan in favour of rivals Tommy Goodwin, Jimmy O'Neill and Noel Dwyer.

The move to Preston should have revitalised Alan's career. Instead it hindered his claims for a recall to the Irish team. Throughout his first three seasons at Deepdale Alan remained on the sidelines while English goalkeeper Fred Else stood between the posts. But when North End were relegated from the English First Division in 1961, Jimmy Milne was appointed manager and Alan was given the chance to establish himself in the Preston line-up. He wasted little time proving his goalkeeping credentials and by the time the Lilywhites lined up for

the 1964 Cup final against West Ham United, Alan was Preston's undisputed number one. However, Wembley remained an unhappy venue for Alan and eight years after his first appearance beneath the twin towers he experienced another painful defeat, as West Ham struck a late winner to claim the Cup.

Alan's upturn in form at Preston had brought about his return to the Republic team and he won his third cap, against Austria, in April 1962. It was the start of a run of nine games in the team for Alan, during which time he helped Ireland to the European Nations Cup quarter-finals. However, when it came to the qualifiers for the 1966 World Cup, Alan was omitted from the squad. Both Pat Dunne and Noel Dwyer would enjoy spells in the team during the mid-1960s and it was only towards the end of the decade that Alan could consider himself a fixture in the Republic line-up. Thereafter, Alan, by now in his thirties, began to enjoy his best form at a time when the Irish team was enduring a period of poor results.

At club level, Preston had begun to struggle, and the Lancashire side took a brief dip into the third tier of English football before regaining their position in the Second Division at the first attempt in 1971. Alan's international career, however, continued to prosper. In 1972 he became the first keeper to captain Ireland when he led the team out to face the USSR at Lansdowne Road. But just when it seemed his career was on the brink of a well-deserved Indian summer, Alan's playing days were brought to an abrupt end after a challenge during a match for Preston against Bristol City at Deepdale left him with a serious injury to his right shoulder.

No longer able to take his place in goal, Alan embarked upon a career in coaching. Preston and the Republic of Ireland were quick to appreciate the value of their experienced former player. Alan worked as a coach both at Deepdale and with former team-mate John Giles, who had become Republic manager in 1973. Alan also enjoyed a brief reign as international manager himself when he took control of the Ireland team for one match in 1980. A spell as manager of Preston followed and there have been several other coaching jobs on both sides of the Atlantic. But it is as a top class goalkeeper that Alan Kelly will be remembered. In the 1990s Alan's achievements with the Republic of Ireland were recognised when he was inaugurated into the FAI Hall of Fame, a fitting tribute to a master of the goalkeeping art.

A bulwark at the back for Ireland, providing a rare blend of guile and steel.

1957–1969

 40 CAPS **2** GOALS

BORN ● Cork, 4.10.36
DEBUT ● v England (H) 19.5.57
CLUBS ● Millwall, Sunderland, Bolton Wanderers

At the peak of his form Charlie Hurley would have improved any international football team. Fortunately for the Republic of Ireland, Charlie was born in Cork and although he spent the latter part of his childhood in Essex, he is every inch an Irishman. Throughout the 1960s Charlie was a bulwark at the back for Ireland, providing a rare blend of guile and steel in a team that was all too often struggling. For followers of the boys in green, Charlie became a reassuring presence at centre-half. He was a commanding figure, combining power in the air with an assured touch and the confidence to carry the ball out of defence. Had he played today, Charlie would have been considered a natural 'libero'.

Charlie Hurley

Charlie spent his teenage years in England and began his football career in South-East London with Millwall after he was spotted playing for Rainham Youth Centre by Lions scout Bill Voicey. He arrived at The Den to join a team in the midst of a ten-year run in the Third Division (South) and after a short spell in Millwall's junior ranks, he got his chance in the first team at the age of 17. Charlie wasted little time in winning over the notoriously critical Millwall crowd and he became a firm favourite at The Den. Over the next four seasons he made 105 League appearances for the Lions and his increasingly mature displays earned him many glowing reviews.

Reports of Charlie's progress had made their way to the FAI selection committee, and in 1955 he was called into the Republic squad for the match against Spain on 27 November. Injury, however, intervened and denied Charlie a teenage debut. The most galling aspect of this episode was that the offending knee complaint had been sustained in a match for the Army Catering Corps whom Charlie was representing while on National Service. Eighteen months later Hurley was able to forget this embarrassing international false start and commence his Republic of Ireland career in a World Cup match against England at Dalymount Park. England had beaten the Republic 5–1 at Wembley 11 days earlier and Charlie – who was still playing his club football in the lower

reaches of the Football League – was faced with the awkward prospect of marking Manchester United centre-forward Tommy Taylor. The new boy met the challenge head on and barely gave Taylor a touch in a match which ended in a 1–1 draw.

A £20,000 transfer to Sunderland followed shortly after Charlie's international bow but in his first season on Wearside (1957-58) the Rokerites were relegated to the Second Division. Sunderland would not regain their top-flight status until 1964, by which time Charlie had established himself as the team's skipper and defensive kingpin. His international career had also blossomed and when the Republic began their European Nations Cup matches in 1962 Charlie was appointed team captain. Thereafter Charlie shared the honour of leading the team with fellow defender Noel Cantwell.

Although Charlie's most significant contributions were defensive, he could also pose a threat in attacking situations. During his 12-year career with Ireland he scored two goals, both of which came during a rare appearance at centre-forward against Norway in May 1964. By the late 1960s Charlie was one of a small and diminishing number of world class players available to the Republic of Ireland. But while he was undoubtedly an extremely talented footballer, what set him apart from his team-mates was his ability to instil confidence in those around him.

In 1969 Charlie's career entered its final chapter. Jackie Carey's decision to relinquish his vaguely defined coaching role had left the Republic in need of somebody to prepare the team for a round of World Cup qualifying matches in 1970. Charlie was the man chosen and he was named player/coach/captain for a short spell prior to the appointment of Mick Meagan. However, it was a period of great turmoil for Irish football. Charlie's tenure brought little success and coincided with the end of his international playing days. His club career lasted two more seasons, and 42 League appearances, all of which were spent as player-manager of Bolton Wanderers. He then entered management full-time with Reading. It would be some time before Ireland would see the likes of Charlie Hurley again. In 1989 he was rightly admitted to the FAI Hall of Fame.

MICK McGRATH

1958–1967

22 **0**
CAPS GOALS

BORN	Dublin, 7.4.36
DEBUT	v Austria (A) 14.5.58
CLUBS	Blackburn Rovers, Bradford Park Avenue

Mick McGrath is all-too frequently placed in the pigeonhole marked 'honest, reliable, hardworking' – a category that overlooks his significant constructive and creative skills. From the wing-half position, Mick was a constant threat, combining his well-documented work ethic with excellent close control and a rare ability to deliver the 'killer ball'.

Jackie Carey was one man in no doubt as to McGrath's talents, and in August 1954 the former Republic of Ireland international – then boss of Blackburn Rovers – signed the 18-year-old midfielder from Dublin club Home Farm. McGrath had already established quite a reputation as a schoolboy footballer, following impressive displays in an international under-18s tournament in Germany the previous season. The new boy made occasional first-team appearances during his first three seasons at Ewood Park but it was in 1957–58 – a promotion-winning season for Rovers – that he made the step up to regular first-team status.

A Second Division runners-up medal was quickly followed by a call-up to the Republic of Ireland senior squad for a two-match tour of Poland and Austria. Jackie Carey had been appointed coach for these fixtures and, had been given the authority, by the selection committee, to make changes to the line-up for the second game against Austria. He took the opportunity to blood 22-year-old McGrath. The game proved a disappointment, with Ireland losing 3–1, but the debutant made an impressive entrance and looked the most inventive man in green.

Mick would remain in the Republic of Ireland squad for the next nine years – appearing in 22 of the 34 games played during that period. And although he was never a goalscorer during his international career, Mick's cultured play created many chances for others and helped him maintain his place despite competition from the likes of Ronnie Nolan, Ray Brady and Johnny Fullam. A typical example of McGrath's ability to deliver a defence-splitting pass came against Poland at Dalymount Park in 1964 when he slipped a perfectly weighted ball into the path of Blackburn team-mate Andy McEvoy who drove home off a post.

McEvoy was one of a number of Blackburn strikers to benefit from McGrath's first-class midfield service but in 1966, and after 268 League appearances, the Dublin-born wing-half left Ewood Park to join Fourth Division Bradford Park Avenue on a free-transfer. Mick added four caps to his tally following the move to Yorkshire but after just over a season with Park Avenue he retired from full-time professional football.

The Republic of Ireland team of the late 1950s and early 1960s was no place for a promising forward wishing to enhance his reputation.

Scoring chances were few, while the tactics were defensive at best, negative all too often. In such an environment, Andy McEvoy's achievements must be looked upon as nothing short of remarkable. Andy was a footballer of tremendous talent who could score goals of the highest order and was parsimonious in the penalty area. He possessed fine ball skills and had a rare ability to see and deliver a killer pass. However, for all his undoubted quality, Andy McEvoy was rarely able to show his best form in a green shirt.

A first-class career, which began with Bray Wanderers, blossomed at Blackburn Rovers towards the end of the 1950s. Andy had arrived at Ewood Park at the behest of Rovers manager, and former Irish international, Jackie Carey. But despite the presence of Carey and another compatriot, Mick McGrath, it took him several years to settle in Lancashire. In 1959, Andy's perseverance paid off when he got a two-goal haul on his first-team debut against Luton Town. It was the start of a prolific goalscoring career with Rovers and after a brief flirtation with the wing-half position Andy provided Rovers with a regular supply of goals from inside-forward.

In 1961 Andy's progress was rewarded with an international debut against Scotland at Hampden, which was quickly followed by a second cap in the return fixture in Dublin four days later. Both matches ended in heavy defeats and for Andy, who had once again been played out of position at wing-half, it was to be a false start to his international career. When he eventually returned to the Republic of Ireland line-up in 1963 (for a third cap against Scotland) Andy was at the start of a rich vein of form which, over the next two seasons, would see him net 66 League goals for Blackburn and enjoy an unbroken run of 11 international appearances.

A European Championship match against Spain in Seville in 1964 saw Andy, at last, take up his rightful position at inside forward. And although Spain eventually emerged as 5–1 victors, the Blackburn striker did not disappoint, grabbing an early goal with an astute volley from a Giles pass. For the remainder of his international career Andy found himself playing the key role in a perpetually changing forward line which boasted few players of genuine quality.

Declining fortunes at Blackburn Rovers saw Andy disappear from the international scene in 1967 and, although he enjoyed good form with Limerick towards the end of his playing days, he was unable to add to his 17 caps and seven international goals. Andy McEvoy died in Bray in 1994 aged 56.

ANDY McEVOY

1961–1967

17 CAPS **6** GOALS

BORN Dublin, 15.7.38
DEBUT v Scotland (A) 3.5.61
CLUBS Blackburn Rovers

It was the activity in his brain rather than in his boots which set Giles apart.

1959–1979

59	**5**
CAPS	GOALS

BORN • Dublin, 6.11.40
DEBUT • v Sweden (H) 1.11.59
CLUBS • Manchester United, Leeds United, West Bromwich Albion, Shamrock Rovers

Rarely has a single player been as important to a football team as John Giles was to the Republic of Ireland in the 1960s and 1970s. Giles was the complete midfielder; combining polished ball skills and immaculate distribution with a strong competitive streak and an uncanny ability to find space on the field. But it was the activity in his brain rather than in his boots which set Giles apart. Even in the midst of midfield battle, he needed barely a nanosecond to assess his options before deciding whether to pass, run or shoot, and invariably he chose the right one.

John Giles

Giles had arrived on the international scene as an 18-year-old Manchester United outside-right, having made just two first-team appearances for the Reds. But despite this lack of senior experience his debut against Sweden at Dalymount Park proved memorable. The visitors – who had been World Cup finalists a year before – had raced into a two goal lead when, after 13 minutes, a Swedish clearance fell to Giles 30 yards from goal. He took aim and sent an unerring volley into the net. It was the start of a long and significant international career.

Though meteoric, John Giles's rise to star status was not completely unexpected. The Gileses were a well-known soccer family in Dublin. John's father Dickie had played for Bohemians and Dolphins before becoming manager of Drumcondra. His uncle Matt and cousin Christy had also played for League of Ireland clubs. John himself had been a schoolboy international and was a Home Farm junior when he was spotted by Manchester United scout Billy Behan in 1955. Success came relatively quickly at United but after helping Matt Busby's team to the 1963 FA Cup, John decided that his future lay elsewhere. A £37,500 transfer to Second Division Leeds United brought raised eyebrows from many quarters but it was to prove an astute move.

At Manchester United, John had played mainly on the wing, but he was brought into the Leeds team in his favoured midfield position. Under the guidance of manager Don Revie, Giles added the combative qualities that his game had lacked and in his first season at Elland Road he helped the Yorkshire club to the Second Division Championship. It was the first of many trophies for a Revie team which would go on to become one of Europe's leading clubs during the late 1960s and early 1970s.

But success with Leeds United would have an adverse effect upon Giles's international career. Cup runs, both at home and in Europe, resulted in a hectic fixture schedule and meant it was not always possible for the Republic of Ireland to gain John's release for international matches. By the mid-1960s he was universally regarded as his country's star player and, in an era when there were precious few top-class footballers wearing the green of Ireland, expectation became unreasonable. If Giles was unavailable or failed to deliver a match-winning performance he would be vilified, with critics declaring that he only cared about his club. Tension between Giles and the selection committee was growing too, and the situation reached a watershed in 1969 when the Leeds midfielder was inexplicably dropped for the World Cup tie against Denmark in Copenhagen. Not only was Giles out of the team but he was also not even considered good enough to merit a place in the squad. It was a farcical situation. Giles reacted by making himself unavailable for the next squad and though he soon returned, the selection committee had made a formidable enemy. Over the next two years, Giles would play a key role in the successful campaign to reform Ireland's antiquated selection process.

John's international appearances would continue to be restricted by Leeds' success during the early 1970s, although the situation improved under manager Liam Tuohy who only expected Giles to turn out for World Cup and European Championship duty. Tuohy's reign, however, was short-lived, and in 1973 Giles's Ireland career entered its final phase when he took over as player-manager of the national team. It proved a difficult managerial tenure but whatever the problems off the field the manager remained his country's most important player well into his late thirties. In 1979 Giles – who was combining his international job with the manager's post at Shamrock Rovers, after a spell in charge at West Bromwich Albion – played his last game for Ireland. Giles had enjoyed a long international career but it is difficult not to feel that without the vagaries of Ireland's curious selection procedures of the 1960s, he would have achieved so much more.

FRANK O'NEILL

1961–1971

20 **1**
CAPS GOALS

BORN ● Dublin, 13.4.40
DEBUT ● v Czechoslovakia (H) 8.10.61
CLUBS ● Shamrock Rovers

In 1959 Frank O'Neill joined fellow winger and Home Farm product Joe Haverty at First Division Arsenal. While Haverty prospered, O'Neill floundered and after just two first-team appearances for George Swindin's Gunners he headed back to Dublin. Shamrock Rovers had been sufficiently impressed by Frank's performances for Arsenal's second string to pay a record League of Ireland fee to take the 21-year-old outside-right to Milltown. It was a bold move, with Frank a relative unknown in Ireland at the time, but any reservations were soon dispelled.

Frank quickly found the measure of LOI football and his skilful wing play brought him to the notice of the international selection committee during his first season with the Hoops. The committee – desperate for success after painful back-to-back defeats against Scotland had left no hope of qualification for the 1962 World Cup – was keen to give Irish-based players a chance. Frank was drafted into the team for the final two qualifiers (both against Czechoslovakia) alongside club-mate Ronnie Nolan. But there was to be no dream debut. Ireland failed to make any impression against superior opposition, losing 3–1 in Dublin and 7–1 in Prague. It would be two-and-a-half years before Frank got another chance in the green shirt of Ireland.

While Frank's international career cooled on the back burner, he continued to enjoy great success with Shamrock Rovers – collecting seven FAI Cup winners' medals in his first eight seasons and helping the Hoops to a League and FAI Cup 'double' in 1963-64. Consistent form in Rovers' 'double' campaign earned Frank a recall to the national team at the start of the 1964-65 season and for the remainder of the decade he was a regular in the Republic line-up.

However, it was Frank's misfortune that his international career coincided with a disappointing period in Ireland's footballing history. While he, together with all the players and officials, must take his share of the responsibility for this general malaise, he should also be applauded for his part in several notable triumphs. Most famously, it was Frank who delivered the free-kick which forced Spain's goalkeeper Iribar to push the ball into his own net for the single goal which earned a celebrated victory at Dalymount Park in 1965. Perhaps more significantly, Frank should also be remembered as one of the key members of the players' committee that challenged the merits of the selection committee and proposed a single manager/selector in the summer of 1971.

It is impossible to say whether Frank's role in the selection committee debate affected his international career in any way but in October 1971 he won his 20th and final cap against Austria.

'You never got over the excitement of playing for your country,' is Mick Meagan's abiding memory of his nine-year career with the Republic of Ireland. But, in truth, it was not just international football which had the adrenaline pumping for the likeable Dubliner. Mick Meagan has a deep-rooted passion for the game at all levels, and even in his 65th year remains unable to resist the temptation to don his boots for his works team at the Central Mental Hospital in Dublin.

As a schoolboy, Mick had become hooked on soccer after watching the legendary Shamrock Rovers duo of Peter Farrell and Tommy Eglington. Both men would leave Milltown for Everton in 1946 and six years later Mick was given the chance to follow his idols to Goodison Park after impressing in a representative match against a Liverpool district team. However, progress through the junior ranks at Everton was slow and Mick struggled to establish himself in his preferred position of inside-forward. He eventually got his chance in the first team in 1957 after showing his versatility with polished displays at both wing-half and full-back in the reserves.

A reliable and consistent performer, Mick's only weakness was a lack of pace, but this was more than compensated for by effortless control and a full passing range which was obtained with equal assurance by either left or right foot. Throughout most of his 12-year Goodison career, Mick was used at full-back, where his determined defending resulted in many full-blooded duels.

The call to international colours came relatively late for Mick, who was 26 years old when he was selected for his debut as a wing-half in a World Cup qualifier against Scotland at Hampden Park, Glasgow, in May 1961. Ireland lost the game 4–1 but Mick had done enough to retain his place in the line-up for the return match against the Scots at Dalymount Park four days later. Mick would remain in the international squad throughout the 1960s, although like most English-based players he was not always released for matches. This perennial problem, allied to the usual injury set backs, restricted Mick's appearances in the green jersey to just 17 caps.

The 1962–63 season saw Mick play a key role in Everton's championship-winning team but a year later he was on his way out of Goodison Park, heading to Huddersfield Town in an exchange deal for England full-back Ray Wilson. Always a popular player, Mick was made captain at Huddersfield – a job he also enjoyed at his third and final League club, Halifax Town. In the latter years of his playing career in England, Mick was employed as a sweeper, a position that, at last, properly utilised his considerable defensive and constructive talents. However, after a year at Halifax, an Achilles' tendon injury brought Mick's professional career to a close. A switch to part-time football with Drogheda extended his playing days and it was as a League of Ireland player that Mick made his final international appearance.

MICK MEAGAN

1961–1969

17 **0**
CAPS GOALS

BORN Dublin, 29.5.34
DEBUT v Scotland (H) 7.5.61
CLUBS Everton, Huddersfield Town, Drogheda

LIAM TUOHY

1955–1965

8	4
CAPS	GOALS

BORN ● Dublin, 27.4.33
DEBUT ● v Yugoslavia (H) 19.10.55
CLUBS ● Shamrock Rovers, Newcastle United

Despite a career of high achievement in League of Ireland football, Liam Tuohy was only rarely seen in an Ireland jersey. It was not that Liam lacked talent, merely that his sporting prime coincided with that of the mercurial Joe Haverty. Although both men were specialist number 11s, their games were markedly different and it seems the international selection committee was more enamoured of the impish qualities of Haverty than Tuohy's direct, hard-running style.

As a youngster, Liam had topped the under-21 scoring charts for Shamrock Rovers and it came as no surprise when, as a prodigiously talented 20 year old, he made the breakthrough into the first team at Milltown. The young winger quickly became a fixture in Paddy Coad's successful Rovers team of the early 1950s and in his second season in the senior side Liam impressed enough to win a call up to the Inter-League team. Elevation to the full international team followed in 1955 when, in the absence of the veteran Tommy Eglington, Liam was chosen for a match against Yugoslavia at Dalymount.

Three-and-a-half years passed between Liam's first and second caps, but with Haverty unavailable for Ireland's debut in the European Nations Cup, the Rovers man lined up to face Czechoslovakia in Dublin in April 1959. The returnee took his chance in emphatic style, scoring the first goal in a 2-0 win with a header from a Tommy Hamilton cross. Unusually for a winger of 5' 8", Liam posed a significant aerial threat and at Shamrock Rovers he developed a reputation as a far-post specialist. Liam would add three more goals to his international tally in the next six years: all headers.

Despite continued good club form and his performance against Czechoslovakia, Liam won just one more cap before finding himself on a three-year break from international football. Whatever the selectors' doubts, scouts from England seemed more than confident of his talents. Liam had been attracting interest from Football League clubs for many years but with a good job at Guinness and success at Shamrock Rovers, he had no motivation to uproot. However, at the age of 27, for reasons which Liam still cannot explain, he 'got the bug' for professional football and joined Charlie Mitten's Newcastle United. And it was as a Magpie that Liam returned to the national team to win his fourth cap, against Austria in 1962. A goal in that game was followed by further strikes in the next two games, both against Iceland. But even this rich vein of scoring was not enough to satisfy the selection committee and Liam was dropped when Haverty returned for the next match, at home to Scotland.

Two more caps eventually followed but it is difficult to avoid the conclusion that Liam Tuohy was both undervalued and under-used by the Republic's selectors. Surely, with just little ingenuity, both Liam and Joe Haverty could have been accommodated in the Ireland team.

JOHNNY FULLAM ▲

1960–1969

11	1
CAPS	GOALS

BORN	Dublin, 22.3.40
DEBUT	v Norway (H) 6.11.60
CLUBS	Preston North End, Shamrock Rovers

Johnny Fullam was a composed and confident footballer whose value was significantly enhanced by an ability to fill several positions with equal facility. Although primarily a midfielder, Johnny also played at sweeper, centre-half and inside-forward during a long and successful League of Ireland career. However, it was with First Division Preston North End that the versatile Dubliner came to prominence. He had joined the Lilywhites from Home Farm as an 18-year-old and after only 18 months as a professional his progress at Deepdale was rewarded with a

call to Ireland's colours for a friendly against Norway at Dalymount.

Despite Johnny's rapid rise to full international status he never truly became a regular in the Republic of Ireland set-up. A second cap did eventually follow, but only after an absence of close on four years, by which time Preston had been swapped for Dublin and Shamrock Rovers. The move to Milltown proved to be a good one for Johnny Fullam and after helping the Hoops to a League and FAI cup double in 1963-64 he earned his long-awaited recall to the national team.

Throughout the 1960s and 1970s Johnny continued to enjoy success at club level where he proved a man for the big occasion, scoring the winning goal in the replayed cup final against Limerick in 1965 and also registering a memorable score against Real Zaragoza in a Fairs Cup tie. There was an international goal, too, scored against Belgium in 1966, but even that was not enough to earn a regular place in the face of competition from the likes of John Giles, Eamon Dunphy and Mick McGrath.

FREDDIE STRAHAN ▼

1964–1966

5	1
CAPS	GOALS

BORN	Dublin
DEBUT	v Poland (A) 10.5.64
CLUBS	Shelbourne

With no lesser player than Bobby Moore trailing in his wake, Freddie Strahan strode purposefully forward before dispatching a crisp shot beyond England goalkeeper Tony Waiters to register the most unlikely of international goals. It was a strike that any great goalscorer would have been proud of but coming as it did from the boot of an all-action centre-half cum midfielder it was all the more memorable.

Strahan, who had made his name alongside the likes of Tony Dunne and Paddy Roberts in the successful Shelbourne team of the early 1960s, had been called into the Ireland squad in 1964 when Noel Cantwell suffered a back injury. The loss of the skipper resulted in a mass reshuffle and Strahan made his international debut in an unfamiliar right-half position. Unfazed by his new midfield responsibility the newcomer gave an impressive display and retained his place in the team for the next three matches, a sequence which included 'that match' against England.

Strahan would win a recall to the international team for one last game, in 1966, and would also captain the inter-League team, but he would never again attain the heady heights of his goal against the English at Dalymount in 1964.

Like a featherweight boxer his frame belied a steely strength.

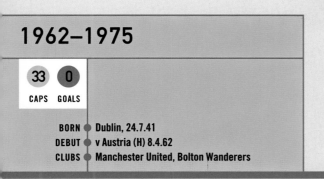

1962–1975

33	0
CAPS	GOALS

BORN ● Dublin, 24.7.41
DEBUT ● v Austria (H) 8.4.62
CLUBS ● Manchester United, Bolton Wanderers

Throughout a 13-year international career Tony Dunne proved himself a master of the art of flank defending. The diminutive Dubliner may have looked less menacing than many of his bulkier defensive colleagues but like a feather-weight boxer his frame belied a steely strength. He had pace too and this utterly reliable defender would regularly dash across field to cover for the positional lapses of errant colleagues. Although a natural left-footer, Tony's value to team and manager was further enhanced by a rare ability to operate on either flank with equal facility.

Tony Dunne

Tony had caught the eye of Football League scouts while helping Shelbourne to an FAI Cup victory over Cork Hibernians in 1960 and shortly afterwards the teenage defender defected to England to join the burgeoning ranks of Irishmen on Manchester United's books. At Old Trafford Tony found the formidable obstacle of Ireland captain Noel Cantwell blocking his path to the Reds' number three shirt. The newcomer was forced to mark time in the reserves while waiting for his opportunity. Once in the team, however, it quickly became apparent that Matt Busby – who had paid just £5,000 to prise Dunne away from Tolka Park – had unearthed a full-back of rare talent and the Dubliner retained his place in the United line-up for more than a decade, making 530 first-team appearances. Busby was beginning to build a great team at Old Trafford when Dunne joined United, and Tony more than earned his place in a side which included the legendary triumvirate of Denis Law, George Best and Bobby Charlton. But with such attacking talent in the team, Tony was largely unconcerned with the business of breaking forward, preferring instead to deliver a simple pass to a United midfielder or striker. Some ultra-critical observers felt that he should have made better use of his pace to reap havoc in opponents' penalty areas, but such nitpicking concerned neither player nor manager.

Tony's priority was to guard the left flank and he did this with much élan. Having made the breakthrough at Manchester United, he was, at international level, once more hindered by the familiar figure of Noel Cantwell, who was the man in possession of Ireland's number three jersey. But in 1962, with the national team increasingly keen to use Cantwell's physical presence at centre-forward, Tony won his first cap. In his early days with Ireland, he was played at right-back but his best performances came when paired with United team-mate Shay Brennan. The right-sided Brennan made his debut in 1965. Thereafter, Tony was able to take up his favoured left-back position to reveal the form which served United so well throughout the 1960s. Dunne was a vital member of United's celebrated League Championship-winning teams of 1964-65 and 1966-67 and was also on duty when the Reds enjoyed their greatest triumph, overcoming Benfica 4–1 at Wembley to win the 1968 European Cup.

Always a dogged defender, Tony matured to become an increasingly constructive player and for Ireland, in particular, his raids down the left flank provided several goal assists – one memorable contribution ended with a goal for Jackie Mooney against Poland in 1964. Tony continued to add to his tally of caps throughout the 1960s and was a key player in the Ireland team which narrowly missed out on qualification for the 1966 World Cup finals. However, the pinnacle of Tony Dunne's international career came in 1969 when he was appointed captain of the Republic of Ireland for the first time, this honour coming shortly after he had been named Ireland's Player of the Year. Tony would skipper his country on four more occasions over the next six years but in June 1972 he withdrew from an international squad for the mini-World Cup in Brazil and fell out with manager Liam Tuohy. Tony had played his last game for Tuohy and was only recalled after John Giles had taken over as manager. Ironically, Tony's return to the international fold came during a tour of South America in 1974. It was to be a brief renaissance and he added only five more caps to his tally.

Tony's period in international exile had coincided with the end of his career at Old Trafford. In 1973 the new Manchester United manager Tommy Docherty decided that the time was right to allow the thirty-something full-back to move on and Tony joined Bolton Wanderers. Docherty's decision proved somewhat premature, however, and Dunne flourished at Burnden Park, taking on more responsibility when in possession, while maintaining his high standards in defence.

THEO FOLEY ▼

1964–1967

9 **0**
CAPS GOALS

BORN	Dublin, 2.4.37
DEBUT	v Spain (A) 11.3.64
CLUBS	Northampton Town

Theo Foley was one of the many promising Home Farm youngsters to head for England during the 1950s. But his big break did not come with a glamorous First Division club – he began his professional career at Exeter City. A versatile and competitive performer, Theo could fill a number of defensive positions, although his ample strength and speed were best used at at full-back.

Theo was an immediate success at Exeter, but it was only after a move to Third Division Northampton Town in 1961 that he was mentioned as a potential international. He had joined a club in the ascendant – by 1965 the Cobblers had were in the First Division. The international selection committee were impressed and, when Tony Dunne and Noel Cantwell withdrew from a European Nations Cup match against Spain, Theo was drafted into the team.

Theo made his debut at right-back but when Tony Dunne returned, the new boy was left on the sidelines. Occasional appearances followed, but the highlight of his Ireland career came when he was made captain for the match against Belgium in March 1965. Northampton would fade from view in the late 1960s, returning to Division Four by the close of the decade, but Theo would enjoy success as coach at Arsenal, Southend and Charlton.

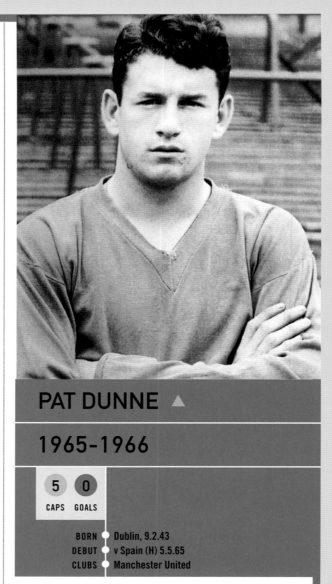

PAT DUNNE ▲

1965–1966

5 **0**
CAPS GOALS

BORN	Dublin, 9.2.43
DEBUT	v Spain (H) 5.5.65
CLUBS	Manchester United

Pat Dunne's arrival at Old Trafford in 1964 was impeccably timed. The Dubliner had already suffered the disappointment of failing to make the grade as a teenager at Everton when Matt Busby signed him from Shamrock Rovers for £10,000.

Busby had assembled a formidable squad ahead of the 1964-65 season, but an injury to regular goalkeeper Harry Gregg gave Pat his chance. United swept to the League title and Pat amassed 37 first-team appearances *en route*. A strong and brave goalkeeper, he was a formidable shot-stopper, however his handling of crosses was far from perfect, and he found himself on the sidelines when Harry Gregg returned to fitness. In February 1967 Pat left Old Trafford to join Plymouth where he enjoyed a five-season run in the first-team.

Pat's exploits in United's title-winning season brought a call up to the national team in May 1965, and an impressive debut in the 1-0 World Cup win over Spain led to a run of four games in the line-up. But with Ireland losing three matches in succession, conceding nine goals and failing to qualify for the 1966 World Cup finals, Pat lost his place. Alan Kelly returned to take over the number one jersey and, thereafter, Pat added just one more cap to his tally.

ALFIE HALE ▶

1962–1973

14 CAPS   **2** GOALS

BORN Waterford, 28.8.39
DEBUT v Austria (H) 8.4.62
CLUBS Aston Villa, Doncaster Rovers, Waterford

Alfie Hale was a sharp, quick-witted striker whose greatest asset was the immaculate balance which enabled him to dummy and dribble his way around the pitch unhindered whatever the conditions. His balance was made more remarkable by his insistence on wearing rubber studded boots.

It was with hometown club Waterford that Alfie came to prominence and, after a prolific run of scoring from the left wing, he was selected for an inter-League match in Germany. A hat-trick against the Germans brought a swift move to Joe Mercer's Aston Villa, but Alfie was rarely seen in the Villa first team, although his progress in the reserves did at least lead to a full international debut in 1962. Moves to Doncaster Rovers and Newport County followed, but, after four years in the lower reaches of the Football League, Alfie returned to his native Waterford.

Back on home territory, Alfie enjoyed his best spell with Ireland and in 1968 he was capped in four consecutive internationals. This rare run in the team saw Alfie register his two international goals (against Poland and Austria), both of which were late equalisers at Dalymount Park.

OLLIE CONMY ▶

1965–1969

5 CAPS   **0** GOALS

BORN Mulrany, 13.11.39
DEBUT v Belgium (H) 24.3.65
CLUBS Peterborough United

Oliver Conmy was a tricky, lightweight forward, who enjoyed occasional appearances in the green of Ireland during the 1960s. Although born in Mulrany, Ollie was raised in Yorkshire and it was with Huddersfield Town that he made the breakthrough to senior football. However, in 1964, after just three League appearances in five years for the Terriers he moved to Third Division Peterborough United.

The switch to East Anglia proved a success, and it was as a Posh player that Ollie received all five of his caps. A winger by preference, he took his international bow at inside-forward but failed to make a significant impression as Ireland went down 2–0 against Belgium at Dalymount Park. Ollie returned to the team two years later, by which time Joe Haverty had relinquished his long-held number 11 shirt. And, in a more familiar, left-wing position, Ollie gave a much improved display against Czechoslovakia in the European Nations Cup. The return against the Czechs in Prague saw Ollie produce his best performance in a green shirt, setting-up Ireland's opening goal for Ray Treacy with a jinking run.

JACKIE HENNESSY ▶

1964–1968

5 CAPS   **0** GOALS

BORN Dublin, 1940
DEBUT v Poland (H) 25.10.64
CLUBS Shelbourne, St Patrick's Athletic

Every successful team needs a playmaker – a footballer who can pass with a little savvy and who is not content merely to hoof the ball hopefully forward. In the case of Shelbourne's talented team of the early 1960s, the man directing operations was Jackie Hennessy. A former schoolboy team-mate of John Giles, Jackie was a versatile performer who came into the Shels first-team as a fast and skilful inside-forward, and later found success as a cultured, goalscoring left-half.

A brace of goals for the Republic of Ireland's B team against Iceland in 1960 had alerted the selection committee to Jackie's attacking talents, and four years later he was called into the full international team as an inside-forward. In the interim, Jackie had won much acclaim for his performances for Shelbourne in European competition – scoring against Sporting Lisbon in the European Cup in 1962. He was also a scorer for St Patrick's Athletic in a Fairs Cup tie against Bordeaux in 1964.

EAMON DUNPHY

1965–1971

23 CAPS **0** GOALS

BORN · Dublin, 3.8.45
DEBUT · v Spain (Paris) 10.11.65
CLUBS · York City, Millwall

Eamon Dunphy has made many significant contributions to football, but few, if any, have come on the pitch. A modestly successful playing career began when, as a 16-year-old apprentice, he joined Matt Busby's post-Munich Manchester United. But after three seasons at Old Trafford, Eamon, who had failed to break into the Reds' first-team, left to join York City. It was the start of a 13-year career in England which would see him clock up more than 400 League appearances with York, Charlton Athletic, Millwall and Reading. A spindly, lightweight midfielder with good touch and a full passing range, Eamon was blessed with much footballing talent but little by way of either pace or strength.

Whatever Eamon's deficiencies he was well liked by the international selectors. During his six year international career he won 23 caps. Eamon himself believes that it was 'a lot of caps for a player of my ability,' and he rightly attributes his frequent appearances to the fact that John Giles was regularly unavailable because of club commitments. But former Ireland manager Mick Meagan thinks Eamon is too modest. 'He was a good player, he lacked pace but was a very clever footballer who was an excellent passer of the ball.' Meagan was qualified to judge Dunphy's merits: not only did he give the Dubliner his last cap in 1971, he also played alongside him when, as a 20 year old, Eamon made his debut in a World Cup play-off match against Spain in Paris.

It was off the field, however, that Eamon made his greatest impact. Ireland's selection committee had long been subject to media criticism and in May 1971 Eamon led a players' campaign to replace this archaic, ad hoc system with a manager/sole selector. The players' efforts were partially successful – manager Mick Meagan was given a voice at selection meetings. However, Eamon's hard work had left him exhausted and in the next match – at home to Austria – he asked the newly empowered manager to substitute him. It would be Dunphy's last appearance for Ireland.

Since retiring as a player in 1978 Eamon has forged a successful career as a journalist. With several best-selling books under his belt – including the seminal football diary *Only A Game?* – he now combines regular radio and newspaper work with a role as television pundit for RTE. Never one to engage in the banal or in back-slapping, Eamon's straight-talking analysis led to a well publicised spat with the Ireland manager Jack Charlton during Italia 90. The former Millwall man had dared to criticise Ireland's approach after a group match against Egypt and was vilified for his trouble. The situation deteriorated still further when Eamon attended one of Big Jack's press conferences in Italy only for the manager to tell him he was 'not a proper journalist'. It seemed that in this great game of opinions there was, in Jack Charlton's view, no place for the opinions of Eamon Dunphy.

Shay Brennan's international debut, in 1965, was one of the most controversial and momentous occasions in Irish football history. Brennan, a silky full-back who was at the height of his form with Manchester United, had become eligible for the Republic of Ireland after Fifa had relaxed qualification rules to allow players to represent their parents' nation of birth. The Merrion Square selection committee could ill-afford to ignore Brennan's obvious virtues and with a place in the 1966 World Cup finals at stake, the FAI took the bold step of making him the first player to represent Ireland under the new rule.

Inevitably, the selection of an English-born player brought feverish debate; and the fact that Shay had previously been on the brink of an England cap ahead of the 1962 World Cup only intensified matters. However, the doubters were silenced when the United right-back made a faultless debut against Spain at Dalymount Park in May 1965. Teaming up with club-mates Tony and Pat Dunne, Shay played his part in a celebrated 1–0 victory as Ireland's World Cup campaign got off to a glorious start. Shay retained his place in the team throughout the next 18 months, but found himself on the sidelines when the younger, more attack-minded Joe Kinnear got his chance in 1967.

Shay's international career may have hit a temporary trough, but at United he was enjoying his greatest successes. In possession of two League Championship medals by 1967, the popular defender was in his familiar number two shirt as United steamrollered Benfica at Wembley to lift the 1968 European Cup. Shay had made his United debut ten years earlier in an emotional atmosphere of a very different kind. As a 20-year-old he had taken his senior bow in the first match after the Munich air disaster, scoring twice from an unfamiliar outside-left position in a 3–0 victory over Sheffield Wednesday. Shortly afterwards Shay returned to the Reds reserves. When he was recalled to the first team it was as a specialist full-back. An intelligent player with good passing technique, Shay was a great reader of the game and was adept at jockeying opponents away from danger before striking with a precise tackle.

With such talent and big-match experience on his side it was inevitable that Shay would win back his place in the Republic line-up, and so he did towards the end of the 1960s. New Ireland manager Mick Meagan was suitably impressed by the resurgent Brennan to appoint him captain for his first World Cup match in charge, against Czechoslovakia. In 1970 Shay left Manchester United and went back to his roots to join LOI club Waterford where he enjoyed great success as both player and manager.

SHAY BRENNAN

1965–1970

 19 CAPS   **0** GOALS

BORN Manchester, 6.5.37
DEBUT v Spain (H) 5.5.65
CLUBS Clubs: Manchester United, Waterford

TERRY CONROY ▼

1969–1977

27 **2**
CAPS GOALS

BORN ● Dublin, 2.10.46
DEBUT ● v Czechoslovakia (A) 7.10.69
CLUBS ● Stoke City

Terry Conroy was a quicksilver forward with a welcome ability to provide flashes of crowd-pleasing skill even in the gloomy environs of Ireland's struggling 1970s team. As a teenager, Terry had enjoyed good success with Irish League club Glentoran, where he had shown a prolific goal touch. Then in 1967, the youngster decided the time was right to make the switch to England and joined Stoke City.

After just 18 months of full-time football in England, Terry was given his senior international debut in Mick Meagan's second game in charge, against Czechoslovakia in Prague. The match brought a 3–0 defeat for Ireland, but when Meagan came to make changes to the forward line for the next match Terry kept his place.

Meagan continued to keep faith with the Stoke winger throughout his ten match spell in charge, but it was under Liam Tuohy that Terry enjoyed his best moments. His first international goal came in a World Cup qualifier in 1972 against the USSR at Dalymount. A second goal followed in the next game against France, but thereafter Terry's appearances would be restricted by injuries and the whims of his club. Terry, who, along with Ray Treacy, was renowned as one of the international team's jokers, would go on to become assistant manager during Eoin Hand's time in charge of the Republic of Ireland.

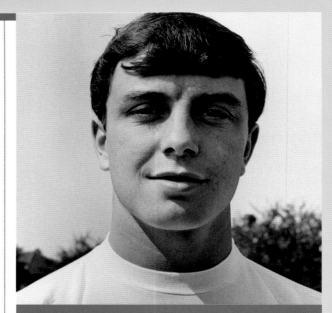

JIMMY CONWAY ▲

1966–1977

20 **3**
CAPS GOALS

BORN ● Dublin, 10.8.46
DEBUT ● v Spain (H) 23.10.66
CLUBS ● Fulham, Manchester City

In May 1966 Jimmy Conway joined First Division Fulham in a deal which also saw his Bohemians team-mate Turlough O'Connor make the switch to Craven Cottage. Just five months later Jimmy was rewarded with a full international cap to add to his amateur honours. A fast, direct winger with an eye for goal, he became a regular in the Ireland team of the late 1960s.

At club level, however, things did not go to plan and by 1969 Jimmy found himself playing in Third rather than First Division football. The fall down the leagues brought an emphatic response from the Dubliner, who finished as the Cottagers' top scorer in 1969–70 and played a key role in the club's successful promotion campaign in 1970–71. With Fulham's return to England's second tier guaranteed, Jimmy celebrated by heading home his first international goal against Italy at Dalymount Park that May.

A cartilage injury struck soon after, followed by a period of international exile, with Jimmy absent throughout Liam Tuohy's 10-match reign. Conway's recall followed the appointment of John Giles as Ireland boss in 1974, and he was included in the squad for the summer tour of South America. Giles's faith was rewarded when the Fulham forward struck his second Ireland goal against Chile. Infrequent international appearances followed during the mid-1970s, but it was as a member of Fulham's 1975 FA Cup final team, alongside England legends Bobby Moore and Alan Mullery, that Jimmy's career hit a late and unexpected high.

John Dempsey was a rare rock of certainty in Ireland's frequently fragile rearguard of the late 1960s and early 1970s. A tough and commanding centre-half, he stood six foot tall and was every inch the no-nonsense stopper. John, London born with a strong Cockney accent, was one of the first players to qualify for Ireland via Fifa's parentage rule but he was no soccer mercenary. Mick Meagan, the former Republic of Ireland manager, remembers meeting Dempsey's father after a game at Stamford Bridge, but instead of the 'Alf Garnett-type character' he had expected, Meagan was introduced to 'an Irishman with a lovely brogue who was clearly very proud that his son was playing for Ireland.'

It was as a Fulham player that John received his first full cap, playing as part of a formidable Ireland defence which boasted Charlie Hurley and Manchester United full-backs Shay Brennan and Tony Dunne. John had joined the Cottagers as an apprentice in 1962 but with the club bound for the Third Division in 1969 he found himself moving across West London to join Chelsea in exchange for £70,000. The switch to Stamford Bridge proved a shrewd move. In his first full season with the Blues, John was an FA Cup winner. He continued to be the man 'shutting shop' for Chelsea's talented squad the following season, 1970–71, as the club embarked upon a successful European Cup Winners' Cup campaign. And it was in the replayed final of that competition that John enjoyed his most memorable moment in a Chelsea shirt when he scored with a perfect volley to give the club a 1–0 lead over Real Madrid. The London club ended the final 2–1 winners after extra time.

At international level, John's career took in some spectacular highs and some equally dramatic lows. There was a goal against Poland at Dalymount Park in 1968 when John was pressed into service as an emergency striker by coach Noel Cantwell. And a year later there was another proud moment for the Dempsey family when, in the absence of Charlie Hurley, 23-year-old John was chosen as captain of the national team for a World Cup match against Denmark in Copenhagen. However, it was not all fantasy football for the burly centre-half. Six months later he became the first Republic of Ireland player to be sent off when he saw red in a World Cup qualifier against Hungary in Budapest. Dempsey had been incensed by a decision by the Yugoslav referee to award the home team a free-kick. When his protestations became too keen he was given his marching orders. Unfortunately, John's problem in Budapest pales into insignificance when compared to the injury setbacks he suffered in the latter part of his career and, in 1972, aged just 26, he played his last game for Ireland.

JOHN DEMPSEY

1966–1972

 19 **1**

CAPS GOALS

BORN Hampstead, 15.3.46
DEBUT Spain (A) 7.12.66
CLUBS Fulham, Chelsea

A strong player who was a mobile and energetic leader of the line.

1966–1979

42 CAPS **5** GOALS

BORN • Dublin, 18.6.46
DEBUT • v West Germany (H) 4.5.66
CLUBS • West Bromwich Albion, Charlton Athletic, Swindon Town, Preston North End, West Bromwich Albion, Shamrock Rovers

As a teenager Dublin-born striker Ray Treacy had been a member of an Ireland schoolboy team that conceded 20 goals in two matches. Fortunately, the combative centre-forward would recover from this setback to make, more significant contributions in the green shirt.

Ray Treacy

Treacy played his junior football for Home Farm but at the age of 15 he became one of the growing legion of exports from the North Dublin club when he signed as an apprentice for First Division West Bromwich Albion. Ray was employed in a number of positions for Albion's under-age teams and for a while it looked like he might establish himself at full-back, a role he also filled for the Irish youth team. But it was at centre-forward that he found his niche and on his 18th birthday he signed his first professional contract with the Midlands club. Two years later in 1966, Ray found himself elevated to full-international status when he was called into the Republic of Ireland team for a friendly against West Germany. It was a meteoric rise for a 20-year-old forward who was still a reserve team player at club level.

Ray continued to make occasional appearances for Ireland during 1966–67, playing alongside the experienced Andy McEvoy, but at West Brom he was making little headway. With his tally of international caps almost equalling in number his senior appearances for Albion, Ray decided to leave the Hawthorns and signed for Second Division Charlton Athletic in 1968. The impact on his game of the move to the Valley was instantaneous and in his first international as a Charlton player Ray applied his head to an Eamon Dunphy cross to claim his first international goal. That goal, against a formidable Czechoslovakia side in Prague, had set Ireland *en route* to an unlikely victory which was completed when Treacy set up the winner for Turlough O'Connor.

It would be five years before Ray scored a second international goal – it came in another memorable victory, this time against France in Dublin. But in mitigation of Ray's disappointing strike rate it must be said that the early part of his international career coincided with the Republic of Ireland's footballing nadir, when the team struggled in all areas of the field. Thereafter Ray was forced to play the second striker's role to the more skilful Don Givens. In any case, Ray offered so much more than just goals. He was a strong player who was a mobile and energetic leader of the line. Ray was also a confident footballer who was a key figure in maintaining team spirit. Not only was he the dressing-room joker he was also a great lover of the traditional post-match sing-songs, at which he became the resident guitar player.

Ray shared his passion for music with his friend and fellow Dubliner John Giles and in 1976 Giles, who was manager of both Ireland and West Brom, took the 30-year-old striker back to the club where he had begun his professional career. A year later Ray left English football to join Giles as his assistant at of Shamrock Rovers. And it was while with the Hoops that Ray made his final contributions in an Ireland shirt, scoring twice against Turkey in April 1978, before making his final appearance against Czechoslovakia the following year. After retiring as a player, Ray enjoyed successful spells in charge of several League of Ireland clubs, most notably at Shamrock Rovers where he led the Hoops to League title success in 1993.

JACKIE MOONEY
1964–1965
Born: Dublin, 1938
Caps: 4
Goals: 1
Debut v Poland (H) 25.10.64
Clubs: Shamrock Rovers

Although not particularly tall, Jackie Mooney's great strength was his aerial ability. At club level, with Shamrock Rovers, he was one of a number of centre-forwards who preyed on the high-quality centres delivered by Liam Tuohy and Frank O'Neill. In 1963–64 he was the League of Ireland's top scorer with 16 goals and the following season he was given his chance in the international team alongside Andy McEvoy. The partnership brought immediate dividends with McEvoy netting twice and Jackie heading home a Theo Foley cross to earn a 3–2 friendly victory over Poland. A second cap followed in the next game, against Belgium, but when a round of World Cup qualifiers kicked off in May 1965 the selectors decided upon a Cantwell-McEvoy pairing in attack.

ERIC BARBER
1965–1966
Born: Dublin, 18.1.42
Caps: 4
Goals: 0
Debut v Spain (A) 27.10.65
Clubs: Shelbourne, Birmingham City

Eric Barber was a mobile and aggressive centre-forward who made his name with Shelbourne in the early 1960s. At Tolka Park, Eric forged a formidable partnership with Christy Doyle and after six seasons of good form with Shels a call to the full international team arrived in 1965. However, Eric's debut performance was much impeded by a bout of toothache and he failed to make a significant contribution as Ireland went down 4–1 against Spain in Seville. An unsuccessful move to Stan Cullis's Birmingham City followed shortly afterwards. While at St Andrews, Eric did earn a second international cap, against Belgium, but alas he enjoyed no better luck when he was asked to play in an unfamiliar position on the wing.

FRAN BRENNAN
1965
Born: Dublin
Caps: 1
Goals: 0
Debut v Belgium (H) 24.3.65
Clubs: Drumcondra

Fran Brennan was a tenacious and whole-hearted defender who could operate at full-back or centre-half with equal facility. His call to the international team came in the spring of 1965 when he was enjoying a run of excellent form with title-chasing Drumcondra. Alas, the red-headed stopper, who deputised for Charlie Hurley, did not enjoy the best of debuts. Ireland, severely depleted by injuries and withdrawals, lost 2–0 to a good Belgium side. Fran Brennan was never to be seen in the green of Ireland again.

TONY O'CONNELL
1966-1970
Born: Dublin, 1941
Caps: 3
Goals: 0
Debut v Spain (H) 23.10.66
Clubs: Dundalk, Bohemians

In 1963 Tony O'Connell was the architect of the League of Ireland's 2–1 win over a Football League team at Dalymount Park. Tony was a skilful and entertaining outside-left and, although he had success with Shamrock Rovers early in his career, he was at Dundalk when he received a surprise international call for a European Championships tie with Spain in 1966. In 1969 he moved to Bohemians, and shortly afterwards wore a second Ireland shirt, albeit as a substitute. Tony was an immediate success at Bohs and in his first season was their top scorer.

BOBBY GILBERT
1966
Born: Dublin
Caps: 1
Goals: 0
Debut v West Germany (H) 4.5.66
Clubs: Shamrock Rovers

With his slicked-backed hair and imposing physique, Bobby Gilbert was an 'old fashioned centre-forward'. No frills, just honest power and a love of aerial challenges and headed goals. He enjoyed his best form at Shamrock Rovers, served by wingers Frank O'Neill and Liam Tuohy. After finishing as the Hoops' top scorer in 1966 with 14 goals, he was elevated to the international team for a friendly against West Germany. Ireland were outclassed. Bobby didn't get a sniff of goal and was given no second chance in the green shirt.

JOHN KEOGH
1966
Born: Dublin, 1942
Caps: 1
Goals: 0
Debut v West Germany (H)
4.5.66
Clubs: Shamrock Rovers

A first-half injury to Theo Foley gave John Keogh the opportunity to make his international debut against West Germany at Dalymount Park in 1966. Ireland lost the game 4–0 and with Tony Dunne, Shay Brennan and Foley all ahead of Keogh in the queue for full-back places there would be no second cap. John, who was one of the first overlapping full-backs to play in the League of Ireland, was a key figure in Shamrock Rovers' many successes of the 1960s.

MICK SMYTH
1968
Born: Dublin, 13.5.40
Caps: 1
Goals: 0
Debut v Poland (A) 30.10.68
Clubs: Shamrock Rovers

A tall (6' 2") and commanding goalkeeper, Mick Smyth was at the peak of his form for Shamrock Rovers when he won his one and only full cap as a substitute during a friendly against Poland in 1968. Smyth's international career, which lasted just 29 minutes, got underway when regular keeper Alan Kelly suffered an injury and had to be withdrawn from the match. At club level, Mick enjoyed rather more success. During spells with Shamrock Rovers, Bohemians and Athlone Town he won every major honour in the domestic game.

KEVIN FITZPATRICK
1969
Born: Limerick, 1943
Caps: 1
Goals: 0
Debut v Czechoslovakia (A)
7.10.69
Clubs: Limerick United

Kevin Fitzpatrick was a reliable and well-respected League of Ireland goalkeeper who played his whole career for Limerick United, his home town team. Kevin's one cap came in a World Cup match against Czechoslovakia in Prague. It was Mick Meagan's first away fixture in charge and the new manager's weakened team – which had been depleted by injuries and withdrawals – went down 3–0 as Czech striker Adamec helped himself to a first-half hat-trick. Alan Kelly returned for the next game and Kevin's tally of caps stopped at one.

BILLY NEWMAN
1969
Born: Dublin, 1947
Caps: 1
Goals: 0
Debut v Denmark (A) 27.5.69
Clubs: Shelbourne

Billy Newman was a careful and constructive midfield player who enjoyed successful spells with Dublin clubs Bohemians and Shelbourne. Although blessed with immaculate technique, Billy was a little slow over the turf and his elevation to full-international status came as something of a surprise. The selection committee, who were in dispute with midfielder John Giles, called Billy into the squad for a World Cup qualifier in Copenhagen but shortly after half-time and with Ireland trailing 1–0 the newcomer was substituted. Billy Newman's international career had lasted just 55 minutes.

CHARLIE GALLAGHER
1967
Born: Glasgow, 3.11.40
Caps: 2
Goals: 0
Debut v Turkey (A) 22.2.67
Clubs: Celtic

In 1967 Celtic's Charlie Gallagher became the first Scots-born player to win a full cap for the Republic of Ireland – an event that led to much celebration amongst the Parkhead faithful. A ball-playing inside-forward with a venomous shot, Charlie enjoyed a significant role in several of the Bhoys' triumphs of the 1960s. His highly accurate corners had proved a regular source of goals for the Glasgow club, and it was from such a set play that Billy McNeill headed the goal which clinched the 1965 Scottish Cup. Charlie qualified as a Republic of Ireland player by virtue of his Donegal-born parents.

AL FINUCANE ▼

1967–1971

11	**0**
CAPS	GOALS

BORN	Limerick, 1943
DEBUT	v Turkey (A) 22.2.67
CLUBS	Limerick

Al Finucane was a studious and well-organised defender who radiated confidence for those fortunate enough to play alongside him. An articulate and popular man, Al began his career as a right-half with his home town club Limerick, but it was only when he switched to central defence that his true talents were revealed. His reading of the game was immaculate and his positional play and foresight helped compensate for a lack of inches which might otherwise have been exploited by some of the more aggressive strikers plying their trade in the League of Ireland during the 1960s.

Although never quite a first-choice selection in the full international team, Al was a regular stand-in for English-based defenders John Dempsey and Charlie Hurley who were often unavailable. In 1969 Al enjoyed his best run in the green of Ireland when he featured in five consecutive line-ups. Four of these matches, however, ended in defeat. The other – Mick Meagan's first match as manager – brought a 1–1 draw against Scotland.

At club level, Al enjoyed rather better fortune and in 1971 he captained Limerick to a first FAI Cup win. Shortly afterwards Liam Tuohy took over as manager of the national team, and for his first game in charge appointed Al as skipper. Alas, Tuohy's team, severely depleted by withdrawals, went down 6–0 against Austria in Linz. Al Finucane's first game as captain turned out to be his last for Ireland.

EAMONN ROGERS ▲

1967–1972

19	**5**
CAPS	GOALS

BORN	Dublin, 16.4.47
DEBUT	v Czechoslovakia (A) 22.11.67
CLUBS	Blackburn Rovers, Charlton Athletic

Eamonn Rogers was a footballer with a talent all too rare in the Ireland team of the late 1960s and early 1970s... he scored goals. Five in 19 games may not seem a prolific strike rate but for a winger, and in the context of a side which went 20 games without a victory, it was an exceptional record. Eamonn came into the international team at outside-left but was also able to operate, with élan, at inside-forward.

As a youngster, Eamonn had played alongside future international team-mates Terry Conroy and Ray Treacy in the Ireland youth team which finished sixth in the UEFA finals of 1965. A League debut for Blackburn Rovers followed shortly afterwards, and the rapid ascent was complete when, aged just 20, the Dubliner was called into the full international team.

Eamonn's debut in the green of Ireland ended in a memorable 2–1 victory against Czechoslovakia in Prague and for the next two years the Blackburn winger remained a key member of the national team. A first international goal came in his third match (against Austria in Dublin), but it was in 1972 that Eamonn truly found his shooting boots, scoring goals in successive matches against Ecuador and Chile during a summer tour of Brazil. However, within four months Eamonn had played his last international. His club career was also in the doldrums following an ill-fated move to Charlton Athletic in October 1971 and, still only 25 years old, Eamonn Rogers made his final Football League appearance.

It is difficult to conceive of Joe Kinnear as anything other than the burly, wise-cracking Wimbledon 'gaffer' and champion of the underdog cause. But the long-time leader of the Dons' self-styled Crazy Gang was himself once a player and an accomplished one at that. Joe, who was born in Dublin's Kimmage district, spent the latter part of his childhood in England, and it was with London giants Tottenham Hotspur that he made his name as an adventurous, attacking right-back in the late 1960s.

As a teenager Joe had captained Watford and Hertfordshire boys but after leaving school he had embarked upon a printing apprenticeship and played part-time for St Albans' City. A successful trial for Spurs at Chesthunt saw Joe join the North Londoners as an amateur while he continued his printing job. Fortunately, the lack of full-time training did not hinder Joe's progress. In 1966 he signed pro and shortly afterwards broke into the Spurs' first team. The following season, 1966-67, the dark-haired Dubliner became a regular in Bill Nicholson's line-up. It was the start of a golden era in Spurs' history and in ten seasons at White Hart Lane Joe played his part in League Cup triumphs in 1970–71 and 1972–73, as well as successes in the FA Cup in 1967, and the UEFA Cup in 1971–72.

While still just a rookie in the Spurs team, Joe was elevated to full-international status as one of three new caps in Ireland's disappointing defeat against Turkey in 1967. Despite the result, Joe had impressed on his debut and for the next three years he would vie with Manchester United's Shay Brennan for the national team's number two shirt. Both players were full-backs of the highest order but where Brennan was patient and steady, Kinnear – nine years Shay's junior – was the more dashing player, ever keen to gallop forward when the chance arose. But Joe was no part-time defender, and with his tigerish tackling he never lost sight of his primary responsibility. A broken leg in 1969 interrupted Joe's progress with both club and country but upon recovery he regained his place in Mick Meagan's international team. Thereafter he played when available until, in 1975, John Giles decided to bring Joe's days in green to a premature end following the team's failure to qualify for the 1976 European Championships.

JOE KINNEAR

1967–1975

26 **0**
CAPS GOALS

BORN | Dublin, 27.12.46
DEBUT | v Turkey (A) 22.2.67
CLUBS | Tottenham Hotspur, Brighton and Hove Albion

club level. He was ravaged by injuries while at Fulham and failed to make an impression at first-team level. He returned to Ireland to play for Dundalk and quickly recaptured his scoring form. But with Don Givens installed in the national team an international recall was slow to arrive.

Liam Tuohy gave Turlough his long-awaited second cap in the 6–0 reverse against Austria in October 1971. Turlough added three more caps to his tally during the mini-World Cup in Brazil in 1972 and also scored a second international goal with a perfect lob from 40 yards against Ecuador. Unfortunately his next appearance, against Chile, ended abruptly when he was sent off for appealing too strongly for a penalty. Shortly afterwards, Turlough returned to Bohemians where he would become the club's record goalscorer. He made two more appearances for Ireland but it is his scoring debut that will live longest in the memory.

TOMMY CARROLL ▼

1968–1973

17 **1**
CAPS GOALS

BORN Dublin, 18.8.42
DEBUT v Poland (H) 15.5.68
CLUBS Ipswich Town, Birmingham City

'A good, solid player who would never let you down,' is how former Republic of Ireland manager Mick Meagan remembers Tommy Carroll. In an era when international squads were often depleted by late withdrawals, Carroll was utterly dependable, happy to play anywhere for his country. He appeared at left-back, right-back, in central defence and in midfield.

Tommy began his career alongside Eric Barber and Tony Dunne at Shelbourne nursery club St Finbarr's. He was still a teenager when he broke through into the Shels' first-team. In seven years at Tolka Park, Tommy played in every position before establishing himself at right-back. In 1964, with League and FAI Cup winners' medals tucked under his belt, he made the move to England, joining Southern League side Cambridge City. After two years of amateur football, Tommy signed for Second Division Ipswich Town and in 1967–68, his second season there, helped them win promotion.

In May 1968, Tommy's efforts at Ipswich were rewarded with his first full cap, adding to earlier amateur and Under-23 honours. Tommy kept his place in the squad for the rest of his career, but was rarely given the opportunity to play in his preferred full-back position, due to the form of Shay Brennan, Tony Dunne and, later, Joe Kinnear. At Ipswich, the emergence of Mick Mills was to hinder Tommy's career so in 1971 he signed for Birmingham City. After little more than a season at St Andrews he was forced to retire because of injury.

TURLOUGH O'CONNOR ▼

1967–1973

8 **1**
CAPS GOALS

BORN Athlone, 22.7.46
DEBUT v Czechoslovakia (A) 22.11.67
CLUBS Fulham, Dundalk, Bohemians

Twenty-one-year-old striker Turlough O'Connor faced a stern test when he made his international debut against Czechoslovakia in Prague.
And the Fulham striker did not disappoint. A weakened Ireland team was given little chance against opponents who had won 2–0 in Dublin six months before. But with five minutes to go, and the score at 1–1, Turlough struck in true 'Roy Race' style, sending an unerring header into the net.

Such an entrance should have signalled the start of a long international career but O'Connor was struggling at

where in the back four, and on occasion was used to good effect in midfield. Tony's greatest asset was his ability to read the game, a strength appreciated by Mick Meagan, who handed him the first of his 14 caps in a World Cup match against Denmark. Tony performed with much élan and at the end of 90 minutes the Danes had breached the Ireland goal only once, via a penalty five minutes from time. For the next three years, under both Meagan and his successor Liam Tuohy, Tony remained a regular in the Ireland squad where his versatility was much valued. But at the age of 28, Tony found himself out of favour at Southampton and joined Third Division Hereford United. Despite helping United to promotion in his second season at Edgar Street, the step down the divisions had, in effect, brought Tony Byrne's international career to a premature close.

MICK LEECH ▼

1969–1972

8	2
CAPS	GOALS

BORN	Dublin, 6.8.48
DEBUT	v Czechoslovakia (H) 4.5.69
CLUBS	Shamrock Rovers

For one glorious season Mick Leech appeared to be the 'natural goalscorer' so long absent from the Republic of Ireland line-up. In 1968-69 the Shamrock Rovers hitman helped himself to 56 goals and offered the promise of a bright international future.

Like all footballers, Mick's game had its weaknesses – he was not the quickest or most industrious player – but for one season his knack of hitting the target was unrivalled. Inside the area he was always looking to shake off his marker. His first touch was immaculate, and he seemed able to deliver a goal-bound shot at any angle.

The inevitable call-up to the full international team arrived shortly after Rovers' 1969 FAI Cup final victory. But Mick was given little opportunity to live up to expectations and was kicked out of the game after 44 minutes. Fortunately he recovered to play in the remaining two World Cup fixtures that summer.

It had been a season to remember for Mick Leech but there would be no repeat performance in 1969–70. With Eric Barber leading scorer at Rovers, and Don Givens grabbing goals and headlines in the national team, Leech began to lose his status as Irish football's great hope. In 1972 he earned a recall to the international team but his chance had gone. Mick won just one more cap, as a substitute, despite continuing to score regularly at club level.

TONY BYRNE ▼

1969–1973

14	0
CAPS	GOALS

BORN	Rathdowney, 2.2.46
DEBUT	v Denmark (H) 15.10.69
CLUBS	Southampton

Tony Byrne was was born in Ireland, but grew up in England and began his career with Millwall before moving on to Southampton in 1964. The move from Den to Dell was the making of Byrne and, although he never truly became a regular in the Saints line-up, he established himself as a reliable First Division performer during ten years with the Hampshire club. An aggressive and competitive player, Tony could operate any-

> *Paddy was a superb reader of the game, who combined both stamina and strength with an enthusiasm for breaking forward.*

1969–1979

50 CAPS   **1** GOALS

BORN ● Dublin, 17.3.45
DEBUT ● v Czechoslovakia (H) 4.5.69
CLUBS ● Shamrock Rovers, Chelsea, Crystal Palace, West Bromwich Albion, Shamrock Rovers

Paddy Mulligan cost Chelsea a record fee for a League of Ireland player when he swapped Shamrock Rovers for Stamford Bridge in October 1969. The previous June, Blues manager Dave Sexton, had visited Dublin to check the form of goalscoring sensation Mick Leech but had been so impressed with Paddy's performance for the Republic of Ireland against Hungary that he made a successful, £17,500 bid for the versatile Hoops defender. It was something of a surprise move for Paddy who, at 24, was older than most of the footballers who were making their way across the Irish Sea. But after adjusting to life as a full-time professional during his first season with the Blues, Paddy's determined approach earned him an extended run in the Chelsea first team during the 1970–71 season.

Paddy Mulligan

Sexton had bought Paddy as a specialist right-back but for Ireland the enthusiastic Dubliner was deployed in a wide variety of defensive roles. He had made his international bow while a Shamrock Rovers player – wearing the number three shirt – in an ill-tempered World Cup tie against Czechoslovakia at Dalymount Park in May 1969. The Czechs, keen to settle an old score after the boys in green had blocked their passage to the 1968 European Championships, were out to intimidate. But Paddy was nothing if not wholehearted and he emerged with much credit despite the match ending in a 2–1 reverse for Ireland. There would be many more international appearances at left-back but Paddy was also used on the right side of defence and even more frequently as one of two centre-halves – usually alongside the imposing figure of Chelsea team-mate John Dempsey.

Paddy's willingness to play in such a variety of positions was indicative of his professional approach to the game which made him a popular figure with both colleagues and supporters alike. This refreshingly enthusiastic attitude was undoubtedly one of Paddy's greatest attributes, but he should not be dismissed as merely an 'honest pro'. Paddy was a superb reader of the game, who combined both stamina and strength with an enthusiasm for breaking forward and, in particular, for overlapping. He was also a good header of the ball and, but for a slight lack of inches, would have made a formidable centre-half at both club and international level.

Although Paddy was a regular in the national team for some ten years, his career at club level did not follow such a steady path. In 1972 he found himself playing most of his football in the Chelsea reserve team, so when south London team Crystal Palace offered a route back to first-team action Paddy made the switch across the capital to Selhurst. However, after three years with the Eagles he was on the move again, this time joining John Giles's West Bromwich Albion. The Hawthorns was to be a happy home for Paddy Mulligan and in his three seasons in the Midlands as an Albion player he made more than 100 League appearances. Giles, who was also the Ireland boss at that time, clearly knew how to get the best work out of Paddy and awarded him 28 of his 50 caps, several of them as captain. Both player and manager would return to their native Dublin with Shamrock Rovers in the late 1970s and it was as a Rovers player that Paddy made his final international appearance, against the USA at Dalymount Park in 1979.

A fiery competitor, Don's commitment to the Irish cause was never in doubt.

1969–1981

56 **19**

CAPS GOALS

BORN — Limerick, 9.8.49
DEBUT — v Denmark (A) 27.5.69
CLUBS — Manchester United, Luton Town, Queen's Park Rangers, Birmingham City, Neuchatel Xamax

What a pity that Don Givens arrived on the international stage at a time when the Republic of Ireland's team was at its lowest ebb and when goalscoring opportunities were rare to non-existent. Fortunately for the Irish selectors, who had cast the teenage striker in such an awkward role, Don proved himself thrifty with the smattering of chances that came his way and he emerged from the first phase of his senior career with an impressive goal tally.

Don Givens

Givens, a centre-forward of obvious potential, had captained the Manchester United youth team but had yet to make an appearance in the Reds' first XI when he was handed his international debut in a World Cup match against Denmark in 1969. A 2–0 defeat against the Danes left Ireland with little hope of qualifying for Mexico, but Givens had shown up well enough to retain his place in the team for the next match against Hungary, in Dublin. The visitors took a first-half lead but, to the delight of the Dalymount crowd, Givens met a Frank O'Neill cross to smash the ball home and get Ireland back on terms. The match would follow an all-too-familiar pattern and, with ten minutes to go, Hungary struck the game's winning goal. In a disappointing qualifying campaign Givens had provided the only cause for optimism among Ireland fans and, when the six-game programme was over, the men in green had scored just three goals and won just one point. Givens' record was rather more impressive and stood at five games played and two goals scored. The young striker had already begun to monopolise his country's scoring and in his first seven caps he claimed all four of Ireland's goals.

Despite Don's impressive international achievements he was still making little headway towards a first-team berth at Old Trafford and in 1970 he was sold to Luton Town for a paltry £15,000. But after just over two seasons and 19 goals for the Bedfordshire side, Don joined Second Division rivals Queens Park Rangers. At Loftus Road, he would enjoy the most settled and productive spell of his career. In six seasons with the West London

club he scored 76 League goals and won 29 caps. Don had kicked off at Rangers in great style, registering 23 League goals as he helped his new club win promotion to the First Division in 1972-73. Back in the top-flight both club and player flourished and in 1975–76 Rangers finished runners-up to Liverpool.

A peerless leader of the line, he combined a crisp first touch with both stamina and aggression. He was also strong in the air and packed a fierce shot. A fiery competitor, Don's commitment to the Irish cause was never in doubt. He was sent off on two occasions while wearing the green of Ireland, both dismissals coming against South American opposition on summer tours, the first for alleged rough play against Ecuador and the second for a misdemeanour against Chile.

After his initial flurry of international scoring, the goal trail ran dry for Limerick-born Givens in the early 1970s. But after an 11-game barren spell, the drought came to a dramatic end as Don registered a hat-trick against the USSR in Dublin. It was the first treble scored by a Republic of Ireland player since Paddy Moore had 'done the trick' 40 years before. A day short of the anniversary of Don's first hat-trick he went one better to grab four against Turkey and in so doing set an individual scoring record for one match for the Republic of Ireland. Don was by now enjoying a productive attacking partnership with Ray Treacy, and with the front two well-supplied by the likes of Steve Heighway, John Giles and Liam Brady, Ireland began to find the net with a little more regularity. In May 1976 Don added another record to his growing collection of achievements when he struck twice against Poland to top Noel Cantwell's tally of 14 and become his country's most prolific marksman with 16 goals.

Don would add three more goals to his account, but as the 1970s drew to a close so did the international career of Ireland's record scorer. In 1978 he left QPR to join Birmingham City and after two seasons at St Andrews, began to ply his trade in the lower reaches of the Football League with Bournemouth and, later, Sheffield United. This somewhat sudden decline had coincided with the emergence of Frank Stapleton as a top-class striker and, though a Stapleton-Givens partnership was employed for a short while, Don's days in green were numbered. The Republic's failure to qualify for the 1982 World Cup signalled the end of Don Givens' international career.

EOIN HAND

1969–1975

 20 **CAPS**   2 **GOALS**

BORN	Dublin, 30.3.46
DEBUT	v Czechoslovakia (H) 4.5.69
CLUBS	Portsmouth

A tough, uncomprimising centre-half who could also play up front, Eoin Hand was somewhat surprisingly used in midfield throughout much of his six-year international career. It was a role that Eoin took to with relish, and the extra security which the Dubliner gave Ireland's rearguard was greatly appreciated by managers Liam Tuohy and John Giles. But Hand was not just a spoiler, as he proved against France at Dalymount Park in 1972, when, after chasing what appeared a lost cause, he delivered a perfect centre for Ray Treacy to score the goal which gave Ireland a first home win in six years.

Eoin's career, which had recovered from an early false-start at Swindon Town as a teenager, began in earnest at Drumcondra where he played at centre-forward. A second chance in England arrived with Second Division Portsmouth in 1968 and after switching to defence Eoin became a regular in the Hampshire club's first-team for seven seasons. And it was as a Pompey player that Eoin won all 20 of his international caps, the first of which came as a substitute for the injured Mick Leech in a bad tempered match against Czechoslovakia in Dublin.

Although Eoin made occasional appearances under Mick Meagan and Liam Tuohy, his best form for Ireland was to come with John Giles in charge. During this period, Eoin proved himself a versatile and whole-hearted performer. He was also a threat from set-pieces, scoring a memorable header against Chile in 1974. The emergence of Liam Brady forced Eoin to move back from his midfield berth to a more familiar defensive position, but when Ireland failed to qualify for the 1976 European Championships his international career was at an end. A return to the homeland followed shortly afterwards, with Hand one of a number of experienced internationals to join Giles's Shamrock Rovers experiment. Thereafter Eoin moved into management as player-coach with Limerick before taking over as manager of the national team from 1980 until 1985.

MICK LAWLOR ▼

1970–1973

5 CAPS   **0** GOALS

BORN   Dublin, 1948
DEBUT   v Poland (H) 23.9.70
CLUBS   Shamrock Rovers

Expectations were always likely to be high for the son of former Ireland international Kit Lawlor. Fortunately for Mick – an effervescent and energetic midfielder who could also play in the forward line – skill was on his side and during a long career in League of Ireland football, Lawlor jnr won every major domestic honour.

Mick began his senior career with Shamrock Rovers and it was as a Hoops player that he accrued all five of his international caps. With English-based players frequently crying off from Ireland matches in the early 1970s, Mick was one of a number of 'locals' to take advantage. A debut against Poland at Dalymount Park was cut short when Mick was injured shortly before half-time, but the new boy had already made a significant impression, coming close to scoring with an effort that struck a Polish post. Mick would stay in the team for the next three games. A fifth cap, also against Poland, came after an absence of two years. Thereafter Mick enjoyed continued success at club level, winning the double with Dundalk in 1978–79 but did not return to the international team.

NOEL CAMPBELL ▼

1971–1977

11 CAPS   **0** GOALS

BORN   Dublin, 11.12.49
DEBUT   Austria (H) 30.5.71
CLUBS   St Patrick's Athletic, Fortuna Cologne

When red-haired midfield livewire Noel Campbell decided the time was right to leave the League of Ireland for pastures new he chose to ignore the well-trodden path to England. Instead he opted to join Fortuna Cologne in West Germany's Second Division. It was a surprising, transfer but the popular Dubliner remained in Germany for eight seasons.

Noel had begun his career as a goalscoring midfielder with St Patrick's Athletic, and it was as a St Pat's player that he broke into the full international team, coming on as a substitute in Mick Meagan's final match in charge in 1971. Though never a regular, Noel made occasional appearances for Ireland throughout the 1970s, enjoying his best run in the team in 1972 when he appeared in all six of Ireland's international matches.

A popular and skilful footballer, Noel was widely regarded as one of the best players to emerge from the League of Ireland during the 1970s. Unfortunately, Noel's international career ended on something of a sour note, when he was sent off after coming on as a substitute in a World Cup match against Bulgaria.

MICK KEARNS ▲

1970–1979

18 CAPS   **0** GOALS

BORN   Banbury, 26.11.50
DEBUT   v Poland (H) 23.9.70
CLUBS   Oxford United, Walsall, Wolverhampton Wanderers

Alan Kelly's retirement from international football in 1973 led to a three-way tussle for Ireland's number one jersey. Both Paddy Roche and Peter Thomas were given their chances between the posts but after much deliberation it was Walsall's Mick Kearns who established himself. Kearns – who qualified for Ireland through his Mayo-born parents – made his debut as a sub in a friendly against Poland in 1970. He played for just 14 minutes but that brief cameo was enough to make the 19-year-old the Republic of Ireland's youngest ever full international.

A second cap arrived three years later, but it was in 1976 that Mick became Ireland's first choice keeper. By then he was in the midst of a six-year spell with Walsall. Fortunately, the 6'3" custodian had little difficulty making the step up from Third Division to international football, producing a memorable display against France at Lansdowne Road in 1977. His fortunes took a turn for the worse after Walsall's relegation to Division Four in 1978–79 and shortly afterwards he lost his place in the Ireland team to Gerry Peyton.

At his best Heighway was capable of lifting the whole team with his fleet-footed wing raiding.

1970–1981

34 **0**

CAPS GOALS

BORN Dublin, 25.11.47
DEBUT v Poland (H) 23.9.70
CLUBS Liverpool, Minnesota Kicks

Steve Heighway was one of the great enigmas of Irish football. How was it that this talented wing wizard could inspire Liverpool to a succession of trophies, yet when red shirt was swapped for green the magic all too often disappeared? In 11 years of international football Steve made 34 appearances and failed to score in any of them. It is true that at club level he played in a team which was both confident and packed full of talented individuals, a situation in marked contrast to the Republic of Ireland set-up he entered in the early 1970s. It must also be said that the Merseysiders' burgeoning fixture list conspired to restrict Steve's tally of caps. But, despite these mitigating factors it is impossible not to feel that Steve Heighway's international career could have delivered so much more.

Steve Heighway

Whatever the disappointments of his days with the boys in green, at his best Heighway was capable of lifting the whole team with his fleet-footed wing raiding. 'Big Bamber' – so nicknamed because of his university education – provided much needed pace in an otherwise pedestrian attack and his direct, high-octane approach was the perfect complement to the considered, patient passing of Giles and Brady. Heighway was also a skilful crosser of the ball and his early centres were gratefully received by Messrs. Don Givens and Ray Treacy.

Liverpool manager Bill Shankly had been quick to recognise the Dubliner's talent and, following his arrival from non-League Skelmersdale United, wasted little time installing the gangly winger in the Reds' first-team. September 1970 was to be a memorable month in the career of Steve Heighway. Following his senior debut for Liverpool, in the League Cup, he found himself included in the Ireland team for the match against Poland at Dalymount Park. His selection was particularly significant, as for the first time the team had been picked by manager Mick Meagan. By the end of his first season as a professional, Heighway had added four more caps to his tally and had scored a goal in the FA Cup final against 'double'-winners Arsenal.

Although Heighway's game undoubtedly relied upon certain instinctive qualities, careful nurturing by the Liverpool coaches helped him to develop into a more complete attacking player. By the mid-1970s he was no longer insistent on bursting down the outside of full-backs, and had improved his effectiveness by adding a willingness to both come inside his marker and drop deep to collect the ball. He had also become a valuable source of goals for the Reds, as the Anfield club set off on a ruthless quest for silverware. A Heighway goal would help claim the 1974 FA Cup, and two assists from the Dubliner ensured a European Cup victory in 1977.

But success for Liverpool did nothing for Ireland's cause, only serving to restrict Heighway's appearances and raise expectations among the fans. The situation reached crisis point in May 1973 when the Reds winger declared himself unavailable for selection for a series of matches during the summer. Heighway claimed he was exhausted after a long season with Liverpool but for manager Liam Tuohy it was a huge disappointment to lose his key attacking player. Shortly afterwards John Giles took over as Ireland boss, but Liverpool's schedule got no easier and the problem persisted.

The new manager did at least oversee Heighway's best performances for Ireland. Under Giles, the Liverpool man was frequently used in a roving striker's role with a brief to attack at will. From such a position, Big Bamber was at his most menacing, as he proved against England at Wembley in 1976 when his trickery earned Ireland a penalty in a memorable 1–1 draw. But as Heighway entered his thirties, he was forced to compete with a new crop of Irish forwards which included the highly-rated Michael Robinson and, in 1981, having left Liverpool to join Minnesota Kicks, he played his last international in a notable 2–2 draw against the Dutch in Rotterdam.

Since hanging up his boots, Steve has enjoyed great success as a key member of the Liverpool youth development programme which has brought through so many talented young players in recent years.

PADDY DUNNING
1970
Born: Dublin, 1951
Caps: 2
Goals: 0
Debut v Sweden (A) 28.10.70
Clubs: Shelbourne

Paddy Dunning got his chance at international level following an impressive display for the League of Ireland against the Scottish League in 1970. Although a centre-half by preference, Paddy had been played at left-back against the Scots from where he nullified the considerable threat posed by Celtic forward Jimmy Johnstone. The following month, Mick Meagan called Paddy into the Ireland team for two consecutive European Championship qualifiers against Sweden and Italy. Both fixtures were played on foreign soil and, despite the manager opting for defensive line-ups, both ended in defeats. Paddy was neither singled out for blame nor criticised for his performances but at 19 years old he had played his last full international.

JOHN HERRICK
1971–1973
Born: Cork, 1947
Caps: 3
Goals: 0
Debut v Austria (A) 10.10.71
Clubs: Cork Hibernians, Shamrock Rovers

John Herrick was a tough-tackling left-back and a key player in the strong Cork team of the early 1970s. He was one of a number of League of Ireland players to make his debut in Liam Tuohy's first game in charge – an ill-fated 6–0 reverse against Austria in Linz. Two more appearances in the green shirt followed, both as substitute for Tommy Carroll. In the last of these (a World Cup tie in 1973), John played a key role in a memorable 1–1 draw against France at the Parc des Princes.

PADDY ROCHE
1971–1975
Born: Dublin, 4.1.51
Caps: 8
Goals: 0
Debut v Austria (A) 10.10.71
Clubs: Shelbourne, Manchester United

Paddy Roche was a goalkeeper of immense natural ability whose greatest flaw was a lack of confidence. At his best the slightly built Dubliner was a custodian of the highest quality, although his reputation was somewhat tarnished after a spate of media criticism after a 'mistake' while playing for Manchester United against Liverpool in 1975–76. Paddy had joined the United from Shelbourne and it was as a 20-year-old Shels player that he made his international debut in Liam Tuohy's scratch team that leaked six goals against Austria. Fortunately, the experience left no lasting scars and Paddy recovered to enjoy an excellent run of form upon his return to the international line-up in 1973.

DAMIEN RICHARDSON
1971–1979
Born: Dublin, 2.8.47
Caps: 3
Goals: 0
Debut v Austria (A) 10.10.71
Clubs: Shamrock Rovers, Gillingham

Despite a modest international record, Damien Richardson was a striker without any obvious weaknesses who enjoyed successful spells on both sides of the Irish Sea. Strong on the ground and good in the air, Damien proved himself a reliable goalscorer in the League of Ireland during the late 1960s but it was not until 1972 that he made the move to England. A transfer to Preston North End had fallen through three years earlier and Damien was 24 years old when he joined Fourth Division Gillingham. By then the Dubliner was already a full international and during a nine-year spell at Priestfield Stadium he added two more caps to his tally.

MICK GANNON
1971
Born: Dublin, 2.2.47. Caps: 1 Goals: 0
Debut v Austria (A) 10.10.71. Clubs: Shelbourne

Mick Gannon was a diminutive but tenacious left-back who enjoyed a long and successful career in the League of Ireland with Dublin clubs Shelbourne and Shamrock Rovers. A skilful attacker, Mick was on occasion used in midfield, though it was in the number two shirt that he made his international debut, in Liam Tuohy's first game as manager. That match ended in a 6–0 defeat against Austria in Linz, and despite consistent displays at club level Mick made no further appearances for Ireland.

MICK KEARIN
1971
Born: Kildare. Caps: 1 Goals: 0
Debut v Austria (A) 10.10.71. Clubs: Shamrock Rovers

Mick Kearin was the kind of all-action midfield player that every successful team needs. A tough tackler, he was always at the hub of things and though he rarely scored he was a vital component in Shamrock Rovers' successful FAI Cup team of the late 1960s. Mick's one and only appearance for the full international team came in the disastrous 6–0 European Championship defeat against Austria in Linz.

JIMMY DUNNE
1971
Born: Dublin, 1.12.47
Caps: 1
Goals: 0
Debut v Austria (H) 30.5.71
Clubs: Fulham

Jimmy Dunne endured a painful introduction to international football. On a miserable Sunday at Dalymount Park, the Dublin-born centre-half stretched to intercept a cross but succeeded only in turning the ball past his own keeper for the most unwelcome of debut goals in a 4–1 defeat by Austria. It was an unfortunate start for a player with a reputation as an astute and constructive passer of the ball. Jimmy, who enjoyed a lengthy career in England with Fulham and Torquay United, was given no second chance in the green of Ireland.

PETER THOMAS
1973–1974
Born: Coventry, 20.11.44
Caps: 2
Goals: 0
Debut v Poland (H) 21.10.73
Clubs: Waterford

But for the small matter of two or three inches Waterford goalkeeper Peter Thomas would surely have become Ireland's regular number one. Peter was a ruthless competitor and an agile shot-stopper who arrived at Waterford from Coventry City in 1967. His impact at Kilcohan Park was instant and in his first season Waterford claimed the League title. In 1970, Peter was named the Irish soccer writers' Personality of the Year and in 1972 – after five years in Ireland – the man from Coventry successfully applied for Irish citizenship. A clean sheet on his international debut, against Poland in Dublin, ensured Peter kept his place for the next match, against Brazil in Rio. Ireland lost that game 2-1 and, although Peter was not held culpable, his international career was brought to an abrupt end.

JOE WATERS
1976–1979
Born: Limerick, 20.9.53
Caps: 2
Goals: 1
Debut v Turkey (A) 13.10.76
Clubs: Grimsby Town

Two caps was scant reward for a footballer of Joe Waters' talent, but it was difficult to argue the Limerick man's case for a regular berth when the players blocking his path were Messrs. John Giles and Liam Brady. A skilful and busy midfield player, Joe enjoyed a long and successful spell with Grimsby Town, whom he joined from Leicester City in 1976. During his time with the Mariners he won both his caps, the first coming at right-back against Turkey in 1976. From this unlikely position, Joe marked his debut with the equalising goal in a 3–3 draw. Despite this bright start he was forced to wait three years for a second cap, which arrived in November 1979 when Joe replaced Gerry Daly in the match against Northern Ireland in Belfast.

RON HEALEY
1977–1980
Born: Manchester, 30.8.52
Caps: 2
Goals: 0
Debut v Poland (H) 24.4.77
Clubs: Cardiff City

Manchester-born Ron Healey began his career as understudy to Manchester City's goalkeeping legend Joe Corrigan, but with little chance of a first-team berth he moved on to Cardiff City in 1974. During a five-year spell as the Bluebirds' number one, Ron made two appearances for the full international team. His debut against Poland in 1977 saw the Ireland defence keep a clean sheet, but despite this promising start it was three years before John Giles called upon the Cardiff keeper again. That match against England, was his only other appearance for the Republic of Ireland. Two years later, Ron Healey's career was ended by injury.

TOMMY McCONVILLE
1971–1973
Born: Dundalk, 1947 Caps: 6 Goals: 0
Debut v Austria (A) 10.10.71 Clubs: Dundalk, Waterford

Tommy McConville was a versatile, committed defender who enjoyed a long and successful career in the League of Ireland. For a time it seemed that he would move to England, with a move to Manchester United strongly rumoured, but the speculation came to nothing and Tommy stayed in Ireland. Shortly afterwards, Liam Tuohy handed him his first full cap – in the 6-0 defeat against Austria in Linz. A move to Waterford and a recall to Tuohy's international line-up for a World Cup match against the Soviet Union at Lansdowne Road followed in 1972. Tommy stayed in the team for the next four matches, but then John Giles took over as manager of the national team and Tommy days in green were over.

EAMONN FAGAN
1973
Born: Dublin. Caps: 1 Goals: 0
Debut v Norway (A) 6.6.73. Clubs: Shamrock Rovers

Eamonn Fagan's international career lasted precisely 11 minutes and, appropriately enough, arrived under the one-match reign of Sean Thomas in 1973. Eamonn, who also won two under-23 caps, was a composed defender who could also operate in midfield.

... his aggressive, energetic approach made him the perfect foil for the likes of Giles and Liam Brady.

1971–1983

52 CAPS **4** GOALS

BORN • Dublin, 9.7.51
DEBUT • v Austria (A) 10.10.71
CLUBS • Bohemians, Manchester United,
West Bromwich Albion, Newcastle United

On 10 October 1971, Republic of Ireland manager Liam Tuohy cast seven fresh-faced debutants into the deep and dark waters of international football. Six of the seven would sink with barely a trace – making just 16 more appearances between them – while only one would prove himself in soccer's most demanding environs. It was no surprise that the player with the bright future should be Bohemians midfielder Mick Martin. After all, Mick's father, Con, had also been an international footballer, winning 30 Republic of Ireland and six Northern Ireland caps during the 1940s and 1950s. The burden of a famous name can weigh heavily upon a young player, but for 'Mick-son-of-Con' it seems to have been carried with ease.

Mick Martin

An early move to England was, no doubt, a key factor in helping Martin Jnr. shake off persistent comparison with his dad. Mick had made his debut for Ireland as a 20-year-old and – after continued good form for club and country – became Irish football's most coveted and highly-rated youngster. Tommy Docherty, the newly-appointed manager of Manchester United in December 1972, was suitably impressed by the tall, energetic utility man and paid Bohemians £20,000 – a record fee for a League of Ireland player – to take him to Old Trafford in January 1973. But Mick's spell under the Doc was far from happy. He had joined a team which had little by way of either confidence or direction at a club where expectations had been raised enormousley high by the great successes of the Busby years.

In his first season as a Red (1972–73), Mick played the anchor-role in midfield and did well enough to hold down a regular place in the team. However, the following campaign saw the Dubliner reduced to a bit-part player as United crashed out of the First Division. Mick stayed long enough to see Docherty's team regain their top-flight status but after just 40 League appearances in two-and-a-half years the time was right for a move. One man more aware than most of Mick's quality was John Giles, man-

ager of Ireland and West Bromwich Albion. A transfer to The Hawthorns duly arrived in the autumn of 1975.

Despite his difficult spell at Old Trafford, Mick had continued to command a place in the Republic of Ireland line-up and during the managerial reigns of both Liam Tuohy and John Giles he won more caps than any other player. Throughout most of his international career Mick was used as the holding player, operating just in front of the back-four. He was a hardworking individual and his aggressive, energetic approach made him the perfect foil for the likes of Giles and Liam Brady. Mick was also used to good effect to mark threatening play makers – as he proved against Portugal's Eusebio in 1972. But Mick was more than just a midfield spoiler: he managed a very respectable total for a midfielder of four goals in his days with the boys in green.

Strong in the air but not one of the quickest over the ground, Mick somewhat inevitably moved back into defence later in his career. The number on his shirt, though, mattered little to Mick Martin and whether at centre-half or inside-forward you could rely on him for a committed, whole hearted performance. These qualities made Mick an ideal candidate for the job of captain and in 1976 John Giles handed his West Brom team-mate the arm-band for the match against Norway at Dalymount Park. It was an honour he would enjoy on four further occasions. Like many tough, all-action ball winners Mick's great strengths could also be his downfall and he was dismissed twice while playing for his country. The second occasion – against Bulgaria in June 1977, when he and Noel Campbell became involved in a four-man brawl – signalled the start of a 23-month exile from international football.

When Mick returned to the international scene it was as a Newcastle United player. He had joined the Magpies in 1978 and would enjoy a successful spell on Tyneside, making 147 League appearances in four seasons. During his time in the North East, Mick remained a regular member of the international squads selected by Giles, and later Eoin Hand. However, in April 1983 he made his last appearance in the green shirt, playing alongside David O'Leary and Mark Lawrenson in a 2-0 defeat against Spain. Mick Martin retired from international football as a veteran of 52 caps... the question now was should it be 'Mick-son-of-Con', or 'Con-father-of-Mick'?

JIMMY HOLMES

1971–1981

30 CAPS **1** GOALS

BORN Dublin, 11.11.53
DEBUT v Austria (H) 30.5.71
CLUBS Coventry City, Tottenham Hotspur, Vancouver Whitecaps

Jimmy Holmes was the Republic of Ireland's youngest ever full-international when he made his debut as a substitute in Mick Meagan's final match in charge of the national team in 1971. At just 17 years and 200 days old, Holmes was still no more than a promising full-back trying to make the grade at First Division Coventry City, but Meagan – a former flank defender himself – had recognised a player of obvious potential.

It was more than a year before Holmes added a second cap to his historic first, but this time the Dubliner was on from the start, playing a key role in a somewhat unexpected 2–1 victory against France in a World Cup qualifier at Dalymount Park. Ireland boss Liam Tuohy was suitably impressed and kept Jimmy in the team for the remainder of his managerial tenure. In defence he was a reliable and consistent performer who combined good positional sense with pace and a biting tackle. Going forward, Jimmy was a sharp, enterprising player, and a keen overlapper. This zest for attacking play made him an ideal candidate to step forward into midfield when Tuohy was in need of added strength on the left side for a World Cup tie against the USSR in Moscow during the spring of 1973.

Jimmy would continue to enjoy the status of international regular following the appointment of John Giles as manager later in 1973, and the Coventry full-back showed his best form during the qualifying campaign for the 1976 European Championships. He also became his country's alloted penalty-taker and took two spot-kicks in consecutive games during 1975-76. The first, against Turkey at Dalymount, was saved by the keeper but Jimmy held his nerve and took the next one, against Norway, and slotted home the second goal in a 3-0 win.

A move to struggling Tottenham Hotspur followed on transfer deadline day in 1977. Alas Jimmy had joined a team destined for Division Two and, despite his goal in the season's final fixture, Spurs were relegated. Jimmy stayed at White Hart Lane and a year later helped the Lilywhites regain their place in the top-flight. However, after enjoying his first full season back amongst English football's elite, disaster struck. A broken leg sustained after 58 minutes of Ireland's European Championship qualifier against Bulgaria in Sofia in May 1979 left the career of Jimmy Holmes in ruins. He patiently worked himself back to full fitness but, although he gained one last cap in a friendly against Wales, he was unable to regain his best form and began to wind down his career with brief spells at several English League clubs.

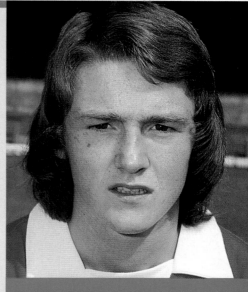

MIAH DENNEHY

1972–1977

12 CAPS   **2** GOALS

BORN	Cork, 29.3.50
DEBUT	v Ecuador (N) 18.6.72
CLUBS	Cork Hibernians, Nottingham Forest, Walsall

Miah Dennehy was a fleet-footed forward who could tease and trick his way past opponents with ease. He had pace and a sharp footballing brain and although he was frequently played on the wing, was at his happiest through the middle.

Miah – who spent eight seasons in England with Nottingham Forest, Walsall and Bristol Rovers – began his career with Cork Hibernians and helped his hometown club to League success in 1971, scoring a hat-trick in a play-off match against Shamrock Rovers. At the end of the following season, the versatile forward was called into Liam Tuohy's squad for the mini-World Cup in Brazil. He would remain on the fringes of the international team, making six appearances during Tuohy's time in charge. Miah scored two goals in Ireland green, the second of which was the opening strike of the John Giles era, arriving in a friendly against Poland.

TERRY MANCINI

1973–1974

5 CAPS   **1** GOALS

BORN	London, 4.10.42
DEBUT	v Poland (H) 21.10.73
CLUBS	Queens Park Rangers, Arsenal

Terry Mancini's stint with the boys in green was an all-too brief episode in a long and colourful career. A tough, no-nonsense centre-half, Terry qualified for Ireland by virtue of his Irish-born mother and made his debut in John Giles's first game in charge. The new manager was clearly impressed and kept the QPR defender in the team for a summer tour of South America. Terry, a renowned dressing-room joker, was unfazed by his elevation to international status at the age of 31 and scored Ireland's only goal in a 2–1 defeat to world champions Brazil in Rio.

After caps in four consecutive matches the stopper with the Italian name lined up in Ireland's colours for his first competitive match, a European Championships qualifier against the USSR at Dalymount Park in October 1974. The match ended in a 3–0 win for Giles's team, but for Terry it had finished sooner than expected when he was sent off for fighting with a Soviet player. It would be Terry Mancini's last appearance in the green shirt of Ireland.

RAY O'BRIEN

1976–1980

5 CAPS   **0** GOALS

BORN	Dublin, 21.5.51
DEBUT	v Norway (H) 24.3.76
CLUBS	Notts County

Ray O'Brien, son of former Drumcondra midfielder Frank, was a wholehearted and attacking left-back. He began his career with Shelbourne, but moved to England in 1973 where, after failing to make the first team at Manchester United, he enjoyed nine years with Notts County.

At Meadow Lane, the combative Dubliner proved a hugely popular player and his committed displays on the left flank won him great acclaim. He was also a regular goalscorer for Notts, and it came as no surprise when Forest manager Brian Clough registered his interest in the tough-tackling full-back. Despite the speculation, there was to be no move across town, and Ray stayed to help County gain promotion to the top-flight in 1981. By then, he had already accrued all five of his Republic of Ireland caps. Ray made all his appearances in friendlies, and his final cap arrived, after an absence of three years, in a match against world champions Argentina in the summer of 1980.

He could pass, had bags of skill and, of course, could shoot with both power and unerring accuracy.

1973–1986

48 CAPS   **13** GOALS

BORN ● Dublin, 30.4.54
DEBUT ● v Poland (A) 16.5.73
CLUBS ● Manchester United, Derby County, Coventry City, Birmingham City, Shrewsbury Town

Gerry Daly's goalscoring record for Ireland was nothing short of phenomenal. 13 goals in 37 starts would be an impressive strike-rate for any international centre-forward but coming, as they did, from the boot of a midfielder it was all the more remarkable. Aside from frontline forwards, no player has scored more goals for the Republic of Ireland. However, it would be wrong to get carried away with the notion that Gerry Daly's only significant contribution was to put ball in net. The wiry Dubliner was a sharp, incisive footballer whose resilience to midfield intimidation belied his slender frame. He could pass, had bags of skill and, of course, could shoot with both power and unerring accuracy.

Gerry Daly

Gerry began with Bohemians but in 1973 booked what appeared to be a fast-track ticket to soccer's big time when he signed for Tommy Docherty's Manchester United in an £18,000 deal. Alas, things did not go to plan and in his first full season at Old Trafford – 1973–74 – the Reds were relegated to the Second Division. By then, though, Gerry was already a full international, having made his debut as a substitute in a friendly against Poland shortly after his transfer to England. It would, however, be some time before the 19-year-old Dubliner enjoyed a run in the Ireland team and a change of managers later in 1973 – from Liam Tuohy to John Giles – meant that Gerry could take little for granted at international level.

At Old Trafford, at least, things began to look up, and in 1974–75 the Reds won back their place in English football's top-flight. Gerry had also started to show his true ability and was beginning to become an increasingly influential figure in Tommy Docherty's exciting young team. Giles could ignore him no longer and – after two substitute appearances – gave Gerry his first start, against West Germany 'B' at Dalymount Park in 1975. Continued good form at club level kept the adroit Dubliner on the fringe of the international team throughout the next season, 1975–76, and following his superb

performance against England at Wembley in September 1976 he became a regular in the Republic of Ireland line-up for the remainder of the 1970s. Gerry – a spot-kick specialist – had scored a penalty against the English to register his first international goal and earn a celebrated draw.

Just as it seemed that Gerry's career was moving back into the ascendant he found himself out of the first team at Old Trafford. In November 1976, Docherty had signed Stoke City striker Jimmy Greenhoff and in the resultant reshuffle Sammy McIlroy had been moved back to midfield. Gerry was the player to lose out and by the following March, Docherty had sold him to Derby County for £180,000. The Scotsman would leave United himself at season's end, also heading for Derby County's Baseball Ground – an irony that, no doubt, failed to amuse Gerry Daly. Despite their awkward past, both player and manager would spend two seasons working together at the Midlands club.

The arrival of Eoin Hand as coach of the national team in 1980 coincided with Gerry's best run of form in the green shirt. The laid-back Dubliner – who scored three times in Hand's first four matches in charge – would prove a highly valued source of both goals and inspiration in an Ireland team which narrowly missed out on qualification for the 1982 World Cup finals. Gerry, by now a Coventry City player, had become an important component in a midfield which boasted the disparate talents of Liam Brady, Tony Grealish and Gary Waddock.

However, by the mid 1980s injuries and loss of form had taken their toll on him, and the name Daly was appearing with less frequency on Republic of Ireland team sheets. A lack of stability at club level did not help his international hopes and following a loan spell at Leicester City in 1982–83, there were transfers to Birmingham City, Shrewsbury Town, Stoke City and Doncaster Rovers. Despite these problems, Gerry retained his scoring touch and was still an occasional international when Jack Charlton took charge of the Ireland team in 1986. It was no great surprise when the first goal of Big Jack's tenure was scored by none other than Gerry Daly. That goal, from the penalty spot against Uruguay at Lansdowne Road, was followed by another in the next match against Iceland, but after just two more substitute appearances Gerry's days in green came to an end.

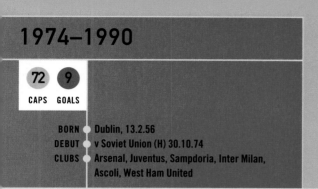

1974–1990

72 CAPS **9** GOALS

BORN	Dublin, 13.2.56
DEBUT	v Soviet Union (H) 30.10.74
CLUBS	Arsenal, Juventus, Sampdoria, Inter Milan, Ascoli, West Ham United

In 1986 Liam's iconic status within Irish football met a new challenge when the FAI appointed Jack Charlton as manager.

After signing off his playing days with a glorious long-range goal for West Ham United in 1990, Liam Brady declared that he was a lucky man. But, in truth, fortune was no significant force in a career which had seen the boy from Dublin's northside prove himself one of the finest midfielders of the 1970s and 1980s.

Liam Brady

Liam was a player of extraordinary talent who provided a rarely-seen blend of effective, entertaining football. A deadly accurate left foot was his primary weapon but his astute brain and unerring vision for a penetrating pass set Brady apart. Although nobody could have predicted the heights Liam would attain, it was no great surprise that football was his first love. Uncle Frank had been a member of the first Republic of Ireland team in 1926, while brothers Ray and Paddy had enjoyed success with Millwall and QPR. Upon leaving school Liam joined Arsenal as an apprentice. But in his early days at Highbury many doubted that the frail, wiry Dubliner would be able to cope in the First Division. Despite Arsenal's best efforts to beef him up, Liam's frame had barely altered when he made his first-team debut, shorts flapping around his spindly legs, as a 17 year old in October 1973. The following season he became a Gunners regular and quickly grew in confidence. Over the next few seasons he became an increasingly influential and popular figure.

Brady's progress had not gone unnoticed by Ireland boss John Giles. A year after making his debut for Arsenal he was called into the international team for a European Championships qualifier against the USSR. On a memorable afternoon at Dalymount Park, the new boy performed with great skill, playing alongside his manager in a famous victory. On the pitch, the Giles-Brady pairing had the purists purring. More importantly, the passing philosophy of Giles the manager was perfect for Liam.

In 1980 Liam made the bold decision to head for Italy. The Arsenal fans were distraught at losing a player who had guided them to four Cup finals in three years, and whose inspirational performance in the 1979 FA Cup win over Manchester United had brought the Gunners their first silverware since 1971. But their loss was Juventus's gain and in two seasons in Turin Liam was twice a League champion. Two seasons at Sampdoria and another two at Inter Milan followed, before Liam joined his last Italian club, Ascoli, in 1986. When he returned to England in March 1987, Liam had made 189 Serie A appearances and had cost combined transfer fees of more than £3m.

Throughout his time in Italy, Liam had remained a key figure for Ireland and in 1985 he became the youngest player to record 50 appearances for the national team when he played against England at Wembley. An undoubted hero to most who followed the boys in green, Liam also had his critics. They said he didn't tackle enough, that he didn't track back and that he only cared about his club football. In truth, most of this backbiting was born out of frustration at Ireland's failure to qualify for either World Cup finals or European Championships.

In 1986 Liam's iconic status within Irish football met a new challenge when the FAI appointed Jack Charlton as manager. Jack liked midfielders to get the ball forward early but Liam's style was to pass from the back, waiting for the right opening. As hard as Liam tried he was never going to be able to disguise his creative instincts enough for Big Jack. There was, however, a brief period of harmony during the qualifying rounds for the 1988 European Championships. Liam appeared in every game. But at the end of the campaign disaster struck. In the dying minutes of the final group match, against Bulgaria, he struck out at his over-eager marker and was shown the red card. The result was a suspension from the first two matches of the finals, although that was later rendered meaningless by a serious knee injury.

Liam's international career was all but at an end. Injuries and the emergence of Andy Townsend would restrict him to a handful of substitute appearances. The final straw came in 1989 when Charlton substituted him after just 35 minutes of a friendly against West Germany. Furious that the manager had humiliated him by hauling him off before half-time, Brady announced his retirement. He would continue with West Ham until the end of the 1989-90 season, since when he has worked as a players' agent and as a manager at both Celtic and Brighton and Hove Albion. Liam is currently the head of Arsenal's Youth Development Programme.

MICKY WALSH

1976–1984

21 **3**

CAPS GOALS

BORN ● Chorley, Lancashire, 13.8.54
DEBUT ● v Norway (H) 24.3.76
CLUBS ● Blackpool, Everton, Queens Park Rangers, Porto

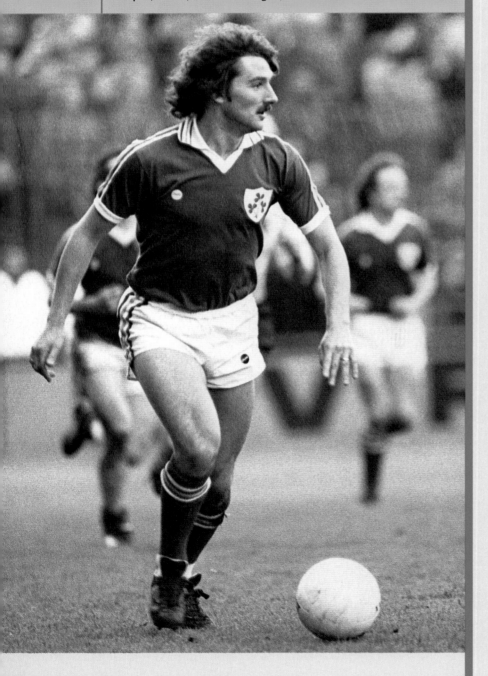

Micky Walsh could have been forgiven if, after his scoring debut for the Republic of Ireland in 1976, he began to dream of a long and goal-filled international career. Unfortunately for Micky, seven months later Frank Stapleton, another aspiring young Irish striker, would also score in his first match with the boys in green and it was he rather than Micky that was given the chance to live the dream. Over a period of eight years, Lancashire-born Walsh would remain a regular squad member, but out of the 56 games Ireland played between his first and last caps he appeared in just nine starting line-ups.

It was not, however, due to any lack of talent that the 5' 10" striker remained more on bench than pitch. Micky was a strong and sharp attacker who possessed a good first touch and a powerful shot. He was also a player with the rare propensity to produce the spectacular, as he proved when he scored a goal for Blackpool that was voted BBC Match of the Day's 'Goal of the Season' for 1974-75. Micky would enjoy a five-year spell at Bloomfield Road but following the Tangerines' relegation from Division Two in 1978 he moved on to Everton in a £325,000 deal. It was a fee that would make him the Republic of Ireland's most expensive player when he replaced Frank Stapleton to win his fifth cap after 54 minutes of a European Championships qualifier against Northern Ireland in September 1978.

The move to Goodison proved a disappointment and, in March 1979, after 20 first-team appearances and just one League goal, Micky was transferred to Queens Park Rangers. The Loftus Road club were in the midst of a relegation battle and had invested a club record fee of £250,000 in their new Republic of Ireland striker. It was a desperate, last throw of the dice, and although Micky responded with three goals in his ten games, it was not enough to save his new club from the drop. He would make just seven more League appearances for Rangers before quitting English football to join Portuguese giants FC Porto in 1981.

The switch to continental football proved a success for him and it was as a Porto player that Micky enjoyed his best form for Ireland. The qualifiers for the 1986 World Cup finals would, however, see him make his last contributions in the green shirt and after scoring the winning goal against the USSR at Lansdowne Road in 1984 he would win just two more caps.

It is Gerry Peyton's misfortune to be remembered chiefly as the patient understudy to record-breaking Ireland goalkeeper Packie Bonner. In a 15-year international career Gerry was rarely absent from the Ireland squad, but featured infrequently in the line-up. Born in Birmingham, the 6'2" custodian had been offered the chance to play for England's under-21 team in 1976 but chose instead to declare for the country of his parents' birth. Gerry's reward duly arrived. At the age of 21 he found himself on the bench for the Republic of Ireland's friendly match against Spain in 1977. At half-time, manager John Giles gave the rookie goalie – who was playing his club football with Fulham in the Second Division – his first taste of international soccer. The match ended in 1-0 defeat for Ireland, but Gerry's confident second-half performance suggested that, at last, Alan Kelly's long-term successor had been found.

For the remainder of the 1970s, the battle for Ireland's number one jersey turned into a two-way scrap between Gerry and the more-experienced Mick Kearns. But the Fulham keeper was nothing if not determined. He had begun his career with Aston Villa as a youngster only to be rejected at the end of his apprenticeship. A year with non-League Atherstone Town followed, after which Gerry made the move back to League football with Burnley in 1976. A solid all-round keeper, distribution was a key strength of the Peyton game and his accurate, long throws were a particularly potent attacking weapon.

Gerry would eventually claim victory over Kearns in 1979 when, after excellent displays against Denmark and Bulgaria, he enjoyed a run of six consecutive matches for the boys in green. He would remain Ireland's first choice goalkeeper throughout the remainder of John Giles's reign as manager and also played in the first four matches under Eoin Hand. Thereafter, the new coach preferred Jim McDonagh. By the time Gerry got another chance Bonner had already made his youthful debut. The emergence of the Celtic player would effectively end Gerry Peyton's days as a regular in the Ireland line-up, but he would remain an important part of the squad and was included in Jack Charlton's final selection for both the 1988 European Championships and the 1990 World Cup finals.

GERRY PEYTON

1977–1992

33	0
CAPS	GOALS

BORN — Birmingham, 20.5.56
DEBUT — v Spain (H) 9.2.77
CLUBS — Fulham, Bournemouth, Everton

Tony's committed, all-action style made him the ideal choice to lead the team.

1976–1985

45 **8**
CAPS GOALS

BORN ● London, 21.9.56
DEBUT ● v Norway (H) 24.3.76
CLUBS ● Orient, Luton Town, Brighton and Hove Albion,
West Bromwich Albion

Tony Grealish brought much needed energy and drive to the Republic of Ireland's all-too-pedestrian midfield of the late 1970s and early 1980s. A direct and hard-running player, his effervescent presence was the perfect complement to the more patient style of Liam Brady. Tony, who could play at full-back too, was a tigerish tackler but was more than just a stopper. He relished the chance to break forward and became a regular goalscorer at international level.

Tony Grealish

Although he was born in England, Tony enjoyed a very Irish upbringing and his parents were both involved in London's Gaelic Athletic Association. As a youngster he had shown great promise at Gaelic football and represented London in the All-Ireland Minor Football Championships. Fortunately, Tony was a true sporting all-rounder and his success at the Gaelic did not preclude him from making good progress at soccer too. In 1972 he joined Second Division Orient as an apprentice and by 1975 had become a regular in the East London club's first-team. At the age of 19, Tony's rapid progress at Brisbane Road was rewarded with a call-up to the full international team for a friendly against Norway.

The Republic of Ireland careers of Joe Kinnear and Tony Dunne had both ended abruptly in 1975, so it was in an unfamiliar full-back role that Grealish made his international debut. The new boy did not disappoint and played his part in a 3-0 victory. Tony kept his place for the next match, a friendly against Poland, but then found himself on the sidelines for two years as John Giles's team made an unsuccessful bid to qualify for the 1978 World Cup finals in Argentina.

Grealish returned to the Ireland team for a friendly against Norway in Oslo, a game which saw him take up his preferred midfield position. The match ended in a 0-0 draw, but the Orient youngster had impressed alongside manager John Giles and was included in the team which faced Denmark in a European Championship qualifier three days later. Tony struck the first of his eight international goals against the Danes and his mature displays on

this mini-tour of Scandinavia earned him a regular place in Giles's squad for the qualifying rounds of the 1980 European Championships.

In 1979 Tony's growing reputation as a skilful and effective midfield player – which had been significantly enhanced by his progress at international level – brought him a transfer to David Pleat's Luton Town. And it was as a Luton player that the energetic Londoner enjoyed his best form for the boys in green. Tony, together with Gerry Daly and Liam Brady, was part of a top-class midfield which was the driving force behind the Republic of Ireland's impressive, though ultimately unsuccessful, attempt to qualify for the 1982 World Cup finals. At the end of the campaign, Tony had missed just one match and had scored goals against Belgium and Cyprus.

The bearded midfielder had become a vital player for Ireland, and nobody won more caps under manager Eoin Hand. Tony, who twice captained the national team during the brief reign of Alan Kelly, was chosen as skipper for Hand's first game in charge. It was an honour he would enjoy on 14 further occasions. Tony's committed, all-action style made him the ideal choice to lead the team and he would wear the skipper's armband at club level too. In 1981 he joined ambitious Brighton and Hove Albion in a £100,000 deal, and two years later led the Seagulls to their first FA Cup final. The Sussex club lost out to Manchester United in a replay but only after a memorable 2-2 draw in the first match at Wembley.

Brighton's Cup form, however, was not matched in the League and at the end of the 1982–83 season they were relegated from the First Division. Tony remained at the Goldstone Ground for one more season before, in 1984, joining John Giles's West Bromwich Albion. In the same year, Ireland began their qualifying programme for the 1986 World Cup. Tony would play a key role throughout qualification, scoring against Switzerland and captaining the team on two occasions. But his efforts were in vain and when Eoin Hand's team failed to book a place at Mexico 86 his international career was at an end.

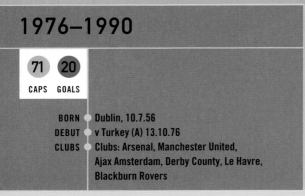

1976–1990

71 **20**

CAPS GOALS

BORN ● Dublin, 10.7.56
DEBUT ● v Turkey (A) 13.10.76
CLUBS ● Clubs: Arsenal, Manchester United,
Ajax Amsterdam, Derby County, Le Havre,
Blackburn Rovers

Frank was the archetypal good pro. He trained hard, constantly improved his skills, rarely lost his cool and was a selfless team player.

Frank Stapleton finished his international career as the Republic of Ireland's record scorer but his 20 goals were not enough to prevent critics from sniping at his strike-rate. They said that he was profligate, lacked pace and his finishing was poor. But these remarks seem churlish when set against the many positive qualities that Frank brought to the ailing Irish attack of the 1970s.

Frank Stapleton

A powerful and determined leader of the line, he possessed a delicate first touch which belied his imposing frame. His control was true and he shielded the ball with calm assurance. Frank was also adept at making clever decoy runs to drag markers away from key areas and make space for team-mates. But his greatest talent was his heading and he was rarely beaten in aerial challenges.

Frank was the archetypal good pro. He trained hard, constantly improved his skills, rarely lost his cool and was a selfless team player. He was also a committed and ambitious footballer. As a youngster he had shown great promise at Gaelic football, before concentrating his efforts on soccer after impressing with Dublin-based junior side Bolton Athletic. He began his career as an apprentice with Arsenal in 1972, joining fellow Irishmen Liam Brady and David O'Leary at Highbury.

Frank quickly adjusted to the demands of professional football and made his first-team debut as an 18-year-old at home to Stoke City in March 1975. By the 1976-77 season, he had become a First Division regular and found himself playing alongside new Gunners signing Malcolm Macdonald. The pair struck up an immediate rapport, scoring 38 goals in their first season together.

Frank's rapid progress could not have been more timely for the Republic. John Giles was desperately short of strikers, and the burden of scoring was weighing heavily on Don Givens. The 20-year-old Stapleton was cast into the international fray in 1976, in a friendly against Turkey. After three minutes he claimed his first goal for Ireland. Frank had done enough to earn a regular place in the squad for the remainder of Giles's reign as manager.

At Arsenal Frank continued to impress and was voted Gunner of the Year in 1977 and 1980. He also played a key role in the club's cup form at the end of the 1970s: Arsenal made it to four cup finals in three years, though their only success came in the 1979 FA Cup when they overcame Manchester United 3–2 in an epic final. The Gunners striker was now at the peak of his form and would prove Ireland's chief source of goals during their qualification programme for the 1982 World Cup. Sadly, Frank's three goals in seven matches were not enough and the boys in green failed to win a place at Spain 82.

In the summer of 1981 Frank had swapped Terry Neill's Arsenal for Ron Atkinson's Manchester United. The move cost United £900,000 but Frank showed his commitment to the Irish national team by insisting upon a clause in his contract guaranteeing that he would be released from club duty when called upon.

In 1983, Ireland manager Eoin Hand chose Frank to captain the national team for a European Championships match against Malta. The new skipper responded with a penalty in an 8-0 win but thereafter the armband proved a jinx and it was 18 months before his name reappeared on the scoresheet. By the time Frank rediscovered his touch, Hand's reign had reached its final phase and in 1986 Jack Charlton took over as manager. The new boss initially kept faith with his predecessor's captain, but the two men had an uneasy relationship over the next four years. Frank remained a potent threat in front of goal, though, and netted three times as Ireland qualified for their first major tournament: the 1988 European Championships. Frank, who had moved to Dutch giants Ajax in 1987, led Charlton's team throughout Euro 88 but injuries and the emergence of Niall Quinn and Tony Cascarino began to restrict his appearances for Ireland.

Frank remained on the fringe of the national team during qualification for Italia 90, making two appearances late in the campaign. A friendly against West Germany in September 1989 gave him a chance to remind Charlton what he could do and he took his chance in style, scoring the only goal of the game. That strike put him level with Don Givens' record of 19 international goals and earned him a place in Charlton's World Cup squad. Frank grabbed one more goal, in a friendly against Malta in June 1990, to make him his country's record goalscorer.

Although never flashy, David liked to pass the ball out of defence and used left and right foot with equal facility.

1976–1993

68 **1**
CAPS GOALS

BORN ● Stoke Newington, London, 2.5.58
DEBUT ● v England (A) 8.9.76
CLUBS ● Arsenal

There was an unmistakable air of composure about central defender David O'Leary and throughout a 17-year international career he remained a serene figure in the all-too-turbulent environs of the Republic of Ireland rearguard. For evidence of his remarkable temperament, one need only recall the nail biting penalty shoot-out against Romania at Italia 90. David, on as a sub for his first appearance at a World Cup finals, was asked to take a spot kick. Others had already declined but the Arsenal man stepped forward.

David O'Leary

It was a remarkable show of spirit from a player who had never scored for his country. When David's turn arrived, the scores stood at 4-4 and he needed to beat the Romanian keeper to earn his team a place in the quarter-finals. Pressure? Not enough to distract our hero, who coolly sent Lung the wrong way before dispatching the ball into the top right-hand corner of the net.

It was a rare moment in the limelight for a player whose conspicuous talent merited far more recognition than it received. David was a dogged defender who combined strength in the air with a superb positional sense. He was also deceptively quick and often appeared to be moving more slowly than his opponent, only to open his stride and cruise ahead to avert danger. The other great strength of the O'Leary game was distribution. Although never flashy, David liked to pass the ball out of defence and used left and right foot with equal facility. It was this passing ability, allied to a distinct absence of any cynicism, which set him apart from other centre-halves.

Although born in North London, David grew up in Dublin and began his career as a junior with Shelbourne. However, by the time he was 15, the captain of the Republic of Ireland's schoolboy team was on his way back to his birthplace to start an apprenticeship with Arsenal. David wasted little time settling in at Highbury, joining Liam Brady and Frank Stapleton at the North London club. Bertie Mee, the Arsenal manager, was immediately impressed and cast David into first-team action as a 17 year old in August 1975. It was the start

of a Gunners career that saw David amass a record-breaking 558 League appearances and win every major honour in English football.

International recognition duly followed, with John Giles awarding Arsenal's 18-year-old prodigy a first cap in a friendly against England at Wembley. David did not disappoint and gave a mature display, keeping Kevin Keegan on a short lead and playing a key role in a creditable 1–1 draw. It was a performance that would earn him a regular place in the Ireland team under Giles, and later Eoin Hand. Giles liked to see his teams pass the ball from the back and, for him, the central defensive partnership of Mark Lawrenson and David O'Leary was perfect. Hand, although less committed to this style of play, also used David when he was available.

However, the appointment of Jack Charlton as international manager in 1986 would bring a sea change to Irish football. And David, who was most definitely not a Charlton player, found himself dropped from the squad for a summer tour of Iceland in 1986. The relationship between player and manager deteriorated still further when, shortly before the tour, the Irish squad became decimated by withdrawals. Charlton went back to David and asked him if he would join up as a late replacement. Thanks but no thanks came the polite reply. David had already booked his summer holiday and, despite Charlton's protestations, he was not going to alter his plans to travel to Reykjavik. It was the start of a two-and-a-half year absence from the green shirt at a time when the accomplished centre-half was at his peak.

David, missed Euro 88 but returned to international duty to play his part in the qualification programme for Italia 90. By now Charlton's preferred defensive partnership was Kevin Moran and Mick McCarthy, but their occasional absences gave Dave the opportunity to prove that he had lost none of his skill. Ireland would, of course, qualify for the World Cup finals, progressing via that shoot-out against Romania to the quarter-finals.

David remained in the squad for the next three years and in 1993 contributed to his fifth World Cup qualifying programme. That same year, he signed off his Arsenal career with winners' medals in both English domestic cup competitions. A transfer to Leeds United followed but injury would put an end to his playing days after just 10 games there. David remained at Leeds, first as assistant manager to George Graham and later as the man in charge.

Mark was as complete a central defender as you are likely to find.

1977–1987

39 CAPS **5** GOALS

BORN • Preston, 2.6.57
DEBUT • v Poland (H) 24.4.77
CLUBS • Preston North End,
Brighton and Hove Albion, Liverpool

Mark Lawrenson was unlike any other centre-half the Republic of Ireland had seen. There had been others who could both defend and pass the ball but what set the moustachioed Lancastrian apart was the aura of assurance he brought to the team. There was something almost cat-like about the way he stalked opposing forwards. Instead of the desperate lunging and excessive physical force favoured by most defenders, Mark would patiently guide his prey away from goal, toying with them before calmly stretching out a leg to claim the ball. It was a routine he carried out with an arrogant swagger, which made his success seem all the more inevitable.

Mark Lawrenson

But the Lawrenson game did not end with merely winning tackles. He was also an extremely constructive player who carried the ball out of defence with the skill and confidence of a top-class midfield player. He had pace too – a useful commodity at both ends of the field, as was his often undervalued heading ability. In short, Mark was as complete a central defender as you are likely to find. The only problem was that a succession of Republic of Ireland managers felt him too gifted a footballer to hide away at number five or six and so pushed him into a more advanced midfield role.

The move forward, however, should not have been too alien to Mark, since it was as a left-winger that he began his career with Preston North End. He had made his debut for the Lilywhites at the age of 17 and quickly became a regular in the first team. Among the Deepdale coaching staff at the time was Republic of Ireland assistant manager Alan Kelly and, after a chance conversation, the former international keeper became aware that Mark was eligible to play for the Irish by virtue of his Irish-born mother. Kelly reported back to Ireland's manager John Giles who wasted little time in handing the 19 year old a call-up to the full international team.

During Giles's time as coach, Mark would make most of his appearances either in midfield or at full-back, though he did enjoy occasional outings at centre-half.

This meant that the dream partnership of David O'Leary and Lawrenson was rarely employed. In 1980 Giles resigned and was replaced by the more pragmatic Eoin Hand. The new manager, however, would persist with the practice of playing Mark in midfield. It was a tactic that bore fruit in Hand's first game in charge, a World Cup qualifier against Holland in Dublin, when the converted defender grabbed the winning goal in a 2-1 victory.

By the early 1980s, Mark, who was now playing his club football for Brighton and Hove Albion, had become one of the most coveted players in the Football League. After four seasons on England's south coast he was on the move once more, heading for soccer's big time with Liverpool FC. There have been few better judges of footballing talent than the Liverpool manager Bob Paisley, so it speaks volumes for Mark Lawrenson's qualities as a central defender that the Kop boss was willing to pay a club-record £900,000 to sign him in 1981.

After an initial spell as a utility man at Anfield, Mark eventually got his chance to play alongside Alan Hansen and the pair quickly forged a celebrated defensive partnership which proved a key factor in Liverpool's domination of English football during the 1980s. After seven years with the 'Pool, Mark had won nine major medals, the undoubted highlights of which were the 1984 European Cup and the 1985–86 League and FA Cup 'double'.

But while Liverpool closed in on the 'double', Ireland were preparing to begin a new and exciting era under the guidance of Jack Charlton. After a couple of friendly matches, which Lawrenson missed, the serious business of qualification for the 1988 European Championships got underway. It was a programme which would bring out the best in Mark and in a match against Scotland at Hampden Park, Glasgow, in February 1987 the tall, elegant defender enjoyed his finest moment in the green shirt. Not only did he score the game's winning goal – after a surging run through midfield – he also outshone his Liverpool colleague Alan Hansen.

Sadly, even before Ireland had qualified for the finals, Mark had succumbed to an Achilles' tendon injury which would ultimately end his career. Jobs in media and management have followed but it will be as a stylish and masterly defender that Mark Lawrenson is best remembered... it's just a pity that he couldn't have played in his best position more frequently for his country.

EAMONN GREGG

1978–1979

8 CAPS **0** GOALS

BORN Dublin, 1953
DEBUT v Poland (A) 12.4.78
CLUBS Bohemians

Eamonn Gregg was a resourceful right-sided full-back who enjoyed a successful League of Ireland career with Bohemians. He was an Under-23 international and a veteran of three European campaigns with Bohs when he was called into John Giles's squad for a friendly against Poland before the qualifiers for the 1980 European championships.

The right-back position had become something of a problem after Joe Kinnear's retirement, and it was in the number two shirt that Eamonn won the first of his eight caps. Despite a 3–0 reverse against the Poles, the new boy impressed enough to stay in the squad for the next 18 months. Eamonn played a part in seven of Ireland's nine internationals in that period but after a run of six consecutive appearances he lost his place following a 4–1 defeat at the hands of Czechoslovakia in Prague.

Within a year, Giles had been replaced by Eoin Hand and David Langan had established himself as the Republic of Ireland's regular right-back. Despite continued good form at club level, there would be no recall for Gregg. Since retiring as a player, the Dubliner has had spells as manager at both Bohemians and Shelbourne.

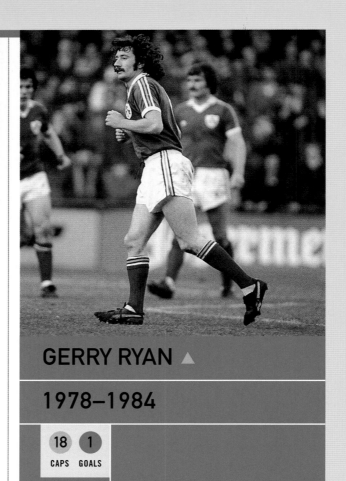

GERRY RYAN

1978–1984

18 CAPS **1** GOALS

BORN Dublin, 4.10.55
DEBUT v Turkey (H) 5.4.78
CLUBS Derby County, Brighton and Hove Albion

Fast, skilful and direct, Gerry Ryan was the type of player often described as an 'old fashioned winger'. He began his career with Bohemians, making his debut in February 1975 and helping Bohs to an FAI Cup triumph in 1976. The following season, Gerry appeared in a UEFA Cup fixture against Newcastle United and his impressive display had several Football League clubs chasing his signature. He moved to Tommy Docherty's Derby County and it was during his one-year spell at the Baseball Ground that the Dubliner won his first cap.

Gerry made his international debut in a friendly against Turkey at Lansdowne Road in April 1978. It would be the only cap he would win as a Derby County player. The following September the pacy outside-right moved on to Brighton and Hove Albion in an £80,000 deal. Gerry played a key role in the Seagulls' promotion to the old First Division in his first season, scoring nine goals in 34 appearances. He claimed his one and only international goal in 1979, a spectacular effort in a 3-1 friendly defeat at the hands of West Germany.

The match against the Germans was a rare appearance in the Republic of Ireland starting line-up for Gerry, who won half of his 18 caps as a substitute. Gerry, who also came off the bench for Brighton in the 1983 Cup final, had his career prematurely ended by injury when he sustained a broken leg in a League match in 1985.

Paul McGee staked his claim for a call-up to the Republic of Ireland team in the most emphatic fashion when, in September 1977, he scored for the League of Ireland against John Giles's full international team at Dalymount Park. Giles took the hint, awarding the Sligo-born forward a full debut in a friendly match against Turkey the following April. The new boy wasted little time making his mark in the green shirt, scoring the second of four Irish goals against the Turks to ensure his continued presence in international squads under Giles.

Despite his swift elevation to full international status, the career of Paul McGee was rarely straightforward. He began with hometown club Sligo Rovers before heading for England as a teenager to try his luck with Hereford United. Paul enjoyed little success, though, and soon returned to Rovers after a short spell at Finn Harps. Back on familiar territory the powerful and pacy forward blossomed. In 1976–77, Paul – who spent his summers playing in Canada – helped Sligo to the League title, scoring 13 goals along the way. Football League scouts began to take an interest and, following 'that' goal for the League of Ireland, the 5'10" striker completed a move to First Division Queens Park Rangers.

It was as a Rangers player that Paul won his first cap but following the club's relegation in 1979 he found himself on the move once more, this time joining Preston North End. While at Deepdale, the winger-cum-centre-forward enjoyed his best form in Ireland green and in 1980 he made his World Cup debut, against Cyprus in Nicosia. It was John Giles's last game in charge, and Paul helped the manager sign off with a victory, striking two goals in a 3-2 win. The arrival of Eoin Hand as coach of the national team in September 1980 sounded the death knell on the international career of Paul McGee. Under the new boss, he managed just 15 minutes with the boys in green.

PAUL McGEE

1978–1980

15	4
CAPS	GOALS

BORN • Sligo, 19.6.54
DEBUT • v Turkey (H) 5.4.78
CLUBS • Queens Park Rangers, Preston North End

DAVID LANGAN

1978–1987

26 **0**
CAPS GOALS

BORN • Dublin, 15.2.57
DEBUT • v Turkey (H) 5.4.78
CLUBS • Derby County, Birmingham City, Oxford United

There have been few more dedicated or unlucky footballers than Davey Langan. Despite a catalogue of career-threatening injuries, the affable Dubliner refused to admit defeat and fought his way back to perform at the highest level. The root of Davey's injury problems can be traced to a World Cup qualifier against France at Lansdowne Road in October 1981. A midfield clash during the first half of that match left the combative full-back with a knee injury. Initially suspecting it to be no more than a strain, Davey played on for the remainder of the game. It would prove his last international action for four-and-a-half years and during his time on the sidelines he would undergo countless operations not only to his knee but also to his back.

Davey's injury jinx struck when he was still only 24 years old but he was already an established international with a reputation as both a fierce competitor and a potent attacker. Ireland fans had taken to him for his courage, his determination and, in most cases, for his surging runs out of defence which so frequently ended with a pin point cross. When Davey had the ball, Lansdowne Road was likely to erupt with a roar of anticipation. He was also a tigerish tackler who expertly trod the fine line between strong defending and excessive force.

Davey Langan began his professional career with Brian Clough's Derby County in 1975 but it was under the management of Colin Murphy that he took his League bow at the age of 19. He quickly established himself as a regular in the first team at the Baseball Ground and in April 1978 was called into John Giles's Republic of Ireland line-up for a friendly against Turkey. Despite continued good form with Derby, Davey won just one more cap under Giles and it was not until Eoin Hand took over that he got the chance to claim a regular place in the international team. In the meantime, the muscular number two had swapped the Baseball Ground for Birmingham City's St Andrews, becoming the Blues' record signing shortly after Derby were relegated in 1980. But then in 1981 came *that* incident against France.

During his long rehabilitation, Langan's contract with Birmingham City came to an end and it was with Jim Smith's Oxford United that he made his long-awaited comeback in 1984. However, it was not until 1986, when he won a recall to the green jersey of Ireland, that Davey's rehabilitation was complete. He had perhaps lost some of his pace but he remained a class act and his crossing created many goals for team-mate John Aldridge. Davey would help Oxford to League Cup success in 1986 and to promotion to the First Division two years later. Alas, after three appearances in Ireland's starting line-up during qualification for the 1988 European Championships, Davey was left out of the final squad that travelled to Germany. It was a bitter pill for the man who had fought back so valiantly from injury.

The international career of Ashley Grimes spanned ten years and the reigns of four managers but, despite his considerable talent, the tall Dubliner was never able to establish himself as a regular in the green of Ireland. Much of the blame for this can be attributed to the versatility which enabled Ashley to perform with equal facility at either full-back or in midfield; a quality that saw him frequently overlooked in favour of more 'specialist' players. But the former Stella Maris junior was no mere 'Jack of all trades' utility man. Ashley was blessed with a supremely accurate left foot and struck the ball both cleanly and truly to deliver either telling pass or unerring shot. A tall, wiry figure with a gawky gait, he also possessed great stamina, which at times made up for a lack of genuine pace.

Ashley, a former Republic of Ireland under-21 captain, arrived on the full-international scene a year after joining Tommy Docherty's Manchester United in a £20,000 transfer from Bohemians, where he had been an FAI Cup winner in 1976. He made his senior debut, along with five other newcomers, in a friendly match against Turkey as manager John Giles attempted to inject some fresh blood into his squad ahead of the 1980 European Championship qualifiers. Ashley proved one of the more successful newcomers, and enjoyed his best run in the national team under Giles – playing in each of the manager's last five games in charge.

At club level, the ginger-haired left-footed player would make more than 100 first-team appearances in seven years at Old Trafford, before moving on to Coventry City. His stay at Highfield Road, however, extended to just one season and in 1984 he joined David Pleat's Luton Town. It was a transfer that would bring Ashley a winner's medal in the League Cup when he came on as a substitute in the Hatters' victory over Arsenal in 1988. But by then his days in green were already at an end. The reign of Eoin Hand had seen Ashley make just two appearances in competitive fixtures and although he claimed his only international goal in one of these matches, he was unable to convince the manager that he merited a regular place in the line-up. The arrival of Jack Charlton as coach of the national team in 1986 gave hope of an Indian summer for the international adventures of Ashley Grimes but after just two more appearances the sun finally went down on the Republic of Ireland career of a skilful and underrated footballer.

ASHLEY GRIMES

1978–1988

18 CAPS **1** GOALS

BORN Dublin, 2.8.57
DEBUT v Turkey (H) 5.4.78
CLUBS Manchester United, Coventry City, Luton Town

SYNAN BRADDISH
1978
Born: Dublin, 1958
Caps: 2
Goals: 0
Debut v Turkey (H) 5.4.78
Clubs: Dundalk

Synan Braddish was an elegant midfielder who began his career with Dundalk before embarking on an unsuccessful stint at Liverpool in 1978. The following season saw the Dubliner return to Dundalk where he played a key role in helping the club to their League Cup victory in 1981. Synan's international career was a short-lived affair, and extended to just two appearances in friendlies during 1978.

JEROME CLARKE
1978
Born: Drogheda, 1951
Caps: 1
Goals: 0
Debut v Poland (A) 12.4.78
Clubs: Drogheda United

Jerome Clarke was a hard-running forward whose international career lasted just 12 minutes. His Republic of Ireland debut came in a friendly against Poland when he replaced player-manager John Giles during a 3-0 defeat against Poland in Lodz.

MAURICE DALY
1978
Born: Dublin, 28.11.55
Caps: 2
Goals: 0
Debut v Turkey (H) 5.4.78
Clubs: Wolverhampton Wanderers

Dublin-born Maurice Daly was a Home Farm product who enjoyed one season of first-team action with Wolverhampton Wanderers in 1977–78. A fast and attacking left-back, Maurice made both his international appearances in the spring of 1978 as John Giles attempted to unearth new talent for the forthcoming European Championship qualifiers.

NOEL SYNNOTT
1978
Born: Dublin, 1952
Caps: 3
Goals: 0
Debut v Turkey (H) 5.4.78
Clubs: Shamrock Rovers

Noel Synnott was a fiercely competitive centre-half who came to prominence in John Giles's Shamrock Rovers team of the late 1970s. The same manager – when deprived of the services of established defenders Mark Lawrenson and David O'Leary – awarded Noel his full international debut in a friendly against Turkey in the spring of 1978. The newcomer did well enough to remain in the team for the next match and the following September made his competitive debut in a goalless European Championship qualifier against Northern Ireland.

TERRY DONOVAN
1979–1981
Born: Liverpool, 27.2.58
Caps: 2
Goals: 0
Debut v Czechoslovakia (A) 26.9.79
Clubs: Aston Villa

Terry Donovan began his career with Grimsby Town but after netting 23 times in 64 League games, the promising young striker left the Mariners to join Aston Villa in an £80,000 transfer. The move to Villa Park was far from successful, although it was during his time in the Midlands that the Liverpool-born forward broke into John Giles's Republic of Ireland team. Terry, whose father Don played for Everton and was also an Irish international, won his first cap in a friendly against Czechoslovakia. A second and final cap arrived two years later during the tenure of Eoin Hand.

AUSTIN HAYES
1979
Born: Hammersmith, 15.7.58
Caps: 1
Goals: 0
Debut v Denmark (H) 2.5.79
Clubs: Southampton

Austin Hayes was a fast and direct winger with excellent ball skills and an eye for goal. Born in London, he made his League debut for Southampton and was still just 20 years old when he was awarded his one and only cap in a European Championship qualifier against Denmark at Lansdowne Road. The new boy played his part in a 2-0 win, setting up the opening goal for Gerry Daly, but would make no further appearances in the green of Ireland. Austin, who also played for both Millwall and Northampton Town, died in London in February 1986.

JERRY MURPHY
1979–1980
Born: Stepney, London, 23.9.59
Caps: 3
Goals: 0
Debut v Wales (A) 11.9.79
Clubs: Crystal Palace

Jerry Murphy was a member of the famous Crystal Palace' team of the 1980s and got his chance for the Republic of Ireland while still only 19 years old. A patient, left-sided midfielder, he made his international debut in a friendly against Wales and did sufficiently well to win two further caps. Jerry's third appearance for Ireland came in John Giles's last match in charge, but despite good form for Palace there was to be no recall to the green jersey.

FRAN O'BRIEN
1979–1980
Born: Dublin, 1955
Caps: 3
Goals: 0
Debut v Czechoslovakia (A) 26.9.79
Clubs: Philadelphia Furies

Fran O'Brien, like his older brother Ray, was a natural-born left-back. He began his career with Bohemians in his native Dublin but spent several summers playing in America. A permanent move to the USA duly arrived and it was as a Philadelphia Furies player that Fran won all three of his full international caps.

JEFF CHANDLER
1979
Born: Hammersmith, 19.6.59
Caps: 2
Goals: 0
Debut v Czechoslovakia (A) 26.9.79
Clubs: Leeds United

Jeff Chandler enjoyed a long and relatively successful career in English football but his days in green were somewhat short-lived. It was as a Leeds United player that the tricky winger won both his caps, and despite excellent performances for Bolton Wanderers during the early 1980s, there was to be no recall.

CATHAL MUCKIAN
1978
Born: Dundalk, 1952. Caps: 1 Goals: 0
Debut v Poland (A) 12.4.78. Clubs: Drogheda United

In 1977–78 Cathal Muckian was Drogheda's leading scoring with 21 goals in 30 games. John Giles duly took notice and called the prolific striker into a scratch Republic of Ireland team to face Poland in April 1978. Cathal would continue to enjoy good form at club level, and in 1979 was a member of Dundalk's League and FAI Cup winning team. Alas there would be no recall to Ireland green for the pacy frontman from Co. Louth.

MICHAEL ROBINSON

1980–1986

24 **4**
CAPS GOALS

BORN	Leicester, 12.2.58
DEBUT	France (A) 28.10.80
CLUBS	Brighton and Hove Albion, Liverpool, Queens Park Rangers

When Michael Robinson was finally given clearance to wear the green of Ireland in the autumn of 1980, the tall, energetic striker was unimaginatively billed as the man to take the place of Steve Heighway. Such weighty expectation, however, was nothing new to this direct front-runner who, as a 20 year old, had made a big-money move from Preston North End to Manchester City. Michael did much to fulfil the hype with an accomplished debut in a World Cup qualifier against France – which saw him have what appeared to be a perfectly good goal ruled out – while playing alongside, rather than in place of, Heighway.

Michael, who had been Ray Treacy's boot-boy at Preston North End as an apprentice, had won the right to represent the boys in green via an Irish-born grandmother, and his call up to Eoin Hand's team had brought the FAI criticism from both the media and football authorities. But the fans, at least, were left in no doubt as to Michael's commitment to the Ireland cause following his excellent form during the qualification programme for the 1982 World Cup. The highlight of this run was a match-winning display in the vital clash against France in Dublin, when the Leicester-born striker scored with a powerful drive and set up a goal for Frank Stapleton with a surging run and low cross.

Although still only 22 years old when he arrived on the international scene, Michael was already with his third club, Brighton and Hove Albion. He had joined the Seagulls following a disappointing spell with Malcolm Allison's Manchester City and during his time at the Goldstone Ground began to recapture the form and confidence which had led Allison to pay Preston North End £750,000 for him as a teenager in 1979. After three years recovering from his City blues on the South Coast, Michael returned to the North-West to join Joe Fagan's Liverpool in a £200,000 deal. It was a transfer that went largely unnoticed by most Reds fans, but it proved a shrewd investment and during his first season at Anfield (1983–84), Robinson helped Liverpool win both the League Championship and European Cup. The following campaign brought a switch to Queens Park Rangers but in 1986, after three years in West London, Michael left Britain to join Spanish club Osasuna.

By then, his days in green were at an end. Despite occasional patches of good form, Michael had struggled to maintain the form which brought him three goals in his first six internationals. And with just one score in the next 18 matches, it came as little surprise that he was unable to force his way into the plans of new manager Jack Charlton.

PIERCE O'LEARY

1979–1980

7	**0**
CAPS	GOALS

BORN	Dublin, 5.11.59
DEBUT	v Czechoslovakia (A) 26.9.79
CLUBS	Shamrock Rovers

If the name didn't give it away, the tall, willowy frame and leggy gait most certainly did: Pierce O'Leary was unmistakably David's younger brother. While the physical similarity was obvious, it was equally apparent that O'Leary senior had been blessed with the greater ability. But Pierce was not without virtue as a defender and although he lacked his older brother's poise and dexterity, he enjoyed a successful career at both club and international level.

Pierce came to prominence in John Giles's Shamrock Rovers team in the late 1970s, and Giles drafted him into the Irish team in 1979. Already an under-21 cap, he made his senior bow in a friendly against Czechoslovakia. Over the next year he made six more appearances – taking in World Cup and European Championship qualifiers. He appeared alongside his brother twice but after Giles left, he played just one match under Eoin Hand.

A move to Celtic in 1984 saw the versatile defender claim a Scottish Cup winners medal in 1985, but an injury in 1988 forced him to hang up his boots.

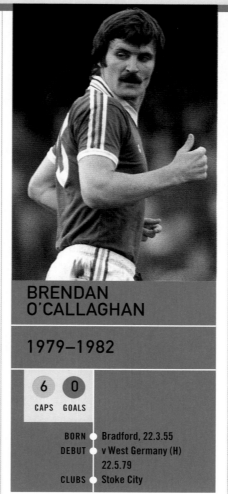

BRENDAN O'CALLAGHAN

1979–1982

6	**0**
CAPS	GOALS

BORN	Bradford, 22.3.55
DEBUT	v West Germany (H) 22.5.79
CLUBS	Stoke City

Brendan O'Callaghan was a tall and powerful target man who, despite his imposing frame, displayed sharp reflexes and a deceptive turn of pace. A Yorkshireman by birth, he qualified for the Republic of Ireland under the parentage rule and was first drafted into the senior squad by John Giles in 1978.

Brendan had earned his chance with the boys in green after scoring 16 goals for Stoke City in their 1978–79 promotion season, and made his full international debut in a friendly against West Germany at Lansdowne Road. All six of his caps would come in non-competitive matches, spread equally between the reigns of John Giles and Eoin Hand.

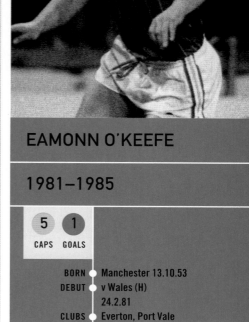

EAMONN O'KEEFE

1981–1985

5	**1**
CAPS	GOALS

BORN	Manchester 13.10.53
DEBUT	v Wales (H) 24.2.81
CLUBS	Everton, Port Vale

Eamonn O'Keefe's rise from non-League soccer to international status was nothing short of meteoric. The muscular Mancunian had been playing part-time football for Mossley in the Northern Premier League when he made a £25,000 switch to Gordon Lee's Everton in July 1979. An aggressive, all action striker, Eamonn quickly made his mark at Goodison, and in 1981 earned a call-up to Eoin Hand's Ireland team.

In January 1982 Howard Kendall sold him to Fourth Division Wigan Athletic and in two seasons at Springfield Park, Eamonn failed add to his debut cap. It was only when he stepped up to Division Three with Port Vale in 1983–84 that he could bring an end to his three-year international exile. Eamonn celebrated his return to Eoin Hand's team for the Japan Cup match against China with his one and only goal for Ireland. Three more caps followed in quick succession, but in 1985, aged 32, his international career ended. Eamonn would, however, continue to score goals with great regularity as he wound down his career with first Blackpool and later Cork Celtic.

JOHN DEVINE ▼

1979–1984

13	0
CAPS	GOALS

BORN Dublin, 11.11.58
DEBUT v Czechoslovakia (A) 26.9.79
CLUBS Arsenal, Norwich City

John Devine, a lean and pacy right-back with a well-honed attacking instinct, looked, for a short time in the early 1980s, to be the man to bring both class and consistency to the Republic of Ireland's troublesome number two jersey. He had arrived on the international stage with an impeccable pedigree, having ousted Pat Rice from the Arsenal line-up while making his way from Gunners apprentice to first-team regular in just three years.

He won his first cap in 1979 in a friendly against Czechoslovakia. But he made just one more appearance for Ireland before, in 1980, Eoin Hand took charge of the national team. David Langan was the new manager's choice at right-back, and it wasn't until the Birmingham City player suffered an injury in October 1981 that John was given a chance in his favoured position.

The qualifiers for the 1984 European Championships saw Devine enjoy his best run in Hand's team, playing in four of the last six fixtures. But his performances for Arsenal had become inconsistent and in 1983 he left Highbury to join Norwich City. John was a regular member of Eoin Hand's squad during his first season at Carrow Road but in his second season with the Canaries his form dipped and he moved to Stoke City, where a broken leg ended his career in 1986.

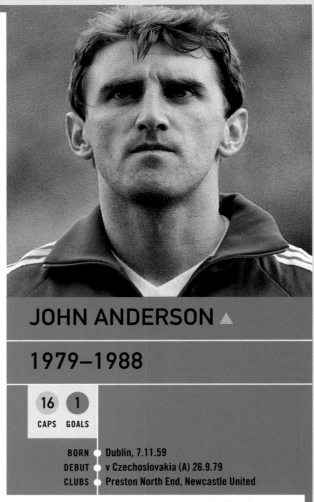

JOHN ANDERSON ▲

1979–1988

16	1
CAPS	GOALS

BORN Dublin, 7.11.59
DEBUT v Czechoslovakia (A) 26.9.79
CLUBS Preston North End, Newcastle United

John Anderson was a strong, dependable right-back whose international career spanned most of a decade, but brought just 16 caps. At various times, the former Stella Maris junior found himself in line behind David Langan, John Devine and Chris Morris in the queue for Ireland's number two jersey and, despite consistent club form, he never claimed a regular place.

John began his professional career under John Giles at West Bromwich Albion but he was sold to Preston North End for £45,000 in August 1979 by Ron Atkinson. Three months later Giles, as Ireland manager, gave him his senior debut as a sub against Czechoslovakia in a friendly. But it proved to be a false start and, although John scored in his second match for Ireland, he was restricted to a handful of friendlies and tour matches during the first seven years of his international career.

By the time John lined up for his first competitive Ireland match Jack Charlton had taken charge of the national team. It was not the first time they had worked together, as their paths had crossed at Newcastle United in 1984. With Langan injured, Charlton recalled his former charge to the international team for three vital European Championship qualifiers in 1986 and 1987. John was rewarded when he was included in the party which travelled to the finals in West Germany in 1988. He did not appear in any of Ireland's three matches and, with the more attack-minded Chris Morris in the team, John added just one more cap to his tally.

Gary Waddock must surely have spent his spare time inverting horse shoes and kicking black cats, such was the poor fortune which dogged the latter stages of his international career.

Despite his ill-luck, the flame-haired midfielder remained an enthusiastic and dependable figure throughout a ten-year run with the boys in green.

A Londoner by birth, Gary made his Ireland debut as a teenager during Alan Kelly's one-match reign as national coach in 1980. He had come to prominence with Queens Park Rangers, where his powerful tackling and energetic displays had made him a firm favourite with the Loftus Road crowd. In 1982 Gary was a member of the Rangers team that lost out in a replayed Cup final defeat against Tottenham Hotspur. The following season he was instrumental in the West Londoners' successful promotion campaign. Progress at club level brought further reward for the 5' 10" ball winner when he earned a regular place in Eoin Hand's team for the qualifying rounds of the 1984 European Championships, but just when it seemed he could do no wrong, the bubble burst in dramatic fashion.

In 1985 Gary sustained a serious knee injury that kept him out of the game for more than a year. He eventually recovered but, unable to win back his place at QPR, moved on to Belgian club Charleroi before completing his rehabilitation with Millwall. Eighteen appearances in 1989–90, and a testimony from Lions team-mate Tony Cascarino, earned Gary a somewhat unexpected recall to Ireland green. It seemed, with Italia 90 fast approaching, that the experienced and revitalised Waddock had timed his return to perfection.

Jack Charlton played Gary in two warm-up matches ahead of the World Cup, and included him in an initial squad for Italy. However, just as the stage was set for a 'footballer triumphs in the face of adversity' story, the manager announced the final changes to his squad. Charlton had decided to leave Gary behind, instead taking Alan McLoughlin. It was a desperate disappointment for a player who had overcome so many obstacles to regain his fitness. Gary would make just one more appearance in Ireland green, although he would continue to play at club level into his late thirties with initially Bristol Rovers and, later, Luton Town.

GARY WADDOCK

1980–1990

21 CAPS   **3** GOALS

BORN ● Kingsbury, London, 17.3.62
DEBUT ● v Switzerland (H) 30.4.80
CLUBS ● Queens Park Rangers, Millwall

In his younger days, he was also a potent attacker with a penchant for overlapping.

1979–1991

53 CAPS   **1** GOALS

BORN ● Forest Gate, London, 11.12.58
DEBUT ● v USA (H) 29.10.79
CLUBS ● Tottenham Hotspur, West Ham United

Chris Hughton was a graceful and stylish full-back who remained unfathomably underrated despite a career of high achievement at both club and international level. At his peak, in the mid-1980s, the East London-born defender was a reassuring presence on the Republic of Ireland's left flank, bringing the same professionalism to the number three jersey that Tony Dunne had in the 1960s and 1970s. Like his predecessor, Chris was blessed with pace and a strong competitive streak – qualities which made him a formidable opponent. In his younger days, he was also a potent attacker with a penchant for overlapping.

Chris Hughton

Before embarking on a career as a professional footballer, the young Hughton had completed an apprenticeship as a lift operator, but it was a trade he would never need to call upon. In 1979, still only 20 years old, he devoted himself to full-time soccer with Tottenham Hotspur and was immediately called into the senior team. At the end of his first season at White Hart Lane, Chris had made 39 consecutive League appearances in a star-studded line-up which included such luminaries as Glenn Hoddle, Ossie Ardiles and Ricardo Villa. The new boy had been given his chance at right-back but, although a natural right-footer, it was on the opposite flank that he made his name with the Lilywhites.

In 1981 Spurs triumphed in a replayed FA Cup final against Manchester City and as usual the man guarding the left wing for Keith Burkinshaw's team was the diminutive but muscular Chris Hughton. Both club and player would repeat their FA Cup success in 1982, beating QPR in the final, and two years later a third Cup-winners' medal arrived when the White Hart Lane team overcame Anderlecht in the final of the UEFA Cup. It would prove the highlight of Hughton's club career, but by then he had already won 19 caps and was a regular in Eoin Hand's Republic of Ireland line-up.

Chris had arrived at international level just months after breaking into the Spurs team and took his bow in a friendly against the USA in Dublin. While the match may have lacked any competitive importance, the debut of

this young and relatively unknown full-back was of immense significance. Chris Hughton had become the first black man to play for the Republic of Ireland. He had kicked off his international career under John Giles, but would remain a regular member of international squads over the next 12 years, playing for Alan Kelly, Eoin Hand and Jack Charlton.

By the time Charlton arrived as national coach in 1986, Chris had begun to lose a little of his pace and had become more of a conscientious stopper than an attack-minded wing-back. It was an approach which was ideally suited to the pragmatism of the new manager; a man unimpressed by defenders dribbling the ball out from the back. For both club and country, Chris had forged an effective and industrious left-wing partnership with Tony Galvin, and the pair were key figures in Ireland's qualification for the 1988 European Championships. The Spurs duo would appear in all three matches played by the boys in green at the finals in West Germany.

Chris would also travel to the 1990 World Cup finals but by then he had lost his place in the Spurs team and was struggling for form. The emergence of first Jim Beglin and later Steve Staunton did nothing to help Chris's cause at international level, and in the latter part of his Ireland career he was often used at right-back.

In the autumn of 1990 Hughton brought the curtain down on a 12-year run at White Hart Lane and returned to his East End roots to sign for West Ham United in the old Second Division. Chris helped the Hammers to promotion in his first season at Upton Park but when his former Spurs nemesis Mitchell Thomas arrived the following summer things did not bode well for Chris. A move to Brentford arrived, but after 32 appearances for the West Londoners and several injury problems he decided the time was right to hang up his boots.

Shortly after retiring as a player, Chris was offered the chance to join the coaching staff back at White Hart Lane when former team-mate Ossie Ardiles took over as manager in 1993. It turned out to be an unhappy time for Ossie but, for the man he hired, success did eventually arrive. Chris, who has worked under three managers at the Lane, was appointed assistant manager during Gerry Francis's reign and from 1998 fulfilled the same role alongside George Graham.

After just ten appearances for Manchester United, Kevin was called into the Republic of Ireland's senior team.

1980–1994

71 **6**
CAPS GOALS

BORN Dublin, 29.4.56
DEBUT v Switzerland (H) 30.4.80
CLUBS Manchester United, Sporting Gijon, Blackburn Rovers

Kevin Moran was a powerfully built, fearless Dubliner who enjoyed a long and often painful career with the boys in green. Kevin was a player who could always be relied upon to throw himself forward, willingly greeting flying boots and striker's elbows in the team cause. The origins of Moran's gutsy approach, which earned him both war wounds and plaudits, can be found in Gaelic football; a game at which the raven-haired defender excelled long before he gained fame and fortune under the Association code.

Kevin Moran

Kevin, who won an All-Ireland medal with Dublin, could so easily have been lost to first-class soccer altogether had it not been for the astute judgement of Manchester United scout Billy Behan. It was the Reds' talent spotter who recommended that Dave Sexton sign the 21-year-old defender following his impressive displays for non-league Pegasus (a University College Dublin team). The United manager took heed and Kevin – who was still more famous for Gaelic football than soccer – arrived at Old Trafford in 1978. A year later he made his professional debut, although it was not until 1980–81 that he enjoyed an extended run in the first team. In his early years with the Reds, Kevin was frequently employed as a forceful presence in midfield but following the decline of Martin Buchan and Gordon McQueen and the arrival of Ron Atkinson as manager in 1981, the Irishman moved back to his favoured position in central defence.

After just ten League appearances for Manchester United, Kevin was called into the Republic of Ireland's senior team for a friendly against Switzerland during the one-match reign of Alan Kelly in 1980. The arrival of Eoin Hand as national coach shortly afterwards did nothing to hinder the progress of the Manchester United defender, who became an instant regular under the new manager, playing in five out of the eight qualifiers for the 1982 World Cup.

Ireland were blessed with an abundance of riches at centre-half during the 1980s but despite intense competition Kevin retained his place in the line-up for many years and at various times played alongside Mark Lawrenson, David O'Leary, Paul McGrath and Mick McCarthy. At Old Trafford he had been paired initially with Gordon McQueen, whom he partnered in United's FA Cup final win over Brighton in 1983. But when the Reds reached Wembley again two years later, Ron Atkinson opted for the all-Dublin Moran/McGrath combination. However, McGrath would have to play much of the game without Kevin, who gained notoriety after becoming the first player to be sent off in an FA Cup final when his mistimed, though not malicious, challenge felled Everton midfielder Peter Reid during the second half.

The appointment of Jack Charlton as Ireland manager in 1986 brought about Kevin's best form in the green shirt, and in 1988, after a run of three goals in four games, he was appointed captain for the first time. It was an honour that the teak-tough stopper would enjoy on a further 12 occasions. Kevin, who had played a key role in qualification, was also included in the squad which travelled to the 1988 European Championships in West Germany and appeared in each of Ireland's three games. By then, however, he had played his last game for Manchester United, with Alex Ferguson handing him what proved to be a premature free transfer.

Kevin kicked off the 1988–89 campaign with Spanish club Sporting Gijon, but at season's end he was on his way back to Lancashire to join Blackburn Rovers. It proved a hugely successful move and in five seasons at Ewood Park the veteran centre-back made 147 League appearances, captaining Rovers to promotion in 1992. Kevin remained a key figure throughout Jack Charlton's reign and was an ever-present at Italia 90. Four years later, aged 38, he was included in the Ireland squad that travelled to the World Cup in the USA. Alas, injury prevented him from adding to his impressive collection of caps. After that tournament Kevin decided to call a halt to his playing days. His full-blooded contributions would be greatly missed.

JIM McDONAGH

1981–1985

25 **0**
CAPS GOALS

BORN ● Rotherham, 6.10.52
DEBUT ● v Wales (H) 24.2.81
CLUBS ● Everton, Bolton Wanderers, Notts County, Wichita Wings

The presence of a familiar and reliable goalkeeper can do wonders for a football manager's biorhythms and stress levels. In the case of Eoin Hand, who spent five-and-a-half years as Republic of Ireland boss, Jim McDonagh was the custodian who did most to save the 'gaffer' from sleepless nights and involuntary twitching. The Yorkshire-born six-footer was already a veteran of 300 League appearances when he made his senior international debut, aged 29, in a friendly against Wales in 1981. The match, Hand's fifth in charge, ended in a 3-1 reverse, but the new number one was not held culpable. A month later he made his World Cup bow against Belgium at the Heysel stadium, Brussels.

Jim, who had played for the England youth team as a teenager, qualified for the boys in green through parentage and began his professional career with hometown club Rotherham United. But it was a move to Bolton Wanderers, in August 1976, that propelled his career into the ascendant. For three years Jim was an ever-present for the Trotters and, after helping the Lancashire side into the First Division in 1979–80, he became the subject of much transfer interest before making a £250,000 switch to Gordon Lee's Everton ahead of the 1980–81 season. It proved, however, to be a short stay on Merseyside. After one year and 40 League appearances, the custodian was returned to Burnden Park, Bolton, by new Toffees boss Howard Kendall. Despite the brevity of his Goodison sojourn, it was as an Everton player that Jim had made his breakthrough into Eoin Hand's Ireland team. Frequent transfers thereafter – there were eight of them in all – had little bearing on Hand's selection of McDonagh, who remained his preferred keeper for four-and-a-half years.

Agility and courage were Jim's great strengths; his great misfortune, however, was that these qualities were also displayed in abundance by another Republic of Ireland keeper. Packie Bonner, who was then an aspiring wannabe, had made occasional appearances in the early 1980s but in 1985 got his first chance of a run in the team. The Celtic goalie played in four consecutive matches until illness let Jim back into the line-up for the final five games of Hand's tenure. He responded in great style to record three consecutive clean sheets. It was, however, not enough to convince new international coach Jack Charlton that Jim was the man who could not only guard goal but also protect him against anxiety and insomnia.

Kevin O'Callaghan was a skilful and versatile forward who, despite conspicuous talent, struggled to live up to the expectation that somewhat inevitably arrived after he had made his senior international debut at the age of just 19. Hype, however, was nothing new to the Dagenham-born winger who had played his first League game for Millwall as a 17 year old and who had joined Ipswich Town for a club record £250,000 two years later.

Kevin, who was primarily an outside-left, could operate anywhere across the forward line and became an instant regular in Eoin Hand's Republic of Ireland squad, playing in three consecutive friendlies in 1981. However, it was not until he won his ninth cap in the final match of 1982 that he was named in the starting line-up for a competitive international. The breakthrough had arrived in a match against Spain in the preliminary rounds of the 1984 European Championships and was followed by appearances in each of Ireland's remaining six qualifiers. It was a sequence of matches that would see Kevin produce his best form in a green shirt, culminating in a goalscoring performance against Malta in November 1983. It was to be the first and last goal he would claim in international football.

For the remainder of Eoin Hand's reign, Kevin was involved only as a substitute – a role he had also filled frequently at Ipswich. In January 1985, after 115 League games for the Suffolk club, he moved on to Second Division Portsmouth and it was as a Pompey player that he won the last of his caps. His final appearance in Ireland green arrived under Jack Charlton in a friendly against Brazil. Although still only 25 years old, Kevin had been overtaken by the emergent talents of both Tony Galvin and Kevin Sheedy and after 21 caps his international career was at an end.

KEVIN O'CALLAGHAN

1981–1987

 21 **1**
CAPS GOALS

BORN Dagenham, 19.10.61
DEBUT v Czechoslovakia (H) 29.4.81
CLUBS Ipswich Town, Portsmouth

Ronnie was a midfielder of poise and dexterity whose magnetic control and transcendent authority would have made him a certain choice for any international team.

1981–1995

53 CAPS **3** GOALS

BORN ● Dublin, 25.9.61
DEBUT ● v Czechoslovakia (H) 29.4.81
CLUBS ● Liverpool, Southend United

In Ronnie Whelan's case, the statistics do not lie. He played nearly 500 first-team games for Liverpool, scoring 73 goals and amassing a vast and impressive collection of silverware. He was neither flattered nor undeserving of the success he enjoyed as a member of one of the greatest club sides in football history. The skilful Dubliner, however, was rarely given the recognition that his contribution to 12 major trophy successes warranted and throughout much of his career he remained curiously under-rated. Ronnie, whose father Ronnie Snr. had won two full caps for the Republic of Ireland in the 1960s, began his career at Home Farm, making his League of Ireland debut on his 16th birthday. Three years later Liverpool manager Bob Paisley swooped to take the teenager to Anfield.

Ronnie Whelan

Although never a flashy player, Ronnie was a midfielder of poise and dexterity whose magnetic control and transcendent authority would have made him a certain choice for any international team during the 1980s. Fortunately for the Irish, it was they who benefited from the conspicuous talents of this elegant ballplayer. At the age of 19, having made just one first-team appearance for Liverpool, Ronnie took his senior international bow as a sub against Czechoslovakia in a friendly at Lansdowne Road. The next season saw further progress for the talented youngster, who won League Championship and League Cup winners' medals with Liverpool.

Ronnie had marked his first season as a regular in the Reds' senior team with ten League goals, plus a further brace in the League Cup final against Tottenham Hotspur. It was a haul plundered, in the main, from a position on the left of midfield and such impressive form did not go unnoticed by Ireland manager Eoin Hand. By 1983 Ronnie had become a key player in the Ireland 'engine room' although he was never able to reproduce his Liverpool goalscoring record in Ireland green.

Following the appointment of Jack Charlton as manager of the national team in 1986 Ronnie became something of a peripheral figure. However the Liverpool schemer quickly forced his way back into the reckoning. Now in his mid-twenties, he had become a more industrious and resolute player and it was these qualities that appealed most to Charlton.

Ronnie was also a versatile performer and during the qualification campaign for the 1988 European Championships he gave an accomplished performance from an unfamiliar left-back position in the vital match against Scotland in Glasgow. However, it was as a midfielder that he enjoyed his finest moment at international level, scoring a breathtaking goal against the USSR at the finals of the 1988 European Championships. A long throw from Mick McCarthy eluded all the Soviet defenders and fell to Ronnie who leapt into the air to strike a perfect left-footed scissors kick into the corner of the net.

In 1989 Ronnie's loyal service with Liverpool was rewarded when he was appointed captain in the absence of the injured Alan Hansen. The stand-in skipper led the Reds to FA Cup success at season's end but Anfield's glory years were coming to an end and there would be just one more winners' medal added to the Whelan collection. That came in the League Championship of 1989–90. Ronnie's elevation to captain at Anfield had coincided with a similar appointment for Ireland. Following the Republic's qualification for the 1990 World Cup, Charlton had decided that it would be inappropriate for an English-born player to captain the Irish team and so transferred the armband from Mick McCarthy to Whelan. However, when Ronnie was injured ahead of the tournament McCarthy was reinstated as skipper.

Injuries would also restrict Ronnie's appearances during the latter part of his career, although when fit, he remained a regular member of Charlton's squad and in 1994, at the age of 32, he was included in his second World Cup finals squad. However, he would again play no more than a bit part, although there were many pundits who believed his experience would have been put to good use in the key match against Holland.

With Andy Townsend installed as a permanent fixture in the Republic of Ireland midfield, Ronnie made just two more appearances for his country. In 1995 he commenced his managerial career with Southend United – whom he had joined as a player the year before. But after two troublesome seasons in Division One, Ronnie Whelan swapped the Essex coast for the Mediterranean and a one-season spell as coach of Greek club Panionios.

Indomitable, intrepid and imposing, the popular Donegal man became a national hero.

1981–1996

80 **0**
CAPS GOALS

BORN ● Donegal, 24.5.60
DEBUT ● v Poland (A) 24.5.81
CLUBS ● Celtic

Packie Bonner embodied the spirit of the Jack Charlton era more than any other player. Indomitable, intrepid and imposing, the popular Donegalman – who holds the record number of caps for an Irish goalkeeper – became a national hero after his faultless displays at the 1988 European Championships. Packie was a custodian who radiated confidence to those around him and his extensive frame and buoyant personality provided the foundation for Charlton to build his successful team of the 1980s and 1990s. Nitpickers pointed to a supposed weakness on crosses, but while this may have caused an occasional moment of anxiety at club level, it was a problem which rarely surfaced when the big number-one was on duty for Ireland.

Packie Bonner

Packie began his professional career with Celtic, becoming Jock Stein's final signing when he arrived in 1978 from junior side Keadue Rovers. He enjoyed a 17-year career with the Bhoys, appearing in 483 League matches – more than any other goalkeeper in the club's history. In 1980–81, aged 20, Packie was installed as the first-choice keeper at Parkhead and at season's end he collected the first of four League Championship badges. Twelve clean sheets in 36 matches was also enough to catch the attention of Ireland manager Eoin Hand and in May 1981 Packie was called into the senior squad for a tour of Germany and Poland.

On his 21st birthday, Packie – who had won caps at youth and under-21 level – made his debut in the full team. It was to prove an inauspicious start to a career which would attain such highs. Ireland lost the game (a friendly against Poland) 3-0, and the new boy found himself out of the line-up for almost a year. Even when he returned to the team, Packie was a stand-in for Jim McDonagh. It was only in 1985 that the Celtic shot-stopper was given a run of more than two games in an Ireland jersey.

The arrival of Jack Charlton as Republic of Ireland manager in 1986 proved the watershed in Packie's international career. The new manager toyed briefly with the idea of deploying Fulham's Gerry Peyton between the posts but when the serious business of qualifying for the 1986 European Championships got underway, it was the 6'2" Bonner who donned Ireland's number one jersey. Packie proved the perfect goalkeeper for Charlton's tactics; providing not only dauntless shot-stopping and impeccable handling but also a powerful and accurate long kick. With the likes of Frank Stapleton and Niall Quinn as willing targets, these exocet-like deliveries became a key weapon in Ireland's armoury and led to the downfall of many fashionable and fancied opponents.

Packie missed just one of the qualifying fixtures ahead of the 1988 European Championships and played in each of Ireland's three matches during the tournament finals in Germany. The clash against England in Stuttgart brought the best out of the obdurate net guard, who produced a superb save late on to deny Gary Lineker. Ireland would lose just one of their games – a 1-0 reverse to eventual champions Holland – and returned home with a much-enhanced reputation.

In 1990 the Republic of Ireland qualified for their first World Cup finals and, in so doing, made the step-up from likeable underdogs to dangerous wild cards. Bonner, at his assured best, conceded just two goals in the group matches but it was his performance in the second round tie against Romania for which he will always be remembered. After two hours of football the game remained scoreless and went to a penalty shootout. The stage was set for Packie to make his mark, and he did not disappoint. After four successful spot-kicks for each team, the weary Ireland keeper produced a superb save, diving to his right, to deny Romania's Daniel Timofte. Although Charlton's team lost out to Italy in the quarter-finals Packie had played superbly against the hosts and was unlucky to concede the only goal of the game after making an excellent save from Donadoni.

But success in football is nothing if not ephemeral. Four years after his high-jinks at Italia 90, Packie's nadir arrived in the unlikely setting of Orlando, Florida. In the heat of high summer, the Irish crashed out of the USA World Cup after two uncharacteristic defensive errors against Holland, the second of which left the experienced keeper red-faced after he misjudged the bounce of a far-from threatening Wim Jonk long-range shot. Packie would win just three more caps – two as captain – before hanging up his boots to concentrate on a career in coaching with first Celtic and later Reading.

TONY GALVIN

1982–1989

 29 CAPS   **1** GOALS

BORN ● Huddersfield, 12.7.56
DEBUT ● v Holland (A) 22.9.82
CLUBS ● Tottenham Hotspur, Sheffield Wednesday, Swindon Town

Tony Galvin was neither the most skilful nor the most stylish player to wear Ireland's number 11 shirt, but he was undoubtedly one of the most effective. He was the type of footballer commonly described as 'direct', and his refreshingly uncomplicated wingplay was a key factor in the success Jack Charlton enjoyed in the early years of his reign as manager. With Tony there were no frills, no tricks or meandering runs; just large measures of both enterprise and endeavour. However, it would be wrong to portray this energetic Yorkshireman as a mere wing workhorse. Tony – a natural right-footer, although he played most of his career on the left – was a potent attacker who delivered accurate centres with either foot, and his industrious but intelligent forward-play left many a top-class full-back yearning for a more enigmatic opponent to mark.

Like Steve Heighway, his predecessor on Ireland's left flank, Tony is one of only a small number of footballers to have enjoyed the benefits of a university education. After three years of combining a Russian Studies degree with non-League football for Goole Town, he was already in his 22nd year when he got the chance to make the switch to soccer's big time in January 1978. A £30,000 move to Keith Burkinshaw's Tottenham Hotspur, saw Tony join a midfield which already boasted England internationals Glenn Hoddle and Peter Taylor, and which would soon be further gilded by the addition of World Cup winners Ricardo Villa and Osvaldo Ardiles. Somewhat inevitably, the new boy from non-League had to wait his turn for a regular place in the starting line-up. By the early 1980s, though, Tony had made his mark and he was a key player in the Spurs teams which won the FA Cup in both 1981 and 1982, and which claimed the UEFA Cup in 1984.

Tony's success at White Hart Lane attracted the interest of Republic of Ireland manager Eoin Hand, who had discovered that the player qualified to represent Ireland under the grandparent rule. A debut in a European Championships qualifier against the Dutch duly arrived in 1982. Thereafter Tony remained a regular member of the international squad under Hand, but it was following the appointment of Jack Charlton in 1986 that he enjoyed his best days in Ireland green. The Galvin game was perfectly suited to Charlton's pragmatic philosophy, which placed great stock in getting the ball forward early and without fuss. Tony would play a key role in the qualification campaign for the 1988 European Championships, and was included in the starting line-up for all three of Ireland's matches at the tournament finals in Germany. However, by the time the next international fixture came around, he was 32 years old and with Kevin Sheedy providing fierce competition, he added just two more caps to his total. Tony would enjoy spells at both Sheffield Wednesday and Swindon Town – where he was also assistant manager – before injury forced him to hang up his boots in 1989.

EAMONN DEACY

1982

4 **0**
CAPS GOALS

BORN Galway, 1.10.58
DEBUT v Algeria (A) 28.4.82
CLUBS Aston Villa

Eamonn Deacy was a strong and reliable full-back who came to prominence with Galway Rovers in the late 1970s. A move to Aston Villa arrived in 1979, but in four and a half years at Villa Park the left-sided defender made just 33 League appearances. Eamonn's lack of first team opportunities prompted him to move to Derby County for a brief loan spell during 1983, but he decided against making the switch permanent, and shortly afterwards he returned to his native Galway to resume his career in the League of Ireland. By then he had already been capped at senior international level.

All four of Eamonn's appearances for the boys in green arrived in friendly matches during 1982. His debut, as a second-half substitute against Algeria in the Olympic Stadium in Algiers, was followed by caps in each of the next three games on a tour of South America. Unfortunately for Eamonn, Ireland lost all four of the matches he played in, and his last appearance came in the humiliating 2-1 reverse against Trinidad and Tobago in Port of Spain.

MIKE WALSH

1982

4 **0**
CAPS GOALS

BORN Manchester, 20.6.56
DEBUT v Chile (A) 21.5.82
CLUBS Everton

Mike Walsh was a powerful left-sided defender who got his chance in Ireland green when a host of high profile rivals withdrew from a summer tour of South America in 1982. Mike began his career at Bolton Wanderers, becoming a first team regular at Burnden Park in 1978. He made 177 League appearances for Bolton, but in the summer of 1981 moved to Everton in an exchange deal that saw Ireland 'keeper Jim McDonagh move in the opposite direction.

In two seasons at Goodison, Mick was rarely seen in the first team, but it was as an Everton player that he made the breakthrough to international football. His debut cap came in the 1-0 reverse against Chile and was followed by appearances in defeats against Brazil (7-0) and Trinidad and Tobago (2-1). Mick 's fourth and final cap came in a European Championships qualifier against Iceland in Dublin and, at last, he found himself on the winning team, with Ireland recording a 2-0 victory. He would go on to enjoy a successful spell with Blackpool from 1983 to 1989, but was unable to force his way back into the Ireland team.

PAT BYRNE

1984–1986

8 **0**
CAPS GOALS

BORN Dublin, 15.5.56
DEBUT v Poland (H) 23.5.84
CLUBS Shamrock Rovers

It was Pat Byrne's misfortune that his eight-cap international career straddled the management of Eoin Hand and Jack Charlton. After six appearances in the green shirt, Pat had proved himself good enough to gain a first taste of World Cup football – albeit in the 4-1 defeat against Denmark in November 1985. But that match was to be Hand's last in charge, and Pat's days were numbered when Charlton took charge. He would win just one more Ireland cap.

This short international career fails to reflect Byrne's reputation within Irish football as a versatile performer who operated, with good skill, at either full-back or in midfield. A trophy-laden career with Bohemians was interrupted by spells with Leicester City and Hearts, but it was when Pat returned to Ireland to play for Shamrock Rovers in 1983 that he enjoyed his best form. He helped the Hoops to League and Cup successes throughout the mid-1980s.

Pat's virtues were not lost on his fellow players and he was named PFAI Player of the Year in 1983-84. This accolade was followed by the Irish Football Writers' award in 1984-85.

KIERAN O'REGAN
1983–1985
Born: Cork, 9.11.63
Caps: 4
Goals: 0
Debut v Malta (H) 16.11.83
Clubs: Brighton and Hove Albion

Kieran O'Regan was a versatile footballer who could operate at either full-back or in midfield, and who enjoyed a successful career in the Football League with several clubs, most notably Brighton and Hove Albion and Huddersfield Town. All of Kieran's caps arrived during his four-year spell at the Goldstone Ground and came while Eoin Hand was manager of the national team. However, while still only 21 years old, the Cork-born defender won his fourth and final cap as a substitute in a friendly against Spain in 1985.

MICK FAIRCLOUGH
1982
Born: Drogheda, 22.10.52
Caps: 2
Goals: 0
Debut v Chile (A) 21.5.82
Clubs: Dundalk

Mick Fairclough made just two substitute appearances in the senior international team but for a player who had spent several years out of the game with injury, his debut was a huge achievement. The Drogheda-born forward, who was renowned for his ball skills, sustained a serious knee injury while playing for Huddersfield Town and it looked for a time that his career was over. But Mick eventually battled back to full fitness and it was as a Dundalk player that he won both his caps during a tour of South America.

SEAN O'DRISCOLL
1982
Born: Wolverhampton, 1.7.57
Caps: 3
Goals: 0
Debut v Chile (A) 21.5.82
Clubs: Fulham

Midfielder Sean O'Driscoll qualified for the Republic of Ireland under the parentage rule, and won all three of his senior caps during the tour of South America in 1982. Sean, who also won three under-21 caps, would make no further appearances in Ireland green, but went on to enjoy a long career with AFC Bournemouth in England.

JOHNNY WALSH
1982
Born: Limerick, 1957
Caps: 1
Goals: 0
Debut v Trinidad and Tobago (A) 30.5.82
Clubs: Limerick

Johnny Walsh was a member of Eoin Hand's successful Limerick team of the early 1980s, and was called into the senior international squad following a spate of withdrawals ahead of the 1982 tour of South America. A one-club man who started and finished with Limerick, his home-town team, Johnny had already earned inter-League honours by the time he won his only cap in the 2-1 reverse against Trinidad and Tobago.

JACKO McDONAGH
1983–1984
Born: Dublin, 1960
Caps: 3
Goals: 0
Debut v Malta (H) 16.11.83
Clubs: Shamrock Rovers

Jacko McDonagh was an accomplished centre-half who enjoyed a successful career in League of Ireland football with first Bohemians and later Shamrock Rovers. As an under-21 international, Jacko had played alongside the likes of Ronnie Whelan, Packie Bonner and Kevin Sheedy, and in 1983 he got the chance to look up some of his old pals when he was called into Eoin Hand's senior squad for the European Championships qualifier against Malta at Dalymount Park. He took his bow as a half-time replacement for Kevin Moran. Two further substitute appearances followed, both in 1984, but with messrs. Lawrenson, O'Leary, Moran, McGrath and McCarthy all ahead of him in the queue for defensive positions Jacko McDongah's collection of caps remained at three.

LIAM BUCKLEY
1984
Born: Dublin, 14.4.60
Caps: 2
Goals: 0
Debut v Poland (H) 23.5.84
Clubs: Shamrock Rovers,
Waregem

Strong and skilful, Liam Buckley was one of the most feared strikers in League of Ireland football during the early 1980s. He made his name with Shamrock Rovers, whom he joined in 1979. The Dubliner would help Rovers to League success in 1983-84 – scoring 14 goals – and his form was noticed by Eoin Hand, who called him into the senior international line-up for two friendlies in the summer of 1984. In between winning his two caps Liam completed a move to Belgian club Waregem and, thereafter, he received no further international recognition.

GARY HOWLETT
1984
Born: Dublin, 2.4.63
Caps: 1
Goals: 0
Debut v China (N) 3.6.84
Clubs: Brighton and Hove Albion

Gary Howlett was a talented midfielder with an eye for goal, whose professional career enjoyed an action-packed start. By the age of 21, the 5'8" Dubliner had played in an FA Cup final, endured the pain of relegation and had made his senior international debut. The Cup and relegation drama had been provided by Brighton and Hove Albion's 1982-83 season, while the debut cap had arrived in a Japan Cup match against China. Thereafter Gary's career would fail to maintain its momentum and, despite reliable service with AFC Bournemouth and York City, he made no further appearances in Ireland green.

PETER ECCLES
1986
Born: Dublin, 24.8.62
Caps: 1
Goals: 0
Debut v Uruguay (H) 23.4.86
Clubs: Shamrock Rovers

Peter Eccles was a powerful centre-half who was a key member of the Shamrock Rovers team which won five consecutive League titles in the mid-1980s. A product of St Brendan's in Cabra, the red-headed stopper enjoyed the briefest of international careers when he was called upon as a substitute for the last ten minutes of Jack Charlton's second game in charge (a friendly against Uruguay at Lansdowne Road).

TONY MACKEN
1977
Born: Dublin, 30.7.50
Caps: 1
Goals: 0
Debut v Spain (H) 9.2.77
Clubs: Derby County

Tony Macken began his career with Home Farm, but it was as a Derby County player – following spells at Glentoran and Waterford – that he won his one and only senior cap. Tony's international debut had arrived during John Giles's tenure as manager and in October 1977 the Dublin-born utility player joined Third Division Walsall in an effort to gain regular first-team football. He would make 190 League appearances for the Saddlers but was unable to earn a recall to international colours.

ALAN CAMPBELL
1985
Born: Dublin, 10.8.60
Caps: 3
Goals: 0
Debut v Italy (H) 5.2.85
Clubs: Racing Club de Santander

Alan Campbell was a prolific goalscorer who enjoyed successful spells with club sides in three countries after coming to prominence with Shamrock Rovers in the early 1980s. Alan, who was League of Ireland top scorer with 24 goals from 26 games in 1983–84, got his chance in Eoin Hand's senior international team following a move to Spanish club Racing Santander. All three of his caps arrived in friendly matches in 1985, but with Jack Charlton taking over as manager shortly afterwards Alan's days in green were brought to an abrupt ending.

As is often the case with talented playmakers, Kevin was viewed with a degree of suspicion by many pundits.

1983–1993

CAPS **GOALS**
46   9

BORN ● Builth Wells, 21.10.59
DEBUT ● v Holland (H) 12.10.83
CLUBS ● Everton, Newcastle United

The phrase 'sweet left foot' is one of the legion of hackneyed clichés bandied around by modern football commentators, but in the case of Kevin Sheedy it, for once, found legitimate use. Sheedy struck the ball with both unerring accuracy and prodigious power, but most importantly he employed his shamanistic left boot with stealth and intelligence. Not for him the hopeful punt forward or the high-velocity cross to nobody.

Kevin Sheedy

Kevin, who could operate either on the flank or through the middle, was thrifty in possession and his distribution, whether from dead ball or open play, was both precise and imaginative. Penetrating through-balls were something of a Sheedy speciality, as were his wickedly curling centres, which proved a fruitful source of goals at both club and international level.

However, as is often the case with talented playmakers, Kevin was viewed with a degree of suspicion by many pundits. The critics said that he lacked strength, that he was weak in the tackle and that he couldn't head the ball. They were, to a degree, correct in their observations, but surely the attacking talents of the adroit midfielder more than compensated for any defensive shortcomings? Howard Kendall, for one, was in no doubt, and in 1982 the Everton boss paid a tribunal-set fee of £100,000 to take the Welsh-born midfielder across Stanley Park from Anfield, home of rivals Liverpool. Kevin, who began his career at Hereford United, had spent two years clicking his heels in Liverpool's reserves, but soon made a mockery of his paltry price tag. He would prove a pivotal figure in Kendall's successful Everton team of the mid-1980s, playing a key role in League Championship triumphs in 1984–85 and 1986–87, and scoring the clinching goal in the 1985 European Cup Winners' Cup final.

In his first season at Goodison, Kevin's excellent form (he scored 11 goals in 40 games) earned him a call-up to Eoin Hand's senior international squad. A debut cap duly arrived when he came on with eight minutes to go during a European Championship qualifier against Holland at Dalymount Park in 1983. The game ended in a 3–2 defeat for Ireland, and the next match, against Malta, saw Hand make wholesale changes to his team. Kevin was among those to benefit from the manager's tinkering, playing the full 90 minutes and scoring his first goal in Ireland green. However, despite his impressive performance, the Everton player found himself out of the Ireland team for the next year. For the remainder of Hand's reign as manager he would be no more than an occasional international.

The arrival of Jack Charlton as Ireland boss in 1986 brought radical changes and a new tactical approach. Kevin was not among those to profit immediately from the Englishman's new broom. And throughout his first three years in charge, Jack would opt for the more industrious qualities of the indefatigable Tony Galvin over the sorcery of Sheedy. Kevin did, however, make his contribution – albeit in something of a bit-part role – to the memorable 1988 European Championship campaign, playing in a vital qualifier against Scotland and making two appearances at the tournament finals in Germany. Thereafter, the diminutive Evertonian became a regular in Charlton's line-up and he enjoyed his international zenith at the 1990 World Cup finals in Italy.

Kevin would play in all five of Ireland's games at Italia 90, but it was in the 73rd minute of the first match, against England in Cagliari, that he made his greatest contribution. With the boys in green trailing to a scrappy Gary Lineker goal, he won the ball on the edge of the England penalty area, took aim and, with the merest of back-lift, crashed a low drive beyond Peter Shilton to register a deserved equaliser and Ireland's first goal at a World Cup finals. Kevin, though, was not finished. When Charlton's team found themselves facing a penalty shoot-out after the deadlocked second round match against Romania, there was only one choice to take the first spot-kick. Once more the famous left boot of Sheedy did the trick, setting Ireland on course for a place in the quarter-finals against Italy.

However, after the high jinx of Italia 90 the fortunes of both Ireland and Kevin Sheedy began to dip gently. The qualification programme for the 1992 European Championships would end in disappointment and thereafter Kevin – who moved on to Newcastle United in 1992 – began to struggle in the wake of advancing years and niggling injuries. There was, though, to be a final flourish to the international career of this accomplished midfielder. He signed off his days in green with goals in each of his final two matches against Latvia and Wales.

The qualifying campaign for Italia 90 had seen Mick establish himself as not only Republic of Ireland skipper but also Jack Charlton's voice on the pitch.

1984–1992

57 **2**
CAPS GOALS

BORN Barnsley, 7.2.59
DEBUT v Poland (H) 23.5.84
CLUBS Manchester City, Celtic, Olympique Lyonnais, Millwall

There was nothing flashy or indulgent about Mick McCarthy the player. No frills or histrionics, just a large measure of Yorkshire grit and an even larger helping of self-belief. Mick was by no means the complete footballer – he was almost exclusively right footed and his lack of pace was particularly well documented – but his committed, whole-hearted approach more than made up for any shortcomings.

Mick McCarthy

McCarthy began his career with home town club Barnsley, making his League debut in a Fourth Division match against Rochdale in August 1977. He became an instant regular in the centre of the Tykes defence (missing just eight League games out of the next 270), and played his part in helping the club climb from the Fourth to the Second Division with promotions in 1978-79 and 1980-81. But after six seasons at Oakwell, he was keen to move on to a 'bigger' club, and in December 1983 crossed the Pennines to sign for Billy McNeill's Manchester City.

The switch to City brought Mick to the attention of Republic of Ireland manager Eoin Hand and in May 1984, aged 25, he made his international debut in a friendly against Poland. Mick – who qualified for Ireland by virtue of his Waterford-born father – had been surprised by his call-up. With David O'Leary, Mark Lawrenson and Kevin Moran already competing for places at the heart of the Ireland defence, it seemed that Eoin Hand was hardly in need of a new centre-half. But Mick took his chance, giving an assured and disciplined debut performance alongside David O'Leary in a match which ended goalless. The manager was clearly impressed by Manchester City's reigning player of the season, who missed just four of Hand's remaining sixteen games in charge.

The following season (1984-85) saw Mick help Manchester City gain promotion to the First Division, but in the autumn of 1985 Ireland suffered the disappointment of concluding another unsuccessful World Cup qualifying campaign. Eoin Hand resigned as manager and Jack Charlton was appointed as his replacement. Charlton knew McCarthy well – the two men had even

shared the same local pub in Barnsley – but he omitted the Yorkshireman from his starting line-up for his first game in charge, against Wales in March 1986. It proved, however, to be no more than a short-term blip in the McCarthy career, and Mick was back in the eleven for each of the next three games, assuming the captaincy for the last of these (a friendly against Czechoslovakia).

Throughout Ireland's qualifying programme for the 1988 European Championships Jack Charlton's favoured central-defensive pairing was that of Moran and McCarthy. It was a selection that divided the pundits, with many unhappy that Mick had been picked at the expense of the more skilful, but less combative, David O'Leary. The critics, however, could not argue with results and in November 1987 Ireland qualified for their first major tournament: the 1988 European Championships. Mick had played in six of the eight qualifiers and would keep his place for all three of Ireland's matches at the finals in Germany.

McCarthy was also enjoying success at club level. In May 1987 he had left Manchester City to join Scottish giants Celtic in a £500,000 move. Mick's first season at Parkhead was somewhat injury disrupted (he played in 22 of Celtic's 44 League games) but ended in glory when the club claimed the 'double' of Premier League and Scottish Cup. The following campaign brought further success in the Cup, but in the League the Bhoys finished a disappointing third, and at season's end Mick left Parkhead to join French club Olympique Lyonnais. It proved a short-term move, however, and in March 1990 he returned to Britain to join Millwall in England's First Division.

It was as a Millwall player, at the World Cup finals in Italy during the summer of 1990, that McCarthy reached his footballing zenith. The qualifying campaign for Italia 90 had seen Mick establish himself as not only Republic of Ireland skipper but also Jack Charlton's voice on the pitch. Mick understood his manager's tactics and, whether he agreed with them or not, he made sure that they were adhered to. The efforts of both Charlton and McCarthy were rewarded with a run to the last eight of the World Cup and both men returned from Italy as heroes. The captain had been an inspirational figure for the Irish and Charlton was in no doubt as to the value of his contribution, describing him as 'One of the most loyal and trusted players I've ever managed.' It was fitting, therefore, that when Charlton stepped down as manager in 1996, Mick should succeed him.

Only Frank Stapleton has scored more for the Irish, and whatever Cascarino lacks in finesse and pace he more than makes up for in endeavour.

1985–

82	19
CAPS	GOALS

BORN ● Orpington, 1.9.62
DEBUT ● v Switzerland (A) 11.9.85
CLUBS ● Gillingham, Millwall, Aston Villa, Celtic, Chelsea,
Olympique Marseille, AS Nancy-Lorraine

When Pele described football as 'the beautiful game', he clearly did not have Tony Cascarino in mind. Cascarino – lanky, languid, and dentally-challenged – is quite probably the most inelegant footballer to have worn the green jersey of Ireland. However, a striker is judged by goals not technical merit and against this yardstick Tony's record for Ireland is impressive. Only Frank Stapleton has scored more for the Irish, and whatever Cascarino lacks in finesse and pace he more than makes up for in endeavour.

Tony Cascarino

Tony began his career with amateur side Crockenhill, only moving into the professional game as a 19-year-old with Third Division Gillingham in January 1982. The 6'3" striker, who joined the Gills in a swap deal which saw a set of tracksuits and half a dozen balls pass in the opposite direction, proved an immediate success at the Priestfield Stadium, scoring five goals from 19 starts in 1981-82. Tony improved his strike rate the next season, netting 15 goals in 38 appearances and maintained a rate of around a goal every three games for the next two campaigns.

Ireland manager Eoin Hand quickly learned that, despite his Italian name, Tony qualified for the Irish under the grandparent rule and in September 1985 the 23-year-old Cascarino made his international debut in a World Cup qualifier against Switzerland in Berne. The match ended in a disappointing 0–0 draw, but the newcomer kept his place in the line-up for the next two matches. However, when Ireland failed to qualify for the World Cup finals in Mexico, Hand resigned as manager. Jack Charlton was appointed as his successor and, after three successive appearances, Cascarino found himself on the sidelines.

John Aldridge would keep Tony out of the international team for the first two and a half years of Charlton's reign, and it was not until May 1988 that he returned to Ireland green. In the interim he had made impressive progress at club level. He had joined Millwall for £200,000 in the summer of 1987 and in his first season struck 20 League goals, helping his new club to promotion and the Second Division Championship. Jack Charlton, who had led Ireland to the

finals of the 1988 European Championships, was not about to ignore a player in form, and recalled the Millwall striker for a friendly against Poland. Tony took his chance, scoring his first international goal in a 3-1 win. It was enough to earn him a place in the squad for Euro 88, where he made substitute appearances against Holland and the USSR.

Cascarino was an ever-present during Ireland's qualifying campaign for the 1990 World Cup finals. But at Millwall things were not going to plan and with the Lions heading for relegation Tony was sold to First Division leaders Aston Villa for £1.5m in March 1990. The switch to the Midlands was to prove a huge disappointment and Tony failed to find the net in his first eight games for the club. There was further disappointment for Cascarino at the World Cup finals in Italy during the summer of 1990 where, after two games without a goal, he was dropped to the bench for the clash with Holland. Tony would become something of a specialist number 12 for Ireland during the 1990s and no player has made more appearances as a sub for the boys in green.

Tony's miserable time at club level continued during 1990-91, and at season's end he departed Villa Park for £1.1m to begin an equally ill-fated spell with Celtic. After just four goals in 24 appearances for the Bhoys he was on the move again, signing for Chelsea. Tony made a bright start with the Blues, scoring on his debut. However, injuries were to plague his two-and-a-half-year spell in West London and after just eight goals and 40 League appearances he found himself out of contract and facing an uncertain future in the spring of 1994. Fortunately, Jack Charlton had not been swayed by Cascarino's faltering club form and the rangy frontman remained a regular in the Ireland squad.

The 1994 World Cup finals in the USA gave Tony the chance to showcase his unique talents for prospective clubs, but shortly after the Irish arrived he was struck down by a hamstring injury. He missed all three of Ireland's group matches and played just 15 minutes of the second round defeat against Holland. He had done enough, however, to secure a move to French club Olympique Marseille where his career enjoyed a surprising and successful Indian summer. He finished his first season in France as the country's top scorer, before moving on to enjoy further success with AS Nancy-Lorraine. Tony Cascarino had come a long way since his kit and balls transfer to Gillingham and as he approached his 38th year there was still every chance that he would end his career as Ireland's record goalscorer.

JIM BEGLIN

1984–1986

15 CAPS   **0** GOALS

BORN ● Waterford, 29.7.63
DEBUT ● Debut v China (N) 3.6.84
CLUBS ● Liverpool

A double compound commuted fracture was the medical diagnosis of the injury sustained by Liverpool's Jim Beglin in a League Cup quarter-final against Everton at Goodison Park in January 1987. Put simply, Beglin had shattered his leg. It was, alas, an injury from which the 23-year-old Irish defender would never fully recover.

Beglin, who had arrived at Anfield from Shamrock Rovers for a fee of £25,000 in May 1983, was a left-back of the very highest quality. He had pace, composure, an assured first touch and although lightly built, was a stern competitor. Jim spent his first season at Liverpool in the reserves, but progressed sufficiently to earn a call-up to Eoin Hand's Republic of Ireland team for two friendlies during the summer of 1984. The following November, the Waterford-born full-back broke into the first team at Anfield and also made his competitive debut for the Republic, in a World Cup qualifier away to Denmark. The match in Copenhagen ended in a 3–0 defeat, but, the newcomer was not held culpable and he kept his place in the line-up for the next four games.

Throughout 1984–85 Jim was regularly called upon to deputise for Liverpool's established left-back Alan Kennedy, and a season of high achievement at club level culminated with his inclusion in Joe Fagan's team for the European Cup final at the Heysel Stadium, Brussels. By autumn 1985 Beglin had become a regular in the Republic of Ireland line-up, while at Anfield he was enjoying an increasingly influential role alongside messrs. Hansen, Lawrenson and Nichol in one of the most talented back-fours English football had ever seen. In such exalted company, Jim's game continued to develop and a propensity for occasional lapses in concentration soon disappeared. A remarkable season was completed when he collected winner's medals for both the First Division Championship and the FA Cup as a member of Kenny Dalglish's 'double' team of 1985–86.

However, just when it seemed that Beglin was destined to wear the number three jersey of both Liverpool and Ireland for many years to come, disaster stuck with *that* injury at Goodison. He was out of action for more than two years and, though he recovered sufficient fitness to make a comeback, he was never able to regain either his sharpness or confidence. In June 1989 Jim moved to Leeds United on a free transfer, but further injury troubles hindered his time at Elland Road and after spells on loan at Plymouth Argyle and Blackburn Rovers he was forced to retire. Fortunately, like Mark Lawrenson, his former Anfield team-mate, Jim has since enjoyed success as a pundit and commentator on both radio and television.

With his flashy ball skills and mane of blonde hair, John Byrne looked every inch the 'fancy Dan' – a throwback to the halcyon days the early 1970s when maverick talents like Rodney Marsh and Stan Bowles entertained the crowds. Byrne was no luxury player, and he combined his repertoire of tricks and flicks with a commendable work rate. He was a versatile player too and could operate in midfield or in the forward line with equal facility. Byrne was at his most effective, though, when playing as a withdrawn striker. From such a position, behind the main frontman, he was able to make good use of his creative talents without exposing his greatest flaw: a slight lack of pace.

Byrne began his career with Fourth Division York City, making his League debut as an 18-year-old substitute in a 2-0 home defeat against Lincoln City in August 1979. He became a regular for the Minstermen the following season, but it was in 1983-84 that he caught the attention of scouts from England's top clubs. Byrne finished the campaign with 27 goals from 46 appearances and in October 1984 moved on to First Division Queens Park Rangers in a £120,000 deal. Four months after making the switch to Loftus Road, Manchester-born Byrne (who qualified for the Republic of Ireland by virtue of his Carlow-born father) won the first of his 23 caps when Eoin Hand called him up for a friendly against Italy at Dalymount Park. He made just two more appearances under Hand, both in friendlies and both as a substitute.

The substitute's role was to become a familiar one to Byrne throughout his international career, with seven of his first ten caps coming from the bench. Jack Charlton would employ Byrne as both striker and midfielder and included him in the final squads for both the 1988 European Championships and the 1990 World Cup. He was unable to make it into the line-up for any of Ireland's matches at either tournament but remained a regular in Charlton's squad until the end of the unsuccessful qualifying campaign for the 1992 European Championships.

At club level Byrne enjoyed a two-year run with French club Le Havre between 1988 and 1990, before returning to England to become something of a Football League nomad during the early 1990s. A spell at Sunderland provided the undoubted highlight of this period, with Byrne proving the hero of the Wearsiders' run to the FA Cup final in 1992. Alas, at Wembley, he was unable to maintain a record which had seen him score in each of the previous rounds in the competition and Sunderland lost 2-0. Byrne, who made his final appearance in Ireland green in a friendly against Wales in February 1993, retired from League action at the age of 35.

JOHN BYRNE

1985–1993

23 **4**

CAPS   GOALS

BORN Manchester, 1.2.61
DEBUT v Italy (H) 5.2.85
CLUBS Queens Park Rangers, Le Havre AC, Brighton and Hove Albion, Sunderland, Millwall

McGrath is quite probably the greatest defender to have worn the green jersey of Ireland.

1985–1997

83 CAPS   **8** GOALS

BORN ● Ealing, 4.12.59
DEBUT ● v Italy (H) 5.2.85
CLUBS ● Manchester United, Aston Villa, Derby County

The life and times of Paul McGrath would make the perfect sporting biopic. It is the classic tale of triumph against adversity, a story that begins in a Dublin children's home and ends with our hero as the most capped player in the history of the Republic of Ireland. McGrath, a man of fierce appearance but modest personality, was forced to contend with frequent problems throughout his career, most notably a serious knee complaint.

Paul McGrath

Paul McGrath is quite probably the greatest defender to have worn the green jersey of Ireland. Strong in the tackle, good in the air, quick (in his younger days) and with great distribution he lacked nothing as a central defender.

Despite his conspicuous talents, McGrath made a somewhat truncated journey into football's big time. He began with junior team Pearse Rovers before moving on to non-League Dalkey United. He quickly became Dalkey's star player and in the autumn of 1981 stepped up to the League of Ireland with St Patrick's Athletic. He proved a revelation at St Pat's too and was voted PFAI Player of the Year for 1981–82. Scouts from England descended and even before he had completed his first season with St Pat's, the then 22-year-old stopper was on the move again, joining Manchester United in April 1992 for a bargain £30,000.

McGrath took his League bow against Spurs in 1982, but it was not until the second half of the 1984–85 season that he won a regular place in Ron Atkinson's team. International recognition also came Paul's way during 1985 and in February he made his Ireland debut as a sub in a friendly against Italy at Dalymount. The match ended in a 2–1 reverse for the Irish but the newcomer gave a polished display against the World Cup holders and won caps in each of the next three games (all friendlies). However, when the qualifiers for the 1986 World Cup resumed in May 1985, McGrath found himself out of the team. The disappointment of international rejection was quickly forgotten, when he claimed an FA Cup winner's medal after a commanding display in United's ten-man victory over Everton in 1985.

McGrath was recalled to the Ireland team following the appointment of Jack Charlton in February 1986 and played in 13 of the new manager's first 14 games in charge. Big

Jack, however, felt that a player of such talent should not be hidden away at centre-back and found McGrath a new and pivotal role within his team plan. Paul would play as a midfield sweeper, occupying a position just in front of central defence. The switch proved a success. Ireland booked a place at the 1988 European Championships, with McGrath scoring in each of the last two qualifying matches against Luxemburg and Bulgaria. He would play in two of Ireland's three games at Euro 88 and was, according to many good judges, his country's player of the tournament.

However, McGrath's progress with Ireland served only to highlight his significant problems at club level. Alex Ferguson had taken over as United manager in November 1986 and his relationship with McGrath was strained from the start. The situation was not helped by a string of knee injuries that restricted the Irishman's first-team appearances during 1988. United believed these persistent knee problems would soon bring an end to McGrath's career and in the summer of 1989 he was sold to Graham Taylor's Aston Villa in a cut price £450,000 deal. Many Villa fans suspected that their new signing – now 29 years old – was merely winding down his career. But the doubters were to be proved wrong. United had sold McGrath too soon and, while his famous 'dodgy knees' meant he was not always able to train, he maintained his fitness through a special programme of exercises devised by the Villa physio and enjoyed a seven-season run in the first team at Villa Park.

As he entered his thirties, Paul had become acknowledged as one of the most accomplished footballers of his generation. In 1992–93 he was voted PFA Player of the Year and helped Villa to runners-up spot in the new Premier League. At international level he helped Ireland to the final stages of both the 1990 and 1994 World Cups.

In his latter years, Paul reverted to his favoured position at centre-half and it was from there that he gave his greatest performance for Ireland, in the 1–0 victory over Italy at USA 94. Playing against the sprightly Roberto Baggio he produced an immaculate display, which included an improbable sequence of five blocks and tackles in the space of no more than 20 seconds. McGrath continued to command a place in the Ireland line-up until the end of the qualifying campaign for Euro 96. He would play on with Villa until the autumn of 1996, whereupon he moved on to enjoy spells at first Derby County and later Sheffield United, before hanging up his boots in 1998. It would be many years before football would see the like of Paul McGrath again.

Aesthetics can be misleading and Niall's gangly frame disguises an intelligent and skilful footballer.

1986–

68 CAPS   **16** GOALS

BORN ● Dublin, 6.10.66
DEBUT ● v Iceland (A) 25.5.86
CLUBS ● Arsenal, Manchester City, Sunderland

In a sport which is dominated by image, Niall Quinn's long and successful career is a refreshing triumph of substance over style. Quinn, 6'4" tall and lightly built, cuts an ungainly figure, a player who seems awkward in possession and lumbering when not. Aesthetics, though, can be misleading and Niall's gangly frame disguises an intelligent and skilful footballer.

Niall Quinn

As you would expect, given his height, Niall is an expert header of the ball, but he is more than just a targetman. He has an excellent first touch, passes with élan and leads the line tirelessly. Niall is also capable of the occasional spectacular goal too – nonebetter than his superb curler for Manchester City against West Ham United in 1996.

Niall kicked off his career as an apprentice with Arsenal in 1983 and made the breakthrough to the Gunners first team in December 1985. Niall's debut – against a Liverpool team that would eventually win the 'double' that season - was, to put it tritely, a blinder. The 19-year-old Dubliner scored in a 2-0 victory and was a constant menace to Liverpool's classy central defensive pairing of Alan Hansen and Mark Lawrenson. However, it was to prove something of a false start, and though Niall kept his place in the team for the next nine games, he failed to add to his goals tally.

In the spring of 1986 George Graham took over as Gunners manager and Quinn was forced to prove himself all over again. Initially, at least, the signs were promising, and in Graham's first full season in charge Niall enjoyed his best run in the Arsenal first team – playing 35 games and collecting a League Cup winners' medal. But he scored just eight goals and at season's end the manager invested £800,000 in Leicester's Alan Smith. It was a move which sounded the death knell on Niall Quinn's days at Arsenal.

But while his club career faltered, Niall was at least making progress with Ireland. The young Gunner had won his senior cap against Iceland in May 1986 and became a regular on the Ireland bench thereafter. He made three substitute appearances in the qualifying rounds of the 1988 European Championships and earned a place in the squad. Niall's only action at Euro 88, however, was as a second half sub for Frank Stapleton in the game against England.

Niall left Highbury to join Manchester City for £800,000 in March 1990 and proved an instant success, scoring four times in his first nine games. The following April he was recalled by Charlton after an absence of more than a year. It was a timely return, for without him the Republic had qualified for the 1990 World Cup finals. Niall was included in the squad for Italia 90, but, with messrs. Aldridge and Cascarino the first-choice strikers, he was on the bench for the opening game against England. A substitute appearance followed in the second match against Egypt before Quinn at last made the starting line-up. He played the full 90 minutes of the final group game against Holland and scored the equaliser which sent Ireland into the second round of the World Cup. Quinn would retain his place for the remainder of Italia 90, playing a full role in a run to the quarter-finals.

Niall continued to impress with his performances for City in the early 1990s. He scored 20 goals for the Blues in 1990-91, and averaged a goal every three games during his first three seasons at Maine Road. He was by now Ireland's first choice striker, netting twice and playing in all 12 qualifying matches ahead of the 1994 World Cup finals. However, on 29 November 1993, in a match against Sheffield Wednesday, he ruptured a cruciate ligament and was forced to sit out not only the World Cup finals but also a year of his career. To his credit, Niall made a full recovery from this horrific injury, but his bad luck was not yet over.

Season 1995-96 was to provide a double disappointment. Firstly Ireland missed out on a place at Euro 96 after a play-off defeat against Holland, and then, in May, City were relegated from the Premier League. Niall had played his last game for the Blues, and in August he was sold to newly-promoted Sunderland for £1.3m. But his ill-fortune continued, and after 12 games and two goals, he was struck down by another serious injury which kept him out of action for the remainder of the League campaign. Without Niall, Sunderland struggled and, at season's end, were relegated.

Niall fought his way back to fitness in 1997-98, regaining his place in the Ireland team and scoring 14 League goals as Sunderland progressed to the play-off final. However, at Wembley, Peter Reid's team suffered the heartache of defeat on penalties. The following season Sunderland won promotion as Champions of the Football League and at the age of 32 Niall Quinn was back where he started: the English top-flight. And after a six-year spell dominated by injuries and relegations, it was no more than the likeable Dubliner deserved.

MICK KENNEDY
1986
Born: Salford, Lancashire, 9.4.61
Caps: 2
Goals: 0
Debut: Iceland (A) 25.5.86
Clubs: Portsmouth

Mick Kennedy was an aggressive, left-sided midfielder who got his chance in Ireland green during the early days of Jack Charlton's reign in 1986. Mick, who began his playing days with Halifax Town in 1978, would wear the colours of 10 different League clubs during a 16-year career as a pro but it was as a Portsmouth player that he made his senior international bow. His two caps came in successive victories over Iceland and Czechoslovakia.

BARRY MURPHY
1986
Born: Dublin, 1.4.59
Caps: 1
Goals: 0
Debut v Uruguay (H) 23.4.86
Clubs: Bohemians

Central defender Barry Murphy was an experienced League of Ireland player when he got the call to international colours for Jack Charlton's second game as manager. The Bohemians stopper, by then aged 27, was given his chance for the boys in green when both Paul McGrath and David O'Leary withdrew from the squad for a friendly against Uruguay. Barry would play the full 90 minutes against the South Americans but, despite a solid debut in a match which ended 1-1, it was to prove his one and only cap.

KEN DE MANGE
1987–1988
Born: Dublin, 3.9.64
Caps: 2
Goals: 0
Debut v Brazil (H) 23.5.87
Clubs: Liverpool, Hull City

Ken De Mange was a combative midfielder and former Home Farm junior who began his professional career with Liverpool in August 1983. He would fail to make the first-team at Anfield but, following a loan period at Scunthorpe United in 1986-87, he was somewhat surprisingly elevated to the Republic of Ireland senior squad. Ken made his debut for the boys in green as a second-half substitute in the 1-0 victory over Brazil at Lansdowne Road. A second cap, also as a sub, arrived during a three-season run with Hull City.

KELHAM O'HANLON
1987
Born: Saltburn, 16.5.62
Caps: 1
Goals: 0
Debut v Israel (H) 10.11.87
Clubs: Rotherham United

Rotherham United goalkeeper Kelham O'Hanlon made his Republic of Ireland debut in a 5-0 win over Israel ahead of the 1988 European Championships. However, despite keeping a clean sheet, Kelham was unable to displace Gerry Peyton as Packie Bonner's understudy.

PAT SCULLY
1988
Born: Dublin, 23.6.70
Caps: 1
Goals: 0
Debut v Tunisia (H) 19.10.88
Clubs: Arsenal

A contract at Arsenal and an international debut at 18 years old suggested a bright future for Pat Scully. Alas, youthful promise was never translated into senior success. After winning his cap as a sub for Chris Morris, Pat returned to the Arsenal reserve side and to the Ireland under-21 team to continue his footballing education. With his passage to the Arsenal first team blocked by the likes of Tony Adams, David O'Leary and Steve Bould, Pat moved on to Southend United without making the first team at Highbury. A no-nonsense centre-half, Pat's commitment was never in doubt, but without the pace to succeed at the highest level, he was never likely to displace Moran, McCarthy, McGrath and company.

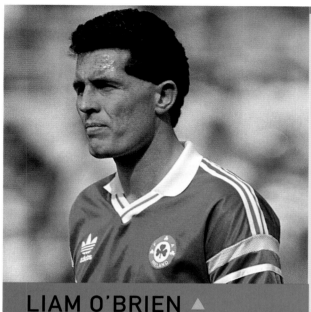

LIAM O'BRIEN ▲

1986–1996

16	0
CAPS	GOALS

BORN ● Dublin, 5.10.64
DEBUG ● v Uruguay (H) 23.4.86
CLUBS ● Shamrock Rovers, Manchester United,
Newcastle United, Tranmere Rovers

Liam O'Brien was already a full international when he crossed the Irish Sea to join Manchester United for £50,000 in October 1986. The 6'1" midfielder had made his Republic of Ireland debut in Jack Charlton's second game in charge after impressing in Shamrock Rovers' 1985-86 League and FAI Cup 'double'-winning team. A clamour for his signature had ensued, and Liam had chosen to head for Old Trafford.

A silky performer who delivers passes with both accuracy and consummate ease, Liam had all the qualities needed to establish himself as playmaker for both club and country. But for all his virtues, the Dubliner was unable to oust Robson, Whiteside, Strachan and co. from the United starting line-up. At international level, too, Liam remained on the fringe of things and in November 1988 he joined Newcastle United in a £275,000 deal.

Injuries would disrupt the early part of Liam's time on Tyneside but in 1992–93 he fulfilled his early potential to become the midfield fulcrum in Kevin Keegan's First Division title winning team. Unfortunately for Liam, his best form had coincided with Jack Charlton settling on a midfield of Houghton, Townsend, Keane and Staunton.

In January 1994 Liam moved on to Tranmere Rovers after making just six Premier League appearances for the Geordies. At Rovers, he retained his position as an occasional player for the Republic, but is difficult not to feel that 16 caps in an 11-year international career is scant recognition for a player of undeniable talent.

TOMMY COYNE ▼

1992–1997

22	6
CAPS	GOALS

BORN ● Glasgow, 14.11.62
DEBUG ● v Switzerland (H) 25.3.92
CLUBS ● Celtic, Tranmere Rovers, Motherwell

Tommy Coyne's greatest moment in Ireland green came in the famous victory against Italy at the 1994 World Cup finals in New York. The Glasgow-born centre-forward played as a lone-striker against the Italians, and it was his tirelessly running at a defence which included the Milan pair of Franco Baresi and Paolo Maldini, that paved the way for a much-celebrated 1-0 triumph.

Tommy, who played in two of Ireland's first three matches at USA 94, had arrived late on the international stage: making a scoring debut as a 29-year-old in a friendly against Switzerland in March 1992. He had come to Jack Charlton's attention as a Celtic player and declared for Ireland under the grandparent rule. In 1993, Tommy spent a seven-month spell with Tranmere Rovers but following the tragic death of his wife he returned to Scotland and, after a short absence from the game, signed for Motherwell. It was as a 'Well player that he appeared at USA 94.

Tommy is an orthodox number-nine who is adept at holding the ball up and is strong with his back to goal. He can also finish, as he showed in emphatic style with a well-taken goal against Holland in a friendly in 1994. Tommy made three appearances for Ireland during the qualifying rounds for the 1996 European Championships, and scored twice in the 4-0 win against Liechtenstein in October 1994. However, despite continued good form for Motherwell, he won just two caps under Mick McCarthy.

The disparity between John's domestic and international form had become even more marked following a £750,000 move to Liverpool in January 1987.

1986–1996

69 CAPS **19** GOALS

BORN ● Liverpool, 18.9.58
DEBUT ● v Wales (H) 26.3.86
CLUBS ● Oxford United, Liverpool, Real Sociedad, Tranmere Rovers

When John Aldridge arrived on the international scene in 1986 it seemed, at last, that the Republic of Ireland had found the prolific finisher they had always lacked. More complete footballers than Aldridge had played at centre-forward for Ireland, but none could match his talent for the crucial business of putting ball in net. He was, to use glib tabloid-speak, a 'natural goalscorer'.

John Aldridge

Anticipation was the key to Aldo's game, and his eye for the main chance, allied to an uncanny ability to hit the target whatever the angle, made for a potent combination. However, despite an impressive strike rate at club level, John struggled to score during his early years with Ireland.

Aldridge qualified under the grandparent rule and made his debut against Wales in the opening game of the Charlton era. International football had come relatively late in Aldridge's career. He was after all 27 years old and a veteran of more than 200 League games with Newport County and Oxford, but a scoring ratio of better than one goal in every two games could not be ignored. However, to universal surprise, John failed to score in his first 20 internationals.

Aldo's goal famine was, in the main, the result of Jack Charlton's game-plan, which relied heavily on pressuring opponents and compressing the play into key areas of the field. The role of Aldridge was critical to this tactic. It was his responsibility to close down defenders and to follow the ball into the corners when it was played into the space behind the full-back. The plan was a huge success, and John, despite his lack of goals, was a crucial factor. He played in seven of Ireland's eight qualifiers for the 1988 European Championships and appeared in all three matches at the tournament finals in Germany.

The disparity between John's domestic and international form had become even more marked following a £750,000 move to Liverpool in January 1987. In 1987-88 he struck 26 goals in 36 League appearances to help 'Pool to the Championship. The following October, with the goals still flowing at club level, John at last broke his duck for Ireland when he struck in a 4-0 victory against Tunisia in Dublin. But there was to be no sudden glut of goals and it was

another year and seven blank appearances before he scored again. John's second goal arrived, along with his third, in a World Cup qualifier against Malta in November 1989.

The autumn of 1989 had seen Aldo leave Liverpool to join Real Sociedad of Spain for £1m. His stay on the continent lasted two seasons, during which time he struck 33 times in 63 appearances, and it was as a Sociedad player that he travelled to the 1990 World Cup finals. Charlton's tactics, however, had changed little since the European Championships two years earlier, and Ireland's number-nine worked tirelessly in all five games at Italia 90 without scoring. In fact, so great were his exertions, that he was substituted in each game and even quipped that his legs would be 'like stumps' by the time Charlton had finished with him.

In July 1991, at the age of 32, Aldridge decided that the time was right to end his sojourn in Spain and he returned to his native Merseyside with Tranmere Rovers for a fee of £250,000. The popular view was that the move was a stepping stone to retirement. Aldo, they said, was on his way out. The moustachioed striker, however, had other ideas and took the concept of an Indian summer to ridiculous extremes with a seven-year run in the Rovers first-team.

The move to Prenton Park would also precede John's best run of scoring for Ireland. He struck six goals in ten games during qualification for the 1994 World Cup finals and made three appearances during the finals in the USA, the most memorable of which came in the first-round match against Mexico. John began the game on the bench, but with Ireland trailing 2-0 he was set to replace Tommy Coyne until the officials intervened to prevent him doing so until an administrative hitch had been resolved. Aldo lambasted the FIFA man and after a six-minute delay during which time Ireland were down to ten men, he was allowed onto the pitch. And, 16 minutes after entering the fray, an intensely fired-up Aldridge scored with a well-taken header which proved decisive to his team's progress to the second round.

John won nine more caps for Ireland after returning from USA 94, and in stark contrast to the opening phase of his international career, he scored five times to end his days in green with a highly respectable total of 19 goals. Aldridge won his final cap came against Macedonia in October 1996, and four months later he took over as player-manager at Tranmere. He would continue to torment First Division defences with Rovers until, at the end of the 1997-98 season, aged 39, he decided to hang up his boots for good.

John nonchalantly held opponents at bay while waiting for the perfect moment to release the ball.

1988–1995

34 **5**
CAPS GOALS

BORN Manchester, 1.10.64
DEBUT v Romania (H) 23.3.88
CLUBS Leeds United,
Sheffield Wednesday

John Sheridan was an adroit playmaker who brought both skill and an air of calm authority to the Republic of Ireland midfield of the late 1980s and early 1990s. He was a player who was rarely hurried and who passed the ball with unerring accuracy and intelligence.

John Sheridan

John was strong too, and nonchalantly held opponents at bay while waiting for the perfect moment to release the ball. Defence-splitting passes were undoubtedly the Sheridan speciality, but he was also a more than capable finisher himself, and counted a powerful right-footed shot among his armoury.

However, despite his obvious talents, John was frequently overlooked by Republic of Ireland manager Jack Charlton, whose formation in the early years of his reign did not always have room for a ball-player in midfield.It was with Charlton's former club, Leeds United, that John began his career, making his League debut against Middlesbrough in November 1982, and adding 26 more appearances by season's end. A broken leg in 1983 brought a temporary halt to the Manchester-born midfielder's progress, but in 1984-85 he was ever-present for Leeds and was rewarded with a call to the Republic of Ireland under-21 team. It was, however, not until March 1988 that John made the step up to the senior international line-up, by which time he had played almost 200 first-team games for Leeds United. His debut, in a friendly against Romania at Lansdowne Road, had arrived shortly after Ireland had clinched qualification for the 1988 European Championships in Germany. The newcomer made an impressive start to his international career, winning caps in four consecutive matches and scoring in a 3-1 win against Poland in Dublin to book a place in the final 20-man party for Euro 88.

However, having established himself in Jack Charlton's squad, John struggled to move beyond the status of fringe player and in the three-and-a-half years after his debut he made just eight appearances in the starting line-up. Charlton's tactic of employing Paul McGrath in a holding role in front of the back four meant that there was intense competition for the remaining central midfield place, a situation not eased by the rapid rise of Andy Townsend and Roy Keane. As a result, John made just one substitute appearance at the 1990 World Cup finals, coming on for the last 12 minutes of the quarter-final defeat against Italy.

Sheridan had travelled to Italia 90 as a Sheffield Wednesday player, having joined the Owls for £500,000 in November 1989. The switch to Hillsborough had, however, only come about after a somewhat bizarre four-month spell at Nottingham Forest. John had arrived at the City Ground in a deal which had not been ratified by Forest boss Brian Clough, and the controversial manager refused to put John in his team, selling him to Ron Atkinson's Wednesday before he had played a game. The move back to Yorkshire would revitalise Sheridan's career and, although his new team were relegated in 1989-90, he was an ever-present during the following campaign as they won promotion at the first attempt. A memorable season was completed when John struck the winning goal in Wednesday's League Cup final victory against Manchester United.

In June 1993, John – who had helped Sheffield Wednesday to both domestic Cup finals in 1992-93 – was recalled to the Republic of Ireland line-up after an absence of more than 18 months. His comeback came with a substitute appearance in a World Cup qualifier against Latvia, which was followed by another run-out from the bench when Spain visited Lansdowne Road four months later. The match against Spain ended in a 3-1 defeat, but John had struck his team's goal and was back in Jack Charlton's plans. Ireland duly qualified for the 1994 World Cup finals and, after impressive performances in pre-tournament friendlies, Sheridan found himself not only in the squad but also in the starting XI for the opening match against Italy in New York. The Sheffield Wednesday midfielder would play in all four of Ireland's games and returned from the finals with his reputation much-enhanced. John remained a key player for the Republic of Ireland throughout the qualifying campaign for the 1996 European Championships. However, at the age of 31, his international career came to an end following the Euro 96 play-off defeat against Holland at Anfield. It was, many felt, a somewhat premature retirement for a player who relied on neither pace nor energy, and who had been greatly underemployed by the boys in green.

Houghton's goals against Italy and England were deserved reward for a footballer who was arguably the most consistent performer of the Charlton era.

1986–1997

 73 **6**

CAPS   GOALS

BORN   Glasgow, 9.1.62
DEBUT   v Wales (H) 26.3.86
CLUBS   Oxford United, Liverpool, Aston Villa,
Crystal Palace, Reading

'Bloody hell! This one's going in,' exclaimed Jack Charlton as Ray Houghton lobbed the ball over Italian goalkeeper Gianluca Pagliuca to strike the only goal of Ireland's opening game at the 1994 World Cup finals. Raymond – as Charlton was wont to call him – did not often score for Ireland, but for the second time in his international career he had struck a goal that would live long in the memory.

Ray Houghton

Six years earlier, he had found the net with an equally famous winner, when he had headed Ireland into an early lead against England at the European Championships.

Houghton's goals against Italy and England were deserved reward for a footballer who was arguably the most consistent performer of the Charlton era. Ray played on the right side of midfield and possessed a rare blend of skill and work-rate, which satisfied both the manager's zeal for industry and the supporters' yearning for entertaining football. He was the archetypal modern wide-player: he could tackle, he could pass and he could shoot, he had great control and even took his defensive duties seriously.

Ray, who was born in Glasgow but spent his adolescence in London, qualified for Ireland by virtue of his Donegal-born father. Ray made his international debut, along with club-mate John Aldridge, in Charlton's first game in charge and kept his place in the line-up for each of the next seven games. He would play a key role in Ireland's qualifying campaign for the 1988 European Championships, missing just one match *en route* to the finals.

Ray's impressive start at international level, however, was in contrast to the struggles he had faced as a youngster with West Ham United. The 5'7" Glaswegian had joined the Hammers as a youth player but, despite impressive form in the club's reserves, made just one first-team appearance in three years at Upton Park. In July 1982 Ray moved across London to sign for Second Division Fulham on a free transfer. His stay with the Cottagers proved a success and in September 1985, after three seasons of first-team action, he moved to First Division Oxford United for £150,000. Ray's progress at both club and international level had been noted by English football's top teams and, shortly after the

start of the 1987-88 season, Liverpool manager Kenny Dalglish handed Oxford United a profit of £675,000 to sign the 25-year-old midfielder. The switch to Anfield brought rapid dividends and in May 1988 Houghton, who had made 28 appearances and scored five goals in his first season with the Reds, collected a League Championship medal.

Title success with Liverpool was quickly followed by further glory as a member of Ireland's team at the 1988 European Championships in Germany. Ray played in all three of Ireland's games and scored his first international goal with a much-celebrated header after five minutes of the opening game against England. It was not only a goal which brought the Irish a sweet victory over Bobby Robson's highly-fancied England team, but also one which made Houghton a hero in his adopted country.

Ray appeared in all eight qualifying matches for the 1990 World Cup and was also ever-present at the finals in Italy. He was by nature an attack minded player but under Charlton he was appreciated as much for his tenacity and stamina than for his accurate centres or dribbling skills.

At Anfield Ray enjoyed a somewhat freer role – a fact reflected in his strike-rate of a goal every five games or so. He would accrue an impressive collection of silverware during his five years with Liverpool: claiming a second League Championship trophy in 1989-90 and FA Cup medals in 1989 and 1992. However, in the summer of 1992 Anfield boss Graeme Souness moved Ray on, selling him to Aston Villa for £900,000. It was a decision that disappointed Liverpool fans, whose suspicions that the 30-year-old had been sold prematurely proved well-founded. Ray went on to enjoy a successful three-season spell at Villa, with whom he was a League Cup winner in 1994, before winding down his career with spells at Crystal Palace and Reading.

Houghton remained a vital player for Ireland throughout the early 1990s. He missed just one of the qualifiers for the 1994 World Cup and, of course, at the finals scored against Italy with *that* famous lob. Ray played in all four of the Republic's matches at USA 94, but thereafter his place came under threat from a youthful Jason McAteer. However, despite advancing years and niggling injuries, he won 11 more caps before bringing the curtain down on his international career with a substitute appearance in the World Cup play-off match against Belgium in 1997. Ireland lost the match 2-1 but Ray, ever the big game player, signed off his days in green by scoring Ireland's goal.

CHRIS MORRIS

1987–1993

35 CAPS **0** GOALS

BORN	Newquay, 24.12.63
DEBUT	v Israel (H) 10.11.87
CLUBS	Celtic, Middlesbrough

The first five years of Chris Morris's career had been far from spectacular, but in 1987-88 the skilful, right-sided full-back made a dramatic step into soccer's big time following a £125,000 move to Glasgow giants Celtic. Chris, who began his career with Jack Charlton's Sheffield Wednesday, had emerged from junior football as a fast and tricky winger, but it was only after he switched to the number-two jersey at Hillsborough that his true potential was revealed. He was to become one of a new-breed of attacking full-backs and, while defensively he was no more than adequate, going forward the tall Cornishman was a revelation. Chris possessed pace in abundance and, with his background at outside-right, was also a talented dribbler. So when, in 1987-88, new Celtic manager Billy McNeill decided to opt for a formation based around a sweeper and wing-backs, Morris was the perfect choice to assume duties on the Bhoys' right flank.

In his first season at Parkhead Chris – who had joined the Old Firm club shortly after future international team-mate Mick McCarthy – was a revelation. Not only was he an ever present, he was also one of Celtic's most potent attacking weapons and at the end of the campaign the Hoops had claimed both the League and Cup to record their first 'double' for 11 years. Chris's enterprising attacking play had not gone unnoticed by his former Wednesday boss Jack Charlton, and in November 1987 he was called into the Republic of Ireland team for a friendly against Israel at Dalymount Park. Morris could not have timed his entrance on to the international stage any better. Ireland had just clinched a place at their first major tournament finals – the 1988 European Championships – and Charlton was looking to add an attacking full-back to his squad. Chris quickly formed an impressive partnership with Ray Houghton on Ireland's right flank and, after five consecutive appearances, travelled to Euro 88 as the team's first choice right-back. In the space of one year, Chris Morris had gone from squad player at Sheffield Wednesday to a 'double'-winning international.

Jack Charlton did not need another full-back. He already had Chris Morris, Denis Irwin and Steve Staunton. However, one thing Jack's team of the early 1990s did lack was pace. And pace was something that Wimbledon left-back Terry Phelan had in abundance. Terry, who is undoubtedly one of the quickest players to have worn the green jersey, would become a vital player for Ireland during the latter years of Charlton's reign, frequently providing cover for more pedestrian defensive colleagues. Manchester-born Phelan began his career at Leeds United, but in July 1986 was released by the Yorkshire club after just 14 appearances. A successful season at Fourth Division Swansea City followed and then, in 1987, the 5'8" full-back joined Wimbledon's Crazy Gang. Terry's tenacious tackling and mercurial attacking play made him a big hit with the Dons' small band of fans, and in his first season in SW17 he helped the club to their famous FA Cup final win over Liverpool at Wembley. International recognition, however, was slow to arrive. And with messrs. Hughton, Morris, Langan and Staunton all, at various times, ahead of Terry in the queue for full-back places, it was not until September 1991 that he made his senior Republic of Ireland debut.

In the autumn of 1992 Phelan, who had by then accrued eight caps, joined Peter Reid's Manchester City for £2.5m. The move to Maine Road made Terry the most expensive defender in Britain, and coincided with his best spell in Ireland green. Up until 1992, prospects of a regular place in Jack Charlton's team had not looked good. However, when Jack decided to push Steve Staunton forward into midfield, the number three shirt suddenly became vacant. Terry would play in ten of Ireland's 12 qualifying matches for the 1994 World Cup and travelled to USA 94 as the team's first choice left-back.

Terry began the 1994 World Cup well enough, playing his part in the much-celebrated victory over Italy in New York. However, a second tournament booking in the next match, against Mexico, left him suspended for the final group game versus Norway. Full-back partner Denis Irwin had suffered a similar fate and the pair were replaced with 19-year-old Gary Kelly and Staunton. A draw against Norway proved enough for Ireland to progress to a second round match against Holland, but Charlton now had to decide which of his full-backs to leave out. In the end Jack chose to play Phelan over Irwin. However, with 11 minutes played, Terry hesitated and under hit a back-pass to Packie Bonner, gifting the Dutch the game's opening goal. Henceforward, Denis Irwin became Ireland's regular number three.

Terry would continue to make occasional appearances for the boys in green throughout the mid-1990s, but after spells at Chelsea and, later, Everton he fell victim to the twin perils of injuries and advancing years. As the 20th century drew to a close, it looked increasingly likely that his tally of caps would remain at 38.

TERRY PHELAN

1991–

 38 **0**

CAPS **GOALS**

BORN   Manchester, 16.3.67
DEBUT   v Hungary (A) 11.9.91
CLUBS   Wimbledon, Manchester City, Chelsea, Everton

Staunton is a footballer blessed with a touch of wizardry in his left-boot.

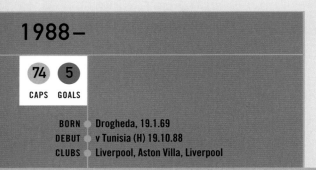

1988–

74	**5**
CAPS	GOALS

BORN   Drogheda, 19.1.69
DEBUG   v Tunisia (H) 19.10.88
CLUBS   Liverpool, Aston Villa, Liverpool

When Steve Staunton decides to hang up his boots and retire from international football, there is every chance that he will do so as the Republic of Ireland's most capped player. But despite a career of high achievement, which has also seen him collect winners' medals in all three of England's major domestic competitions, the left-sided defender-cum-midfielder enjoys a relatively low profile. Stephen's lack of celebrity, however, has more to do with image than talents.

Steve Staunton

On the field, Staunton often appears austere and he makes little effort to play to the gallery. He is deeply competitive though, and approaches the game with a seriousness that would have made even Bill Shankly proud. But while smiles are rare from the alliteratively named Dundalk man, his performances give much cause for celebration.

Staunton is a footballer blessed with a touch of wizardry in his left-boot. His speciality is the low, driven centre – a ploy which frequently creates mayhem in opposing penalty areas. Steve also shoots at high velocity and, though not a prolific scorer, his goals tend to be of the long-range and spectacular variety. However, for all his attacking talents, it was as a teak-tough left-back that Steve made his name with Liverpool in the late 1980s. He had arrived at Anfield from Dundalk in 1986 and, after an eight-match loan spell at Bradford City, made his League bow for the Reds in a 1-1 draw at home to Tottenham Hotspur in September 1988. The following spring, Steve became Liverpool's first choice number-three and his tenacious defending was a key factor in the Merseysiders' late surge up the First Division table. The 1988-89 League season would end in disappointment, though, with Liverpool pipped to the title by Arsenal in the final match, but for Steve and his team-mates there was at least the consolation of an FA Cup final victory over Everton.

Steve's rapid progress at Anfield was mirrored at international level, and in October 1988 the 6ft-tall defender made his full international debut against Tunisia at Lansdowne Road. The match ended with a 4-0 victory for Ireland and the newcomer kept his place for a World Cup qualifier against Spain in Seville four weeks later. Steve would play in four of the five remaining Italia 90 qualifiers

and, having helped Liverpool to the League title in 1989-90, he was included in Charlton's 22-man squad for the World Cup finals in Italy. At 21 years old, Staunton was Ireland's youngest player at the finals, but he was already established in the team and played in all five games.

However, in the summer of 1991, Steve's already success-laden career took an unexpected twist when Liverpool boss Graeme Souness sold him to Aston Villa. The £1.1m transfer of the still improving Staunton was one the Reds would regret during the 1990s. In his second season at Villa Park, Steve missed just three games and scored four times to help his new club to runners-up spot in the new Premier League. In the autumn of 1992, Ireland had kicked-off their qualifying programme for the 1994 World Cup finals. Steve began the campaign in his familiar left-back position but, with Kevin Sheedy injured, he was asked to step forward into left-midfield for the third match against Spain in Seville. It was a role he had filled occasionally at club level and he performed with élan in a 0–0 draw.

Steve would continue in midfield throughout the qualifiers for USA 94, scoring goals against Northern Ireland, Albania and Lithuania *en route* to the finals. It remains his best run of form at international level and his efforts were rewarded when he was named FAI Player of the Year in 1993. Steve was assigned the number-11 shirt for the 1994 World Cup finals and played on the left wing in all four of Ireland's matches. However, owing to his fair complexion, he suffered more than most in the heat of Orlando and was substituted in both games played there.

Steve would continue in midfield during the Euro 96 qualifying campaign, missing just one game ahead of the play-off defeat against Holland at Anfield. However, Staunton is in truth a more accomplished defender than midfielder, and at Aston Villa, with whom he won a League Cup winners' medal in 1994, he tended to operate in the back-line. The appointment of Mick McCarthy as Ireland manager in 1996 saw Steve revert to defence at international level too, where his experience has been vital since the retirement of messrs. McGrath and Moran. Staunton would also take his career back where it started in terms of clubs when, in the summer of 1998, he returned to Liverpool FC in a free transfer move under the Bosman ruling. Much had changed at Anfield in seven years, and in his first season back the Reds leaked goals at an alarming rate to finish seventh. However, few would bet against either Steve or 'Pool regaining the glories of years gone by.

MARK KELLY ▼

1988–1990

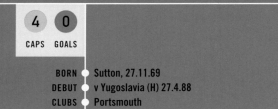

4	0
CAPS	GOALS

BORN ● Sutton, 27.11.69
DEBUT ● v Yugoslavia (H) 27.4.88
CLUBS ● Portsmouth

Mark Kelly was a skilful and adventurous winger who had a penchant for running with the ball and for attacking his maker on the inside. However, he was lightly built and was frequently the victim of crude challenges from frustrated full-backs tired of seeing his heels. Such rough treatment would bring a premature end to Mark's promising career at the age of just 24.

Surrey-born Kelly began his playing days as an apprentice with Portsmouth, making his League debut in a First Division match against West Ham United in February 1988 and international recognition soon followed. Mark had played for England at youth level, but chose to declare for the Republic of Ireland after talking with the ever-persuasive Jack Charlton.

He made his senior Ireland bow in a friendly match against Yugoslavia prior to the 1988 European Championships. He would miss out on a place in Charlton's squad for Euro 88, but became a regular for Portsmouth during 1988-89. However, after just 24 appearances in the starting line-up for Pompey he sustained a serious knee injury which would eventually end his career. He had won just four caps.

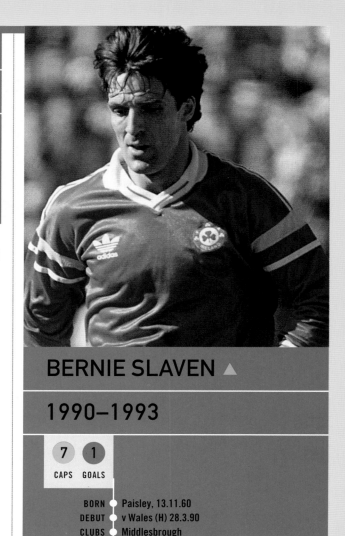

BERNIE SLAVEN ▲

1990–1993

7	1
CAPS	GOALS

BORN ● Paisley, 13.11.60
DEBUT ● v Wales (H) 28.3.90
CLUBS ● Middlesbrough

It is difficult to overestimate Bernie Slaven's status on Teesside. Bernie was an idol to the Ayresome Park faithful; the Boro fans appreciated his goals when there was little else for them to cheer, and he in turn appreciated the adulation bestowed upon him. He had arrived in the North East of England in 1985 after a tour of four clubs in his native Scotland had ended with a rich run of goalscoring at Albion Rovers.

During Bernie's eight years on Teesside, Boro yo-yoed between the first and third tiers of English football. Despite his club's inconsistency, the raven-haired striker remained a reliable goalscorer. In 1989-90 Bernie enjoyed his best spell with Boro, netting 21 goals for a team that struggled to survive in the Second Division. Jack Charlton took note. Upon discovering that Bernie qualified for the Republic, courtesy of Irish grandparents, and persuaded the Scots-born marksman to opt for the green over the blue.

A goalscoring debut against Wales in March 1990 was followed by three more appearances in warm-up friendlies prior to Italia 90. At the 11th hour, Bernie had forced his way into the 22-man squad for the World Cup. Alas, there was to be no *Roy of the Rovers* ending, and Bernie returned from Italy without adding to his collection of caps. Bernie made three more appearances, but, by now the wrong side of 30, he was unable to establish himself in the squad for the 1992 European Championships qualifiers.

On Tuesday 10 November 1987, David Kelly lived the dream. A debut hat-trick against Israel at Dalymount Park silenced all those who had doubted the international credentials of the 21-year-old Walsall striker. And the timing of this dramatic entrance was perfect too. Jack Charlton, who had been so impressed by David's prolific form in the English Third Division, was keen to add another forward to his 1988 European Championships squad, and a goal against Romania in Ireland's next fixture booked the Birmingham born centre-forward a place in the 20-man panel.

David did not add to his tally of caps at the European Championships but returned home much in demand. In August 1988 he left his native Midlands to sign for West Ham United in a £600,000 deal. But it was to be no dream move. The Hammers were struggling, and David was charged with the onerous task of replacing local hero Tony Cottee, who had recently moved to Everton for £2.3 million. During a season that would end in relegation, the Upton Park fans gave David little chance to prove his worth before making him the target of their vitriol. In truth the young Kelly was far from the complete striker, and it had been unrealistic of Hammers' manager John Lyall to expect him to score the goals to keep a poor team in the top flight.

A move to Leicester City in March 1990 would help David resurrect his career, but after his season of First Division struggle with West Ham, many pundits questioned his ability to score goals at the highest level. A spell at Newcastle United followed, and in David's second season at St James' Park he struck 24 goals to help the Magpies to promotion. It seemed that David would now have the chance to prove his quality. But alas it was not to be and he was transferred to Wolverhampton Wanderers before getting a chance in the top flight. At Molineux, David continued to prove his worth in the second tier of English football, but in 1996-97 he finally found himself back in the top flight, this time with Sunderland. However, just as in 1988-89, a frustrating season ended in relegation. A move to John Aldridge's Tranmere Rovers brought a return to the familiar surroundings of the Football League, and the goals inevitably followed once more.

Despite a club career that invites the label 'journeyman', David lacks little as a goalscorer. Good in the air, strong on the ground and hard-working, his only obvious flaw is fragile confidence. Jack Charlton was clearly in no doubt as to David's worth and, although he didn't often make the starting line-up, Kelly was rarely left out of a squad. On each of the three occasions that Charlton picked his players to travel to major tournaments, a place was reserved for David. And six years after making the squad for Germany, David finally got his first taste of tournament football when he came on as a sub for John Aldridge in the World Cup tie against Norway.

DAVID KELLY

1987–

 26 **9**

CAPS   GOALS

BORN Birmingham, 25.11.65
DEBUT   v Israel (H) 10.11.87
CLUBS   Walsall, West Ham United, Leicester City, Newcastle United, Wolves, Sunderland, Tranmere Rovers

Andy was also a charismatic character, and possessed that touch of arrogance so often found in genuinely top class footballers.

1989–1997

70 CAPS **7** GOALS

BORN Maidstone, 27.7.63
DEBUT v France (H) 7.2.89
CLUBS Norwich City, Chelsea, Aston Villa, Middlesbrough

The theory that Jack Charlton's Anglos were no more than footballing mercenaries — opportunists motivated by money alone — was never more clearly refuted than by the whole-hearted performances of Andy Townsend. Andy may have spoken with a cockney accent as London as Big Ben or a signals failure on the Northern Line, but when he pulled on the green jersey his commitment to the land of his grandparents.

Andy Townsend

He was a footballer of great skill and, at his peak in the early 1990s, was the equal of any midfielder playing in England. As an attacking force he combined a fierce left-footed shot with the ability to carry the ball forward with both verve and style. He passed with intelligence too, and, while defensive duties did not come naturally to the young Townsend, he soon evolved into a tenacious competitor.

Andy was also a charismatic character, and possessed that touch of arrogance so often found in top class footballers . His playing days began in non-League football, although he was still only 21 years old when he made the switch to full-time soccer with Southampton in January 1985. Andy would enjoy three full seasons at the Dell, the last of which (1987-88) saw him make 37 first-team appearances. A £350,000 move to Norwich City followed in the summer of 1988 and, after impressive form during his first six months as a Canary, Andy was called into the Ireland line-up for a friendly against France in Dublin. The game ended goalless and the newcomer had not looked out of place in a midfield which boasted Ray Houghton, Liam Brady and Ronnie Whelan. He would miss Ireland's next match, but appeared in each of the proceeding 25 games.

Andy, who had arrived on the international stage in time to play in seven of the eight qualifiers for the 1990 World Cup finals, was quick to adapt his game to comply with Jack Charlton's pragmatic tactics. By the start of the 1990 finals he had become one quarter of a formidable midfield unit that included messrs. Houghton, McGrath and Sheedy. It was a combination that would prove a key factor in Ireland's run to the quarter-finals of Italia 90. Andy's performances against England and Holland were particularly impressive,

and he soon became the subject of intense transfer speculation. Within a week of Ireland's elimination, Norwich had sold their star asset to Chelsea for £1.2m.

Andy became an instant favourite with the Stamford Bridge faithful, and it was to universal approval that he took over the captaincy during his first season with the Blues. The job of leading Chelsea was to prove good experience for a player who would go on to become Ireland's longest serving skipper. Townsend first donned the armband at international level in a 1-0 friendly defeat against Wales in 1992. However, it was not until the start of the qualifying campaign for the 1994 World Cup finals in September 1992 that he was given the job on a permanent basis.

Consistent and impressive performances at both club and international level had seen Andy frequently linked with a move away from Chelsea, with Manchester United seeming, for a long time, to be his most likely destination. However, in the summer of 1992 the Ireland skipper switched to Aston Villa for a then-substantial fee of £2.1m. Villa Park had become something of an Irish enclave during the early 1990s and Andy joined international team-mates McGrath, Houghton and Staunton at the Midlands club.

Townsend was 29 years old when he made the move to Villa, but his footballing zenith was still to come. He would miss just one game during the qualifiers for the 1994 World Cup and provided an assured and creative presence in the Irish midfield. His best form, however, was saved for the finals, and against Italy in New York his polished and energetic display was instrumental in a famous 1-0 victory.

By the start of the 1995-96 season, Andy had been installed as club captain at Aston Villa and in March 1996 he led the Midlanders to a League Cup final win over Leeds United. Both team and player had been successful in the same competition two years earlier, but this time the win provided consolation for the disappointment of Ireland missing out on the 1996 European Championships. Failure to qualify for Euro 96 signalled the end of the Charlton era, and though Andy retained the captaincy under Mick McCarthy, his influence began to wane. Things were changing at Villa Park too, and in August 1997 Townsend was sold to First Division Middlesbrough for £500,000. Andy proved a big hit at the Riverside, helping Boro to promotion in his first season. And it was as a Middlesbrough player that Ireland's long-serving captain won his last cap in the second leg of the World Cup play-off against Belgium.

> ## Denis Irwin is a refreshing reminder that footballers can be both skilful and free from tantrums and histrionics.

1990–

51 CAPS   **4** GOALS

BORN ● Cork, 31.10.65
DEBUT ● v Morocco (H) 12.9.90
CLUBS ● Manchester United

Eamon Dunphy, the journalist and former Republic of Ireland midfielder, dedicated his superb book *More Than a Game* to the 'good pro', a player he describes as the 'hero of professional sport'. The 'good pro' always gives of his best, always accepts responsibility, is always available for a pass and never lets his team-mates down.

Denis Irwin

And if any modern footballer comes close to Dunphy's ideal of the 'good pro' it is Denis Irwin. In an era of spoilt-brat soccer superstars, Denis Irwin is a refreshing reminder that footballers can be both skilful and free from tantrums and histrionics.

As a full-back, Denis has few equals. In defence he is always resolute, patiently holding up opponents before striking to steal the ball away, and in attack he operates with no shortage of skill, moving the ball forward with assurance. He also has a powerful shot and scores his share of goals.

Denis, like his United team-mate, Roy Keane, hails from Cork, but for both men the route to Old Trafford was far from straightforward. Denis had been a promising hurling player, but in 1983 he accepted an offer from Leeds United to sign apprentice forms. At Elland Road he linked up with his future Ireland team-mate John Sheridan, and soon the pair were playing together for Liam Tuohy's Irish junior teams. Under the tutelage of manager Eddie Gray, Denis made steady progress in the white shirt of Leeds, and by 1984 he had become a regular in the first-team. However, the appointment of Billy Bremner as manager in 1985 signalled the end of Denis's time at Elland Road.

A free transfer to Joe Royle's Oldham Athletic revived the fortunes of the 20-year-old Cork man. In his first season at Boundary Park, Denis established himself as a polished first-teamer and in September 1986 he won the first of three under-21 caps. In 1989-90, with Oldham making good progress in both domestic Cups, Denis became the subject of intense transfer speculation. The Latics made it to the final of the League Cup (where they lost to Nottingham Forest), but it was a replayed FA Cup semi-final against Manchester United which was to prove of most significance for Denis. United manager Alex Ferguson had been impressed by the Irishman's perfor-

mance against his star-studded line-up and paid Oldham £600,000 for his services.

Ferguson has made few, if any, better purchases. In his first season at Old Trafford, Denis wore the number two shirt and made light work of the step-up to the top-flight. At season's end he had missed only four League games and had begun his trophy collection with a European Cup Winners' Cup medal after United had overcome Barcelona 2-1 in Rotterdam. The quiet, unassuming full-back may not have burst on to the Old Trafford scene in the way that Ryan Giggs, Eric Cantona and Dwight Yorke would in the 1990s, but the fans would nonetheless come to appreciate the many virtues of Irwin. United would spend the following years incessantly accumulating silverware, and Denis contributed greatly to this success.

Shortly after his arrival at Old Trafford, Jack Charlton upgraded Denis to the full Ireland squad. It was just-reward for a player who had represented his country at every level from schoolboy upward. Chris Morris was the man to lose out as Denis wasted little time establishing residency in his country's number two shirt. The arrival of Paul Parker at Old Trafford in 1991 saw Denis switch to an unaccustomed left-back position, but after a short settling in period he was operating with the same effectiveness he had shown on the right.

The qualifiers for the 1994 World Cup coincided with Denis's best form for United and, despite the emergence of the promising Gary Kelly prior to the finals, it was Denis who travelled to the United States in possession of the number two shirt. Denis performed manfully against the Italians in the Giants Stadium, New York, but, after suspension against Norway, he was displaced from the right-back position. Henceforward, Denis has tended to operate on the left for both club and country, and it was from this position that his Old Trafford career reached its zenith with the Champions League final victory over Bayern Munich in May 1999.

The arrival of Mick McCarthy as manager has done nothing to weaken Denis's international position, and the United full-back remained a key player during the unsuccessful France 98 qualifying campaign, scoring a well-taken goal in the play-off game against Belgium. When the European Championships come around in 2000, Denis will be 34, but it would be folly to bet against him retaining his place in the squad for many years to come. After all, he's the 'good pro'.

Roy's talents as a footballer are matched only by his qualities as an athlete, he possesses unsappable stamina.

1991–

42	**5**
CAPS	GOALS

BORN ● Cork, 10.8.71
DEBUT ● v Chile (H) 22.5.91
CLUBS ● Nottingham Forest, Manchester United

Roy Keane is a footballer who provokes extreme reactions. Manchester United supporters adore him, and to them he is simply 'Keano', their inimitable skipper and midfield enforcer. Others, though, regard the combative Corkman with rather less affection, and his name is often prefixed by expletives by the fans of opposing teams.

Roy Keane

The critics say that his competitiveness often boils over into aggression and that he lacks discipline. But, while a fiery temperament is undoubtedly Roy's greatest weakness, it is a flaw that is often overplayed. You see, winners are rarely popular and, as captain of the most successful team in Britain, Keane has been treated to every available brick bat. His talent, however, is irrefutable.

Keane is a midfielder with few peers. He tackles with gusto, heads the ball prodigiously, passes astutely and scores regularly. As for weaknesses, well, with the exception of that frequently documented propensity for seeing red, there is little worthy of mention. Roy's talents as a footballer are matched only by his qualities as an athlete. He possesses unsappable stamina which, when combined with his competitive streak, makes for a formidable combination.

However, despite his obvious talents, Roy was not among the many Irish youngsters snapped up for apprenticeships by English clubs and began his career with Cobh Ramblers, making his League of Ireland debut at the age of just 17. Word of Roy's progress soon spread, though, and in May 1990 he signed for Brian Clough's Nottingham Forest in a £40,000 deal. Three months after joining Forest, Keane was thrust into first-team action, taking his League bow in the second game of the 1990-91 season away to Liverpool. He remained in the team for the next 34 matches, and a season of high achievement culminated with an appearance at Wembley in the FA Cup final defeat against Tottenham Hotspur. However, for Roy, the disappointment of losing out to Spurs was tempered when, four days later, he made his senior international debut against Chile in Dublin.

By the time the qualifying rounds for USA 94 kicked off in May 1992, Keane had become an established figure in Ireland's midfield, forming an impressive partnership with Andy Townsend. But Ireland's progress toward the World

Cup finals coincided with a period of struggle for Nottingham Forest, and at the end of 1992-93 the club was relegated from the Premiership. Roy, who had made 114 appearances and scored 22 goals for Forest, became the target of a protracted transfer saga, eventually opting to join Manchester United for £3.75m in July 1993. It was a British transfer record fee, and in his first season at Old Trafford Roy helped United to the League and Cup 'double'.

Keane played in all four of Ireland's matches at the 1994 World Cup finals giving a memorable performance against Italy in New York to outshine the Azzurri's midfield. Even in the heat of Orlando, against Mexico and Holland, Roy maintained his all-action style, and his efforts were recognised by RTE viewers who voted him Ireland's player of USA 94.

However, after the high-jinks of the World Cup came a less happy episode in Keane's international career. Over the next two years his appearances in the green jersey became all too rare – he played in just three of Ireland's 10 Euro 96 qualifiers. A series of niggling injuries was apparently the cause of Roy's absence, although his critics argued that it perhaps had more to do with priorities at United.

The appointment of Mick McCarthy as Ireland manager in 1996 offered the chance of a fresh start. However, the United midfielder was sent off in McCarthy's first game in charge. The situation deteriorated still further when, despite being named as skipper for the 1996 US Cup, Roy withdrew from the trip. He returned to the green shirt, after an absence of 15 months for a World Cup match against Iceland in Dublin and found a section of the home crowd had grown hostile to him. But Keane is nothing if not determined and after seven appearances in 1997 he had won back both fans and captaincy. He was also appointed skipper's at United in August 1997. However, after just nine matches his season was over when he sustained a serious knee injury in a challenge on Leeds' Alf-Inge Haaland.

A comeback in the 1998 Charity Shield saw Keane return to United colours looking lean and sharp. Mick McCarthy took note and recalled him for a World Cup clash with Croatia in September. Ireland won 2-0, Roy scored and anybody who doubted his fitness or commitment was emphatically silenced. It was to be a season of high achievement for the former Cobh Rambler who led United to another 'double'. The Reds would also claim the European Cup in 1999, but alas Roy was forced to sit out the final suspended. It had nevertheless been a remarkable recovery for a player whose career had been in jeopardy 18 months earlier.

MIKE MILLIGAN
1992
Born: Manchester, 20.2.67
Caps: 1
Goals: 0
Debut v USA (H) 29.4.92
Clubs: Oldham Athletic

Mike Milligan was the kind of tough-tackling ballwinner who seemed tailor-made for Jack Charlton's Ireland team. He came to prominence as the skipper of Joe Royle's successful Oldham Athletic team of the late 1980s and early 1990s – enjoying two spells at Boundary Park either side of a one-season sojourn with Everton in 1990-91. Despite his good form at club level, Charlton favoured Paul McGrath for the midfield anchor role and Millie won just one cap in a friendly against the USA in 1992.

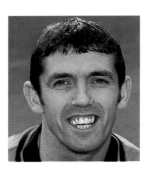

OWEN COYLE
1994
Born: Glasgow, 14.7.66
Caps: 1
Goals: 0
Debut v Holland (A) 20.4.94
Clubs: Bolton Wanderers

Owen Coyle won his only full cap as a substitute for Tommy Coyne in the 86th minute of a World Cup warm-up friendly against Holland in 1994. The Scots-born forward had enjoyed an excellent first season with Bolton Wanderers, playing a key role as the Trotters made progress in both domestic Cup competitions. But at international level Coyle's chance had come too late. By the time he made his bow against Holland, Charlton had all but settled on a thirty-something strikeforce of Aldridge, Cascarino and Coyne for USA 94. Injuries and fitful form denied Coyle the chance to add to his cap, so after just four minutes his international career was at an end.

GED BRANAGAN
1997–
Born: Fulham, London, 10.7.66
Caps: 1
Goals: 0
Debut v Wales (A) 11.2.97
Clubs: Bolton Wanderers

After five clubs in ten seasons Ged Branagan joined Bruce Rioch's ascendant Bolton Wanderers in 1992, and the London-born custodian wasted little time establishing himself as the Trotters' number one. An agile and reliable keeper, Ged has enjoyed an eventful time at Burnden Park – his tenure taking in relegations, promotions and Cup finals – and after much speculation he was included in Mick McCarthy's squad for a rare friendly in 1997. A clean sheet against a strong Wales side at Cardiff Arms Park must have left McCarthy assured that he could call upon Branagan with confidence in future.

BRIAN CAREY
1992–1994
Born: Cork, 31.5.68
Caps: 3
Goals: 0
Debut v USA (H) 29.4.92
Clubs: Manchester United, Leicester City

A tall and commanding centre-half, Brian began his senior career with Cork City where he impressed sufficiently to earn a move to Manchester United. Alas, Brian was never to appear in the Reds' first-team and took his League bow while on loan to Wrexham in 1991. A second loan spell with the Robins in 1991–92 saw Wrexham defeated only four times in 17 games and at the end of the season Jack Charlton brought Brian into the Republic of Ireland squad. A transfer to Leicester City followed, as did two more caps, but McGrath and Moran halted Brian's progress towards a regular place in the Republic set-up.

DAVE SAVAGE
1996–
Born: Dublin, 30.7.73
Caps: 5
Goals: 0
Debut v Portugal (H) 29.5.96
Clubs: Millwall

Dave Savage is a bright, right-sided attacking player who can operate on either wing and is capable of spectacular goals, particularly when cutting in from the left flank. Full international honours came somewhat unexpectedly for Dave, who was selected for five matches in 18 days during the summer of 1996. The most surprising feature of his sudden elevation was that it came after a season of fitful form had ended in relegation for his club, Millwall. Dave's brief international sojourn took in the US Cup, and though his performances were respectable enough, he was outshone by fellow hopefuls Keith O'Neill and Mark Kennedy.

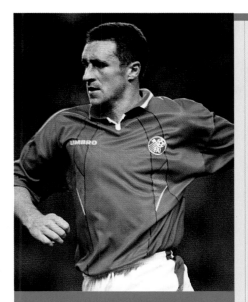

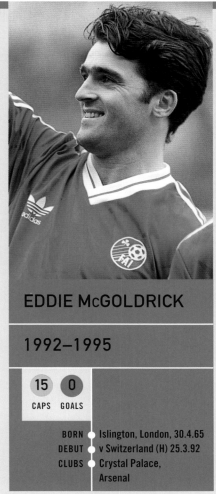

LIAM DAISH

1992–1996

5	0
CAPS	GOALS

BORN	Portsmouth, 23.9.68
DEBUT	v Wales (H) 19.2.92
CLUBS	Cambridge
	Coventry City

Liam Daish was a commanding, central defender who made his international bow under Jack Charlton in a friendly against Wales in 1992. He won a second cap in the next game against Switzerland, but thereafter messrs. Moran and McGrath returned for the serious business of World Cup qualification.

Daish would only return to the team after Mick McCarthy had taken over in 1996. In the four years between his second and third caps, the Portsmouth-born stopper had been transferred from Cambridge United to Barry Fry's Birmingham City and had skippered the Blues to promotion to the First Division in 1994-95. The following season, Liam joined Coventry City for £1.75m and helped the Sky Blues avoid relegation.

Committed displays for Coventry brought Liam his long-awaited recall to the green jersey during the summer of 1996. Unfortunately, Liam's last action for the Republic was to be shown the red card in a US Cup match against Mexico in New Jersey. A knee injury, sustained in training in January 1997, then intervened to end the career of a promising defender.

EDDIE McGOLDRICK

1992–1995

15	0
CAPS	GOALS

BORN	Islington, London, 30.4.65
DEBUT	v Switzerland (H) 25.3.92
CLUBS	Crystal Palace,
	Arsenal

To describe Eddie McGoldrick as a utility player is to dismiss his undoubted talent too cheaply.
Versatility is commonly read as a euphemism for mediocrity, and Eddie's competent displays at both full-back and sweeper did little to help his case as a wide midfielder – the role for which George Graham paid Crystal Palace £1m to take him to Arsenal in 1993. But the big move to Highbury was far from a success and after just 40 games he joined First Division Manchester City.

Eddie, who came to Jack Charlton's attention following a run of good form for Crystal Palace in 1991-92, won his senior cap in a friendly against Switzerland – although after 45 minutes of his debut he was forced off with a knee injury.

Eddie was a regular in the Ireland squad throughout qualification for the 1994 World Cup finals and earned a place in Jack Charlton's 22-man selection for USA 94. However, the London-born midfielder failed to make the Ireland line-up at the finals and shortly afterwards, as his career hit hard times at Highbury, his days in Ireland green drew to a close.

ALAN KERNAGHAN

1992–1996

22	1
CAPS	GOALS

BORN	Otley, 25.4.67
DEBUT	v Latvia (H) 9.9.92
CLUBS	Clubs: Middlesbrough,
	Manchester City

Alan Kernaghan is a powerful, no-nonsense centre-half who first came to Jack Charlton's attention in Middlesbrough's 1991–92 Second Division promotion season. He made his international debut in a World Cup qualifier against Latvia and in the next game partnered Kevin Moran against European Champions Denmark. The new pairing kept a clean sheet, and for the rest of the 1994 World Cup qualifying campaign Alan was the first reserve for Moran and Paul McGrath. In September 1993 he scored his one and only goal for Ireland, against Lithuania, and his hearty celebrations left little doubt as to his commitment.

Alan was included in Charlton's World Cup squad, but throughout the finals the manager preferred to pair Phil Babb with McGrath, and Alan failed to make an appearance. By now he had made a big-money move to Manchester City. However, after a steady start, his form faltered in 1994-95 and he was sent out on loan to Bolton Wanderers. His Ireland career suffered and, although Mick McCarthy made him skipper during the 1996 US Cup, before long he was omitted from the squad.

ALAN KELLY

1993–

20 **0**
CAPS GOALS

BORN ● Preston, 11.8.68
DEBUT ● v Wales (H) 17.2.93
CLUBS ● Sheffield United

It was never going to be easy for goalkeeper Alan Kelly to make his mark at international level. Not only did he face the prospect of displacing the formidable obstacle of Packie Bonner in the Ireland goal, he also had to contend with the added pressure of being the son of a famous father. Alan Kelly's dad is of course Alan Kelly – the former Preston North End and Republic of Ireland goalie. To his credit, though, Alan son of Alan has seemed undaunted by the weight of expectation which greeted his elevation to the senior international team in 1993.

Maturity, however, was perhaps only to be expected from a player who had made his Football League debut as an 18-year-old with Preston North End in the Fourth Division in 1986. Alan helped the Lilywhites to promotion the following season (1986-87), but after a seven-year stint in the first team at Deepdale, Kelly jnr. was sold to Premier League Sheffield United for £150,000 in July 1992. He proved an immediate success at Bramall Lane and in his first season as a Blade, he helped the Yorkshire club to a Wembley FA Cup semi-final against city rivals Wednesday.

Alan, who had won international recognition at youth level, made his senior Republic of Ireland bow as a half-time substitute for Packie Bonner in a friendly against Wales at Tolka Park. The newcomer kept a clean sheet on his 45-minute debut and, while Bonner was back between the posts for the remainder of Ireland's World Cup qualification campaign, Alan had impressed sufficiently to establish himself as the Donegalman's understudy. A second substitute appearance arrived in March 1994, and two months later the 6'2" keeper was included in the starting line-up for a friendly against Germany. Ireland won the game 2-0 and Alan – who had recently suffered the disappointment of relegation with Sheffield United – was rewarded with a place in Jack Charlton's squad for the 1994 World Cup finals in the USA.

Kelly remained on the bench throughout USA 94, but when the qualifying campaign for the 1996 European Championships got under way in the autumn of 1994 he took a rather more active role. With Bonner's international career all but over, Alan had assumed possession of Ireland's number one jersey, and missed just one of the next 11 matches. His early form for the boys in green was nothing short of sensational – remaining unbeaten in six hours of football. However, the Euro 96 qualifying campaign would end in disappointment and following the departure of Jack Charlton shortly afterwards, Alan was faced with the prospect of proving himself to new manager Mick McCarthy. Injury would, alas, prevent him from playing in any of McCarthy's first nine games in charge. Shay Given was the man to benefit from Alan's absence and, although Kelly battled back to make appearances in five of Ireland's France 98 qualifiers, he was unable to re-establish himself immediately as his country's number one.

Never has the phrase 'unlikely hero' been more fittingly employed than when it was applied to Alan McLoughlin on 17 November 1993.

McLoughlin had, until that evening at Belfast's Windsor Park, been no more than a peripheral figure in Jack Charlton's Republic of Ireland squad, featuring only four times in the starting line-up in three years. However, six minutes after coming on as a substitute against Northern Ireland, and with the Republic a goal down, Alan booked himself a place in Irish sporting history. A weak clearance fell invitingly to McLoughlin on the edge of the box, he controlled the ball on his chest and then, as defenders swarmed towards him, unpacked a swerving shot which arrowed beyond the diving Tommy Wright and into the net. It was the goal that would take Ireland to USA 94.

McLoughlin's rise to international hero began at Manchester United. However, he would fail to break into the first team at Old Trafford, and it was only after a move to Swindon Town in August 1986 that his career began to gather momentum. Alan is a midfielder with a distinct preference for attacking. He has a true first touch, passes the ball with guile, and averages five League goals a season. His attacking talents, however, did not become apparent until 1990-91 when he enjoyed a season of high achievement at Swindon under the management of Ossie Ardiles. The Robins would progress to the play-off finals in May 1990 and, at Wembley, Alan struck his 13th goal of the season to give the Wiltshire club a 1-0 victory over Sunderland. But the celebrations were to be short-lived and, after admitting making irregular payments under a previous regime Swindon had their promotion withdrawn.

However, while his club were pleading their case with the football League, Alan was preparing to travel to Italy as a member of Jack Charlton's squad for the 1990 World Cup finals. The Mancunian midfielder, whose parents were both Irish, had impressed Charlton with his performance in a B international against England in March and won his first senior cap in the last pre-tournament friendly, against Malta in Valletta. He would make two appearances at Italia 90, coming on as a substitute against England and Egypt.

At club level, McLoughlin's career turned into something of a blind alley when, shortly after the 1990 World Cup, he made a £1m move to First Division Southampton. Alan would struggle to settle at The Dell and in December 1992, after two years and 24 appearances, he moved down the coast to nearby Portsmouth for £400,000. It was a move that would prove the making of McLoughlin, and his consistent performances made him a hugely popular figure with the Pompey faithful. His international fortunes were also revived following the appointment of Mick McCarthy as Charlton's successor in 1996. Alan would play in seven of the 10 qualifying matches for the 1998 World Cup finals, and, although now in his thirties, he remained a regular in the Ireland squad.

ALAN McLOUGHLIN

1990–

39 **2**
CAPS GOALS

BORN Manchester, 20.4.67
DEBUT v Malta (A) 2.6.90
CLUBS Swindon Town, Southampton, Portsmouth

PHIL BABB

1994–

29	0
CAPS	GOALS

BORN ● Lambeth, 30.11.70
DEBUT ● v Russia (H) 23.3.94
CLUBS ● Coventry City, Liverpool

The career of Phil Babb is an object lesson in the transient nature of sporting success. In his first ten seasons as a professional, Phil has played the role of both hero and villain with equal regularity. At his best, the London-born centre-half is a defender of both poise and athleticism. Strong in the air, lightning fast over the ground, wholehearted in the tackle and constructive in possession. However, consistency has been one quality absent from Babb's game, and, at his worst, hesitancy replaces poise, confidence evaporates and errors become all too frequent.

The best of Phil Babb, in Ireland green at least, came while playing in tandem with Paul McGrath at the 1994 World Cup finals. Babb flourished alongside the veteran Aston Villa defender and their partnership was one of the tournament highlights for Jack Charlton's team. Phil had won just six caps ahead of the finals, and only came into Charlton's plans for USA 94 after making his debut in a round of post-qualification friendlies. The tall, left-sided defender had earned his chance in the green jersey after a series of impressive displays for Coventry City, whom he had joined in July 1992 after spending two seasons at Bradford City where he had played in both defence and attack.

Phil's commanding displays at the 1994 World Cup finals, allied to his continued good form at Coventry City – where he was both reigning player of the year and club captain – made him the subject of intense transfer speculation during the autumn of 1994. The inevitable move eventually arrived, and in September he joined Liverpool for a fee of £3.75m. It made Phil the most expensive defender in Britain, and understandably expectations were high. Liverpool boss Roy Evans had bought Babb to play on the left-hand side of a back-three, but the system proved unsuccessful and Phil, like many of his team-mates, struggled to adapt. Evans eventually relented and in 1997 the Reds reverted to a 4-4-2. However, in the interim Phil's international fortunes had begun to decline and, having played in 19 of Jack Charlton's last 20 games in charge, he appeared in just four of the first 20 under Mick McCarthy.

Babb began to feature with greater regularity in the Republic of Ireland line-up during 1998-99 – playing in four of his country's six games – but at Anfield his prospects were aided neither by the return of Stephen Staunton, or the arrival of new coach Gerard Houllier. It would, however, be wrong to conclude that Phil Babb's zenith has been reached. There may yet be a another ascent in a career which has already taken in its share of highs and lows.

MARK KENNEDY ▲

1995–

20	1
CAPS	GOALS

BORN	Dublin, 15.5.76
DEBUT	v Austria (A) 6.9.95
CLUBS	Liverpool, Wimbledon

All too often, meteoric rises are followed by dramatic descents to rock bottom. However, for Mark Kennedy the decline has been rather more gradual. Mark first caught the eye as a teenager in Mick McCarthy's Millwall team that defeated both Chelsea and Arsenal in the 1995 FA Cup. The Dublin-born six-footer had impressed with his pace and trickery, but had also displayed a sureness in front of goal which hinted at his prolific goalscoring record as a youth team striker.

The inevitable move to the Premiership came in March 1995 when Mark joined Liverpool in a £2m deal. It made him British football's most expensive teenager and after little more than two weeks on Merseyside he made his first team bow, adding five more appearances before season's end. The dream start continued with a senior debut for Ireland in a European Championships qualifier against Austria in 1995. Thereafter, the ascendant trend ceased for Mark Kennedy and injuries, fitful form and the arrival of new players left him marooned in the Liverpool reserves.

At international level Mark fared rather better. By the time he left Liverpool to join Joe Kinnear's Wimbledon in 1998, he had made more appearances in a green shirt than in a red one. Throughout his difficult spell on Merseyside, Mark had managed to retain the self-confidence so essential for an attacking player and was rewarded with the support of Republic boss Mick McCarthy.

KEITH O'NEILL ▼

1996–

12	4
CAPS	GOALS

BORN	Dublin, 16.2.76
DEBUT	v Portugal (H) 29.5.96
CLUBS	Norwich City, Middlesbrough

How Jack Charlton must wish he had been able to call upon a forward like Keith O'Neill. At 6'2" and 12 stone, O'Neill combines a fierce physical presence with a winger's trickery and pace. Mick McCarthy was quick to realise the talent he had at his disposal and O'Neill rewarded his manager's faith by delivering the first goal of the his reign in a friendly against Croatia in June 1996.

A run of impressive form brought Keith four goals in his first seven internationals – two of these strikes coming during a match against Bolivia in the 1996 US Cup. It seemed McCarthy had unearthed a much needed source of goals ahead of the qualifiers for the 1998 World Cup. But after a good start to the 1997-98 season for both club and country, injury struck.

Keith regained fitness and his place in the Ireland squad for the Euro 2000 qualifiers. But since his sojourn on the sidelines, the Middlesbrough frontman has been joined by a growing crop of attacking talent that includes Robbie Keane, Damien Duff, Mark Kennedy and David Connolly. With so many players competing for so few places, it seems likely that Keith's ability to operate as either a winger or a central striker will be to his advantage as Mick McCarthy seeks the right attacking blend to take the Republic to the European Championships in Holland and Belgium.

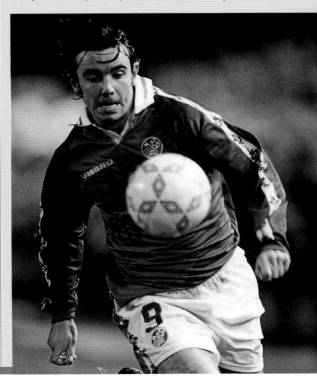

Wilkinson unleashed Kelly on an unsuspecting English top-flight at the start of the 1993–94 season.

1994–

28	1
CAPS	GOALS

BORN ● Drogheda, 9.7.74
DEBUT ● v Russia (H) 23.3.94
CLUBS ● Leeds United

When Gary Kelly arrived at Leeds United in September 1991 he joined a team on course for its first League Championship in 18 years. But for Gary, a teenage forward signed from Home Farm, there was little to celebrate. As an attacker, the slightly-built youngster was a long way down the pecking order after Lee Chapman, Rod Wallace, Eric Cantona and co., and it was only when Leeds boss Howard Wilkinson took the bold step of deploying Gary as an attacking right-back that the world of first-team football opened up to the lightning quick youngster.

Gary Kelly

Wilkinson unleashed Kelly on an unsuspecting English top-flight at the start of the 1993–94 season and the 18-year-old set about his new role with much élan. As a defender, Garry has a tenacity and strength that bely his compact frame and make him a fearful obstacle for any left winger. And although his name rarely features on Leeds' scoresheet, he is a constructive player and is often the platform from which United launch their swift counter-attacks.

An ever-present season with Leeds United in 1993-94 brought Gary many plaudits and, with the Republic of Ireland's World Cup qualification assured, he was called up to the international squad for a series of friendlies in the spring. With the faultless Denis Irwin installed as the team's regular right-back, Gary needed to be at his best to book a place in Jack Charlton's 22-man squad for USA 94. Throughout 1994 he had displayed immaculate timing but never more so than when he struck his first senior goal in a friendly against World Cup holders Germany in Hanover. Jack had seen enough, and the 19-year-old Leeds man headed west for USA 94.

It seemed likely that Gary would see out the entire World Cup finals from the subs' bench, but when Denis Irwin collected a second tournament booking in a heated match against Mexico, Jack Charlton was forced to make changes. The manager's problems were compounded by the fact that Terry Phelan had also picked up a ban. So after just one season of senior football Gary was called into the team for the match against Norway in Orlando and thus became the youngest player to appear for the Republic of Ireland in a World Cup finals. An accomplished display against a forceful, if unambitious, Norwegian team left the Ireland manager with a dilemma... Kelly, Irwin and Phelan were all available for the vital match against Holland. In the end Irwin missed out, and Gary retained his place in the team against a pacy and formidable Dutch forward line that included Marc Overmars, Dennis Bergkamp and Peter van Vossen. The dream for both Kelly and Ireland came to an end with a 2–0 defeat but when blame was apportioned few fingers were pointed in the direction of the squad's youngest member.

A return to League action in 1994–95 saw Gary maintain his consistent form of the previous campaign and for both club and country he was an ever-present. However, in 1996 the Drogheda-born full-back found himself playing for new managers at both club level (George Graham) and for Ireland (Mick McCarthy). Inevitably, Gary had to adapt to new tactics and patterns of play, but to his credit he adjusted to these demands and evolved into a mature and versatile performer. For both Leeds and Ireland, Gary has played on the right of midfield, and for his club he was appointed captain and employed in central defence when Lucas Radebe was on international duty for South Africa during the 1997–98 season.

By August 1998 Garry had won 28 caps, and at 24 years old he had played more games for Leeds United than any other player on the Yorkshire club's books. However, a serious shin injury was to sideline him throughout 1998-99 and, while out of the team, David O'Leary took charge at Elland Road. In the summer of 1999 Gary Kelly faced a difficult battle, not only to regain his fitness but also to prove himself to a new manager.

JASON McATEER

1994–

33 CAPS **1** GOALS

BORN	Birkenhead, 18.6.71
DEBUT	v Russia (H) 23.3.94
CLUBS	Bolton Wanderers, Liverpool, Blackburn Rovers

When Jason McAteer replaced Ray Houghton after 67 minutes of Ireland's match against Italy at the 1994 World Cup finals, he completed a truly meteoric rise. In just two-and-a-half years, the effervescent Scouser had gone from part-time football with non-League Marine to playing on the game's greatest stage. However, what is most remarkable about McAteer's expeditious ascent is not how far he climbed but that he was allowed to start from such a humble footing in the first place.

Jason is a direct, hard-running footballer who possesses both skill and a refreshing enthusiasm for the game. His conspicuous talents were eventually recognised by League scouts, and in January 1992 he made the breakthrough into full-time football with Bolton Wanderers. His League debut arrived during 1992-93 and at season's end he had made 21 League appearances to help the Trotters win promotion to the First Division. Jason was an ever-present the following campaign and played a key role in Wanderers' dramatic run to the quarter-finals of the FA Cup. His progress had been noted by both England and Ireland, but Jason opted to declare for the Republic, and made his bow in the green jersey against Russia at Lansdowne Road in March 1994. He appeared in each of the next 13 internationals, playing in all four of Ireland's matches at USA 94.

McAteer returned from the World Cup to enjoy a spectacular season with Bolton Wanderers, which ended in promotion via the play-offs and an appearance in the League Cup final. Wanderers lost to Jason's beloved Liverpool at Wembley, and the following September he ended 18 months of speculation by joining the Reds in a £4.5m deal. McAteer's marauding midfield play had earned him his big move to Anfield, but it was at right wing-back that he was most regularly employed during his three-year spell with 'Pool. For Ireland, though, he continued to play in midfield and was a regular during the qualifying rounds for Euro 96.

The arrival of Mick McCarthy as manager of the national team in 1996 did nothing to hinder Jason's international career, and in October of that year he scored his first goal for Ireland in the 3-0 win over Macedonia. However, an uncharacteristically crude challenge during the return match the following April earned him a red card and kept the Liverpool man out of the next three internationals. Season 1997-98 was also to bring its troubles for Jason, and in January 1998 he sustained a broken left fibula. But McAteer returned to the Liverpool line-up in May to score twice in a 5-0 win against West Ham United. By September 1998 Jason was back in Ireland green too, playing in the opening Euro 2000 qualifier against Croatia. His days at Anfield, however, would come to an end in January 1999 when, having failed to impress new Reds manager Gerard Houllier, he made a £4m move to Blackburn Rovers. Jason's Ewood Park career began disastrously though, and at the end of 1998-99 Rovers were relegated to the First Division. Both club and player will be looking to make an immediate return to their high aspect of the mid-1990s.

Goalkeepers, according to the experts, get better with age. However, that will not be easy in the case of Shay Given, for already the Donegal man appears to be a custodian without obvious flaw.

He is a mature, competitive performer, and combines impressive athleticism with a mastery of his penalty area which belies his youth. Shay's strengths are many. He is quick off his line, has impressive reflexes, safe hands and an intuitive sense for narrowing shooting angles. Against this, the critics can muster only one area of concern: his height. Shay stands at 6'1" tall but, while it is true that this makes him among international football's shorter keepers, he makes up for any lack of inches with a prodigious spring and has, thus far, shown no real vulnerability from crosses.

Shay began his career as an apprentice with Glasgow giants Celtic, but at the age of 18 – having made the bench but not the team for the Bhoys – he moved south to sign for Blackburn Rovers in August 1994. His League debut, though, came while on loan to Swindon Town at the start of the 1995-96 season. The Lifford-born keeper would make five first-team appearances for Swindon, keeping four clean sheets and conceding just one goal before returning to Ewood Park to take his place in the queue behind Rovers' established number-one, Tim Flowers. A second loan spell followed when, in January 1996, Shay joined Peter Reid's Sunderland. He became an instant hit for the Wearsiders and in 17 appearances kept 12 clean sheets. It was enough to earn him a First Division Championship medal and to tempt Reid to bid £2m to sign him permanently. Blackburn, however, were not interested and Given returned to Lancashire to resume his role as Flowers' understudy.

Shay's sensational form at Sunderland had brought him much publicity, and when Alan Kelly withdrew from the Ireland squad for Mick McCarthy's first game in charge, the 19-year-old keeper found himself elevated to full international status. His debut came in a friendly against Russia in March 1996 and, although Ireland lost 2-0, Given's confidence and talent were obvious. Shay would play in each of McCarthy's first six games in charge. However, his international career would temporarily stall during 1996-97 as he languished in the reserves at Blackburn.

A £1.5m move to Newcastle, where Shay was reunited with his former Ewood Park boss Kenny Dalglish, revived the fortunes of the young keeper during the summer of 1997. He would miss just one of the 15 matches played by the Republic of Ireland in his first two seasons as a Newcastle player and, by the start of the qualifying programme for the 2000 European Championships, had firmly established himself as Ireland's number one.

SHAY GIVEN

1996–

23 **0**
CAPS GOALS

BORN Lifford, 24.4.76
DEBUT v Russia (H) 27.3.96
CLUBS Blackburn Rovers, Newcastle United

KENNY CUNNINGHAM

1996–

22 **0**
CAPS GOALS

BORN ● Dublin, 28.6.71
DEBUG ● v Czech Republic (A) 24.4.96
CLUBS ● Wimbledon

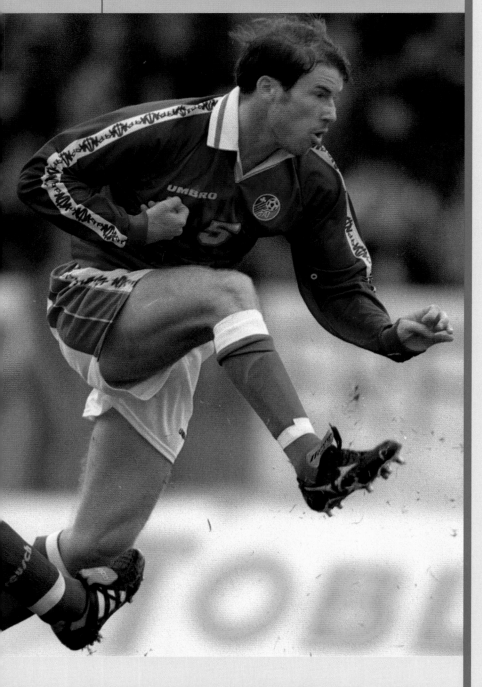

Every successful team has a defensive stalwart, a standard bearer who can be relied upon to maintain dogged resistance come what may. Jack Charlton had the muscular Mick McCarthy to rely upon and Mick, in turn, has the combative Kenny Cunningham. Shortly after taking over as Republic manager, McCarthy handed the 24-year-old Cunningham his debut, and since then the Dublin-born stopper has been a fixture in the Republic of Ireland squad. Kenny is a strong and committed defender, but he is also a disciplined player and rarely lets his determination to win the ball get the better of him. This self-control, allied with a superb ability to time tackles has made Kenny an excellent man-marker; a role he regularly fills at club level.

Kenny began his career as a junior player with Home Farm, and after a spell with Tolka Rovers he was transferred to Millwall for a nominal fee in September 1989. By the end of his first season at the Den, Kenny had broken into the Lions' first-team and was lining-up alongside his future international manager, Mick McCarthy, in England's top-flight. During the next two seasons Kenny emerged as Millwall's regular right-back and by the time McCarthy took over as the club's manager in 1992 he was a fixture in the side. Assured displays for Millwall earned Kenny four under-21 caps and, in April 1994, a move to Premier League Wimbledon.

A joint fee of £1.3m was enough to tempt Mick McCarthy into permitting an all-Irish transfer – Kenny and Jon Goodman moving across South London to join Joe Kinnear's Dons. A record of just one goal in more than 100 games for the Lions failed to reveal Kenny's true attacking worth, but Kinnear recognised that he was getting a constructive full-back capable of both joining and instigating attacks. The ever-innovative Kinnear was not prepared to regard Cunningham as merely a full-back. As well as playing him at both left- and right-back, he employed the former Millwall man at centre-back and wing-back. Whichever position he played in, Kenny rarely let Kinnear down. As a result, was rewarded with the captain's armband on several occasions.

Progress in the Premier League was followed by a full international debut against the Czech Republic in Prague in April 1996 and by the start of the 1997-98 season Kenny had become a regular in McCarthy's starting line-up. It seems the better the opponent, the deeper the Dubliner digs into his defensive resources and the more accomplished becomes his performance. In 1998 Kenny's growing importance to the Republic team was twice rewarded, first when he was handed the captaincy for a friendly against the Czech Republic in March and nine months later when he was named the FAI/Opel International Player of the Year.

The opening phase of Ian Harte's career was intriguing if unconventional, for while the young defender made rapid progress at international level, for Leeds United he was forced to convince a stream of doubters as to his worth. A powerful player who is both strong in the tackle and, for his height (5'9"), formidable in the air, Ian can also be an extremely constructive player and scores his share of goals for both club and country, none better than an exquisite bending free-kick against Southampton in the autumn of 1998.

Ian broke into the Leeds first-team as an 18-year-old in the second half of 1995-96, and in his four appearances for Howard Wilkinson's team that season played at both centre-half and left-back. This ability to defend either flank or centre field was unquestionably the root cause of Ian's difficulties at Elland Road. Many believed him too short to play as an effective centre-half and he was left to compete with Tony Dorigo and Lee Sharpe for the number three shirt at Leeds.

Ian would have been dismayed when David Robertson, another specialist left-back, arrived at Leeds for the start of the 1997-98 season. But by season's end the Drogheda-born youngster had regained his position in the team, enjoying an unbroken 12-match spell at the close of the campaign. The signing of yet another left-back, Danny Granville from Chelsea, in summer 1998 left Ian with a familiar problem, but once more he responded in emphatic fashion. He quickly won back his place and, under the management of David O'Leary, has flourished into a key player for Leeds United.

At international level, Ian's progress has been far less traumatic. Mick McCarthy handed him his debut after he had made just four appearances in the Leeds first-team, and was impressed enough to include the teenager in the Republic's next eight games. Ian rewarded his manager's faith with sterling displays in the qualifiers for Euro 96 and scored two goals in his first six games. In 1998 he won his 15th and 16th caps as a central defender in the World Cup play-off matches against Belgium and, while it is clear that he has a bright future with the boys in green, it is not yet apparent in which position that will be.

IAN HARTE

1996–

19	2
CAPS	GOALS

BORN Drogheda, 31.8.77
DEBUT v Croatia (H) 2.6.96
CLUBS Leeds United

JEFF KENNA

1995–

26	0
CAPS	GOALS

BORN	Dublin, 27.8.70
DEBUT	v Portugal (H) 26.4.95
CLUBS	Blackburn Rovers

Jeff Kenna is a player's player. Whle his skilful and energetic contributions often go unnoticed by media and supporters, his efforts are greatly appreciated by those a little closer to the action. The Dublin-born utility man works selflessly for the team cause, is always willing to receive the ball, never ducks a challenge and is often on hand to bail out errant colleagues. Jeff is by preference a right-sided full-back and although he can also play at left-back or in midfield, it is from this position that his talents are maximised. He crosses well with his right foot and has sufficient pace to move forward without fear of being exposed to counter-attacks.

It was as an apprentice with First Division Southampton in April 1989 that Jeff began his professional career. Within three years, the former Republic of Ireland Schoolboy and Youth international had made the breakthrough into both the Saints first-team and the Ireland under 21 line-up. Jeff would become a regular for Southampton during the 1992-93 season, scoring twice in 29 games, and the following campaign he was an ever-present for the Hampshire club. However, in March 1995 Kenna left the Dell to join former Saints team-mates Alan Shearer and Tim Flowers at Blackburn Rovers for a fee of £1.5m. He arrived at Ewood Park with Rovers *en route* to their first Championship for 81 years and played in each of the last nine games of the season – most of them at left-back.

Just six weeks after signing for Blackburn, Jeff made his senior international debut as a substitute for Ray Houghton in the European Championships qualifier against Portugal at Lansdowne Road. He would make two further substitute appearances before being drafted into the starting line-up to play in midfield for the last two qualifiers, against Latvia and Portugal. Jeff would cement his place in the Ireland team following the appointment of Mick McCarthy as Charlton's successor in 1996, and missed just two of the new manager's first 11 games in charge. He was a regular in McCarthy's line-up during the qualifying campaign for the 1998 World Cup finals, although he was absent for the disastrous defeat in Macedonia in April 1997.

At club level, Jeff showed his best form for Rovers in 1997-98, flourishing under the tutelage of manager Roy Hodgson and playing a key role in the Lancashire club's successful push for a UEFA Cup place. However, the next campaign bought rather different fortunes for both team and player. Jeff would add just one cap to his collection during the course of 1998-99, and at season's end Blackburn were relegated to the First Division.

GARY BREEN

1996–

19 **2**

CAPS GOALS

BORN Hendon, 12.12.73
DEBUT v Portugal (H) 29.5.96
CLUBS Birmingham City,
Coventry City

Gary Breen was one of several players handed the unenviable task of filling the gilded boots of Paul McGrath during 1996. Clearly, no rookie defender could come close to the mark of McGrath, but, of all the candidates, Breen emerged with most credit. In a handful of friendly appearances, Gary proved himself a tough competitor who could also pose an attacking threat – witness his goal against Holland in Rotterdam in June 1996.

When the qualification campaign for the 1998 World Cup began, Gary was installed as Ireland's first choice centre-half and, despite the lack of a regular partner, he performed commendably in the first three games. However, thereafter, both player and team failed to progress as Mick McCarthy would have liked.

The qualifying rounds for Euro 2000 saw Gary resume his place at the heart of the Ireland defence following good form for Coventry City, whom he had joined in February 1997. While Gary may not become a legend in the McGrath/Moran class, he has certainly established himself as a solid defender who, on his day, can nullify even the best international striker.

LEE CARSLEY

1997–

13 **0**

CAPS GOALS

BORN Birmingham, 28.2.74
DEBUT v Romania (H) 11.10.97
CLUBS Derby County,
Blackburn Rovers

Mick McCarthy is a man who appreciates the value of a footballer with a strong worth ethic. So he knew exactly what he was looking for when the industrious Roy Keane was sidelined by a knee injury for much of the 1997-98 season.

After four seasons of toil in the Derby County engine room the spotlight fell on Lee Carsley to provide the energy in Ireland's midfield. Already an under-21 international, Lee was given his senior debut in the World Cup qualifier against Romania in October 1997. His brief was to provide added security for the Irish defence in the face of a potent Romanian attack. A 1-1 draw saw the newcomer emerge with much credit and earned him a regular place in McCarthy's squad.

In February 1999, Lee made a £4m move to Premiership strugglers Blackburn Rovers. However, he was unable to halt the Lancashire club's slide into the First Division. Only time will tell how the step down into the Football League affects the Birmingham-born midfielder's international prospects.

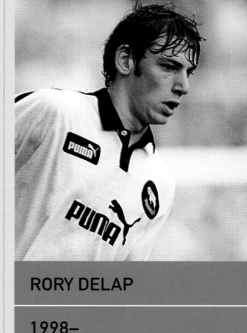

RORY DELAP

1998–

3 **0**

CAPS GOALS

BORN Sutton Coldfield, 6.7.76
DEBUT v Czech Republic (A) 25.3.98
CLUBS Derby County

Versatility is all too often a disguise for the mediocre, but if there is one manager who can distinguish between a genuine talent and a jack-of-all-trades, it is Jim Smith. So when Smith paid £500,000 to take Rory Delap from Carlisle United to Derby County in February 1998, many – including Mick McCarthy – took note.

At Carlisle, Rory had played as defender, midfielder and forward, but at Derby he would be asked to fill the stamina-sapping role of right wing-back. Undaunted by the step up from the Third Division, Rory made his debut in a 2-1 win at Everton and remained in the Rams team until season's end.

Rory's powerful performances in defence, and his qualities as a constructive player, were not lost on Republic manager McCarthy. In the summer of 1998, he was elevated from the under-21s to take part in three friendlies, and though it is too early to predict a glittering international career, the likes of Kenny Cunningham and Ian Harte should take nothing for granted in the years ahead.

ALAN MOORE
1996–

Born: Dublin, 25.11.74
Caps: 8
Goals: 0
Debut v Czech Republic (A)
24.4.96
Clubs: Middlesbrough

Alan Moore is a fast and skilful left winger who came into the Ireland team shortly after Mick McCarthy took charge in 1996. His debut, which came as a 21-year-old in a friendly against the Czech Republic, was deserved reward for impressive displays for Middlesbrough, whom he had helped win promotion to the Premier League in 1995. Alan won eight caps in the space of seven months during 1996, but in the succeeding three years was unable to add to his collection. However, with youth still on his side, Alan retained good prospects of a return to the green jersey.

MARK KINSELLA
1998–

Born: Dublin, 12.8.72
Caps: 8
Goals: 0
Debut: v Czech Republic (A)
25.3.98
Clubs: Colchester Utd, Charlton Athletic

After seven years with Colchester United, Mark Kinsella's career took a brisk step into the ascendant when he joined Charlton Athletic for £200,000 in September 1996. An intelligent midfielder with a good work ethic and an eye for goal, he helped the Addicks gain promotion to the Premier League via the play-offs in 1997-98. He won his first full cap in a friendly against the Czech Republic in March 1998 and retained his place in the Ireland squad when the Euro 2000 qualifiers got underway the following autumn. At club level, however, the Dubliner's career took a somewhat disappointing twist in May 1999 when Charlton were relegated.

CURTIS FLEMING
1998–

Born: Manchester, 8.10.68
Caps: 10
Goals: 0
Debut v Czech Republic (A) 24.4.96
Clubs: Middlesbrough

Curtis Fleming began his career at St Patrick's Athletic and won both under-21 and under-23 honours as a St Pat's player. He moved to Middlesbrough in 1991 and was called into Mick McCarthy's senior international squad for a busy programme of friendly matches during 1996. Curtis, who can play on either flank made his senior Ireland debut against the Czech Republic in April 1996, and over the next seven weeks added six more caps to his tally. However, with competition fierce for the full-back positions in McCarthy's line-up, he made just three further appearances during the proceeding three years.

STEVE CARR
1998–

Born: Dublin, 29.8.76
Caps: 2
Goals: 0
Debut: v Sweden (H) 28.4.99
Clubs: Tottenham Hotspur

The only surprise about Steve Carr's Republic of Ireland debut was that it did not come sooner. The Tottenham Hotspur right-back had been a first-team regular for three seasons by the time he made his senior bow for Ireland. Steve has won many plaudits for his marauding forward play and dogged defending at club level, and it speaks volumes for his determined nature that his game has continued to improve despite playing under three managers during a period of great upheaval at White Hart Lane.

MICKY EVANS
1997–

Born: Plymouth 1.1.73
Caps: 1
Goals: 0
Debut: v Romania (H) 11.10.97
Clubs: Southampton

Micky Evans is a hard-running centre-forward who came to the attention of Mick McCarthy after a rich vein of club form during 1996-97. Micky began the season with home-town club Plymouth Argyle, but after 12 goals in 33 appearances he made a £500,000 move to Premiership Southampton. He added four goals to his tally by season's end and began 1997-98 as Saints' first choice striker. In October 1997 Micky was called into the senior Ireland squad for the World Cup qualifier against Romania in Dublin and duly made his debut as an 85th-minute substitute. Sixteen days later, the newly-capped Evans moved on to West Bromwich Albion.

JON GOODMAN
1997–
Born: Walthamstow, London, 2.6.71
Caps: 4
Goals: 0
Debut v Wales (A) 11.2.97
Clubs: Wimbledon

Jon Goodman is a powerful and pacy striker who can play anywhere across the forward line. His international debut came, somewhat surprisingly, during a season that saw him score just one League goal for his club, Wimbledon. Mick McCarthy, though, had remembered Jon from their days together at Millwall, and handed him a late call to join the Ireland squad for a friendly against Wales in 1997. With Niall Quinn unavailable, Jon kept his place in the team for three World Cup qualifiers in 1997. Alas before the 1997–98 season had got underway, Jon suffered a serious injury that would sideline him for more than a year.

KEVIN KILBANE
1997–
Born: Preston, 1.10.77
Caps: 4
Goals: 0
Debut v Iceland (A) 6.9.97
Clubs: West Bromwich Albion

In June 1997, at the age of just 20, Kevin Kilbane became West Bromwich Albion's record signing. It cost Albion £1.25m to prise the Ireland under-21 left-winger away from Preston North End, but the 6ft-tall Lancashireman quickly proved himself a bargain. Kevin is a powerful and pacy wideman who crosses with accuracy and packs a powerful shot. He was elevated to the senior international team when he was preferred to Mark Kennedy for the number 11 jersey in Ireland's World Cup qualifier away to Iceland in September 1997. A bright future looked in prospect.

ALAN MAYBURY
1998–
Born: Dublin, 8.8.78
Caps: 2
Goals: 0
Debut v Czech Republic (A) 25.3.98
Clubs: Leeds United

Right-sided full-back, and occasional midfielder, Alan Maybury is a former Leeds United youth team captain. He made the breakthrough to first-team football in 1997 and, after three under-21 appearances, won his first senior international cap in the friendly against the Czech Republic in March 1998. Alan spent a spell on loan with Reading during 1998-99, but had to Leeds by season's end, and won a second cap in the friendly against Northern Ireland in May 1999.

GRAHAM KAVANAGH
1998–
Born: Dublin, 2.12.73
Caps: 3
Goals: 1
Debut: Czech Republic (A) 25.3.98
Clubs: Stoke City

Graham Kavanagh is a creative midfielder who began his career at Middlesbrough. However after four seasons on the fringes of the Boro first team he moved to Stoke City for £250,000 in September 1996. Graham has flourished in the Potteries, where his inventive midfield play and fierce shooting have endeared him to the fans at the Britannia Stadium. And although Stoke were relegated at the end of 1997-98, Graham's continued good form earned him a senior international debut against the Czech Republic in March 1998. He added two more caps to his total in 1999, scoring his first goal for Ireland against Sweden in April.

GARETH FARRELLY
1996–
Born: Dublin, 28.8.75
Caps: 5
Goals: 0
Debut: Portugal (H) 29.5.96
Clubs: Aston Villa, Everton

Gareth Farrelly is a player of undoubted talent, but his youthful progress has frequently been halted by injury. His best season at club level, thus far, came in 1997-98 when he played 26 League matches for Everton and scored the goal which saved the club from relegation in the last game of the season. Gareth is a left-sided midfielder with superb passing ability. He began his career with Aston Villa, and it was while at Villa Park that he broke into the senior Ireland team – playing in three friendlies during the summer of 1996. Two further caps were added to his total with appearances against the Czech Republic and Mexico in 1998.

DAVID CONNOLLY ▼

1996–

17	7
CAPS	GOALS

BORN ● Willesden, London 6.6.77
DEBUT ● v Portugal (H) 29.5.96
CLUBS ● Watford, Feyenoord,
Wolverhampton Wanderers

David Connolly is a predatory goalscorer with an instinctive ability to find the target, whatever the angle. The London-born striker burst precociously onto the international stage after a rich run of form for Watford during 1996. David struck eight goals for the Hornets in the last seven games of 1995-96, and in May – at just 18 years old – he made his senior Ireland debut against Portugal. He added three more caps to his total during 1996, and opened his international goals account against the USA.

David was also on target during a World Cup qualifier against Liechtenstein in May 1997, scoring a hat-trick in a 5-0 win in Dublin. Shortly after this performance, though, the 5'8" striker left Watford and signed for Dutch giants Feyenoord under the Bosman ruling. However the switch to Rotterdam was to prove far from successful and, after just two appearances in Feyenoord's starting line-up, he returned to England, to join Wolves on loan for the 1998-99 season. At Wolves, David was paired with Robbie Keane, a player who would block his path at international level.

With Keane installed as the first choice striker for Ireland by the autumn of 1998, Connolly struggled to win back his place in the line-up. But time was still on the side of the quicksilver young Londoner whose goalscoring ratio remains the equal of any current Ireland international.

DAMIEN DUFF ▲

1998–

8	0
CAPS	GOALS

BORN ● Ballyboden, 2.3.79
DEBUT ● v Czech Republic (A) 25.3.98
CLUBS ● Blackburn Rovers

It is still too early to judge which is Damien Duff's best position. As a winger he has the requisite skill and trickery to bamboozle opposing full-backs before unleashing accurate crosses from the deadball line. And when, on rare occasions, Damien has played as a central raider he has shown himself to be not only a good team player but also a composed finisher – witness his two goals in a Premier League encounter against West Ham United in 1997. For most of his first two full season with Blackburn Rovers, however, Damien patrolled the left flank, and it was in this position that Mick McCarthy handed him his debut for the Republic as a 19-year-old.

It has been a rapid ascendancy for the blond-haired forward – Damien's full debut arriving ahead of any under-21 caps. After two friendly appearances in the green shirt towards the end of the 1997-98 season, Damien had impressed his international manager sufficiently to begin the Euro 2000 qualifiers as the Republic's first choice left-winger. However, with the return to fitness of Keith O'Neill, Damien must avoid complacency if he is to retain the number 11 shirt.

At club level, the career of Damien Duff hit its first major setback when Blackburn Rovers were relegated from the Premiership in May 1999. But, with youth very much on his side, there is every chance that Damien will emerge from this adversity as a stronger and more resilient footballer.

The ballyhoo that has accompanied the rise of Robbie Keane has been nothing short of staggering. The young striker had barely kicked a ball in senior football before he was proclaimed as the saviour of Irish football and charged with the job of bringing a return to the glories of the Charlton era. Fortunately, the early signs are that Robbie's talents are as extensive as the hype.

The boys in green have long yearned for a player like Robbie Keane; a player who could inject both sharp finishing and pace into the team's all too pedestrian forward line. However, the lad from Tallagh is more than just a high velocity goalscorer, Robbie is also a skilful footballer with good all-round ability. He is at his best playing just behind the main centre-forward, from where he can drop deep or pull out wide to receive the ball. Robbie's dribbling skills are extravagant and he will often employ a flamboyant trick or flick to beat his marker. But, while entertainment is all well and good, it is goals that win matches and, thus far, Keane has shown himself to be a clinical finisher.

Robbie began his career with Wolverhampton Wanderers and, while still a trainee, made his debut in the opening game of the 1997-98 season. The 17-year-old hopeful took his chance with aplomb, striking both goals in a 2-0 win against Norwich City at Carrow Road and kept his place for the next 11 games. He would play in 38 of Wolves' 46 League matches and ended the season as the club's leading League scorer with 11 goals. Robbie's rapid progress brought great pressure on Mick McCarthy to call the prodigiously talented forward into the senior international team, and in March came the inevitable when, after 46 minutes of the friendly against the Czech Republic in Olomouc, Keane became the second youngest player to appear in the green jersey of Ireland. Two more caps followed during the spring of 1998 – against Argentina and Mexico – and on both occasions the Wolves striker played the full 90 minutes. There would be no summer of rest for Keane, though, and in July he turned out for Brian Kerr's under-18 team which won the UEFA European Championships in Cyprus.

After a first season of such high jinks, it came as little surprise that Robbie began the European Championship qualifying programme as Ireland's first choice forward. And in the second match, against Malta in October 1998, the Lansdowne Road crowd erupted in delight when their 18-year-old idol struck his first international goal. Robbie would score twice in the match, but it was his first – a close range effort from a corner – which caught the headlines, for it was a goal that made him Ireland's youngest ever goalscorer, breaking a record set by John Giles in 1959.

In December 1998 Robbie was named FAI/Opel Young Player of the Year, adding this prize to the PFA Divisional team award he had won the previous May. While still very much a teenager he had become a regular in Mick McCarthy's starting line-up and, though there is still much work to be done, it would be difficult to argue with the assertion of team-mate Niall Quinn that: 'Robbie is going all the way to the top.'

ROBBIE KEANE

1998–

 8 **2**

CAPS   GOALS

BORN Dublin, 8.7.80
DEBUT v Czech Republic (A) 25.3.98
CLUBS Wolverhampton Wanderers

The Big Five

The notion that a committee of administrators and club chairmen should be charged with the responsibility of selecting a national football team is one that seems abhorrent today. However, such 'selection committees' became commonplace in the early days of international soccer, and remained so until well after the Second World War. The Republic of Ireland was one of the last European nations to rid itself of this archaic system, and it was only in 1969 that the manager of the national team gained a voice at selection meetings. By then, 119 matches had been played, and in each case the men in green had been chosen by the men in suits, who possessed little by way of professional experience or qualification

Ireland's selection committee, which was known as 'the Big Five', was elected by the FAI on a season-by-season basis, and comprised five men chosen from the game at all levels – from schoolboy football to the League of Ireland. The committee would meet prior to each international and named not only the squad but also the team. Responsibility for preparing the players then passed to the misleadlingly titled 'team manager'. From 1957 to 1967 this role was fulfilled by former player Jackie Carey. There was, however, rarely enough time for Carey to do more than introduce his charges to one another, and tell them which position they would be playing. His task was made all the more difficult by the fact that Ireland played home matches on Sundays; a situation which meant that most English-based players had usually performed for their clubs the previous day. Withdrawals, some legitimate, others not, were frequent.

By 1969 – with Irish football at its lowest ebb and the boys in green in the midst of a four-and-a-half year, 20-match run without a win – criticism of the selection committee became intense. It was apparent that the criteria for selection had become far from objective. The Big Five were, by all accounts, being guided by personal agendae. Many critics believed that players were often capped merely to increase their transfer value, and after lobbying from club chairmen. The bottom line of course, was that most of this would have been forgotten had it not been for the team's disastrous form on the pitch. But as results deteriorated, pressure mounted.

The final blow for the selection committee came in 1969 and was entirely self-inflicted. John Giles had been the undoubted star of the Republic of Ireland team throughout the 1960s but, for reasons which clearly had little to do with his footballing ability, John was dropped for a World Cup qualifier against Denmark in May 1969. It was an incredible decision, for not only was the Leeds United midfielder left out of the team, he was also not seen as worthy of a place even in the squad. Giles was recalled for the next match, but chose to decline the invitation. The Big Five had made a formidable enemy.

Giles returned to international colours in September 1969, and found that many of his team-mates had also grown tired of the Big Five's selection policies. A players' committee, led by the articulate Eamon Dunphy, and which also included Giles, Alan Kelly and Tony Dunne was formed to protest against the Big Five. They voiced their concerns in a formal statement to the FAI's International Selection Committee and demanded that current manager, Mick Meagan, be appointed sole-selector. In true political style, a compromise was reached, with Meagan granted a voice at selection meetings and also given the power to choose the starting line-up from the squad.

The fight against the Big Five rumbled on and, after another show of player-power in 1971, the era of the selection committee finally came to an end. Henceforth, the team manager was given complete authority to select his squad and his line-up.

MICK MEAGAN

(September 1969–May 1971)

Games in charge: 12
Won: 0
Drew: 3
Lost: 9

In September 1969 Mick Meagan became the first Republic of Ireland manager to be given a voice at selection meetings. It was a watershed in the history of the boys in green, and was due, in the main, to the campaigning efforts of Eamon Dunphy and other senior players. Under the new system, Meagan would make recommendations to the selection committee about whom to include in the squad, before making the final decision on the starting XI himself.

The devolution of selection power from the Big Five represented a major step forward. However, Meagan still had to contend with the problems caused by Sunday fixtures, which meant English-based players travelling to Dublin straight after playing for their clubs on a Saturday. Late withdrawals were commonplace and it was often the case that the manager would have to conduct a roll-call on the morning of the match. Meagan remembers: 'There was never an occasion during my 12 matches in charge when all the players selected turned up.'

The Meagan era began with a 1-1 draw against Scotland, although the new manager's squad was so depleted that he was forced to name himself in the starting XI. It was to be Mick's one and only appearance as an international player-manager, and he took to the dugout for the next match – a World Cup qualifier against

Czechoslovakia in Prague. Meagan gave debuts to four League of Ireland players against the Czechs, but his team were outclassed and lost 3-0. Ireland drew 1-1 with Denmark at Dalymount Park in their next World Cup qualifier, but a run of four consecutive defeats followed.

There was further disappointment for Ireland and Meagan in the qualifying rounds for the 1972 European Championships. The campaign started brightly enough, with a 1-1 draw against Sweden in Dublin, but a 1-0 reverse in the return was followed by home and away defeats against Italy and a 4-1 Dalymount hammering at the hands of Austria. It was a disastrous sequence of results and one which, somewhat inevitably, brought the curtain down on Mick Meagan's managerial tenure. Meagan, however, remembers his time as Ireland manager with great affection: 'I was offered the job with little experience and it was a great opportunity to stay involved with the lads on a more or less full-time basis. But in two years we didn't win a game and, while we had faced tough opponents in every match, they [the FAI] were right to bring in somebody new.'

LIAM TUOHY

(October 1971–May 1973)

Games in charge: 10
Won: 3
Drew: 1
Lost: 6

The £500-a-year job of Republic of Ireland manager was not a particularly attractive one in the Autumn of 1971. The boys in green had gone almost five years without a win, there were precious few top class players available, and withdrawals from the squad were still commonplace. The task of leading the national team, however, was a challenge which Liam Tuohy could not resist, and in October 1971 he signed a three-year contract with the FAI to become Mick Meagan's successor. The new man, unlike his predecessor, would also be the team's sole selector. Tuohy had enjoyed a long and successful career as a goalscoring winger with Shamrock Rovers and Newcastle United, and had been cutting his managerial teeth as player-boss at Dundalk when the Ireland job had become vacant.

Tuohy's first game in charge was a European Championships qualifier against Austria. However, the match had been arranged prior to his appointment and was scheduled for a Sunday. This would have been awkward enough had the game been at home, but it was to be played in Linz. There were no flights available from Dublin on the day of the game, and with English clubs not obliged to release their players from domestic fixtures on the Saturday, Liam was forced to take a scratch team to

Austria. The line-up he fielded included seven new caps and, with the exception of Chelsea's Paddy Mulligan, was entirely comprised of League of Ireland players. Defeat was predictable, but the 6-0 scoreline was nonetheless embarrassing. The debacle in Linz provided a clear lesson for the FAI and throughout the remainder of his reign Tuohy would work closely with the administrators to make sure that, where possible, international matches were played in midweek.

In the summer of 1972 Tuohy's Republic of Ireland travelled to South America for the Brazilian Independence Cup in Recife. It was ostensibly an exercise to help build team spirit and was the first time an Ireland team had entered a close-season tournament of this kind. Somewhat inevitably, Tuohy's squad was hit by a spate of high profile withdrawals, but the trip proved a great success nonetheless. Ireland's first match was against Iran and goals from Don Givens and Mick Leech brought a 2-1 victory to end a 20-match sequence without a win. A 3-2 success over Ecuador followed seven days later and, although Ireland lost their final two matches (against Chile and Portugal), morale had been given a much needed fillip.

The first meaningful competitive action of Tuohy's tenure came with the qualifying rounds for the 1974 World Cup. Ireland began their campaign with two home matches and, though they lost the first of these against a strong USSR team at Lansdowne Road in October 1972, a month later they recorded an impressive 2-1 victory over France at Dalymount. Liam's sharp, intelligent personality seemed to be having the desired effect on the players and confidence was growing. However on 1 December 1972 the manager dropped a bombshell by announcing his resignation. Liam, who was by now also in charge at Shamrock Rovers, had been combining his role as Republic of Ireland boss with his job as an area manager for an ice cream firm. He was also married with four children, and something had to give.

Tuohy was persuaded to stay on as Ireland manager until after a run of three World Cup qualifiers that were scheduled for May 1973, but he could not be coaxed into reversing his decision on a permanent basis. After defeats away to the USSR and Poland, the boys in green produced a memorable away performance to earn a highly creditable 1-1 draw against France in Liam's final match in charge.

The Tuohy reign may have been short, but it was undoubtedly significant. In just ten games, the astute and affable Dubliner had done much to lift the Republic of Ireland team out of the doldrums. His record of three victories was all the more impressive given the fact that he had frequently been without key players – John Giles had played for him just twice. Liam had also been a key influence on the continued modernisation of the FAI, particularly in respect of the importance of fixture planning. He would go on to enjoy good success with the Republic of Ireland youth teams during the 1980s and is currently in charge of Home Farm's renowned youth development programme.

SEAN THOMAS

(June 1973)

Games in charge: 1
Won: 0
Drew: 1
Lost: 0

Following the resignation of Liam Tuohy, the FAI turned to experienced Bohemians manager Sean Thomas to take charge of the national team on a caretaker-basis. Thomas's one match as Ireland manager was a friendly against Norway in Oslo and ended in a 1-1 draw.

JOHN GILES

(October 1973-March 1980)

Games in charge: 37
Won: 14
Drew: 9
Lost: 14

The appointment of John Giles as Republic of Ireland player-manager in October 1973 represented a rare and, somewhat surprising, show of foresight on the part of the FAI. The Leeds United midfielder was still only 32 years old when he took charge of the national team and, although he had no experience of management at club level, he had been Ireland's most influential player for more than ten years. He also had an astute footballing brain and was widely tipped for a bright future as a coach. Giles had not actively pursued the job of Ireland boss – and he had certainly made little effort to curry favour with the decision makers at Merrion Square. But, fearful of the alternative candidates and confident in his own abilities, he had decided to accept the position when it was offered. Giles had been a regular in the international line-up since making his debut in 1959, so was under no illusions about the enormity of the task he was taking on. He regarded the team's sense of inferiority as chief among its many problems, and set about remedying this situation by improving morale and engendering a greater spirit of professionalism within the squad. Giles had learned much from his Elland Road boss Don Revie, and attempted to replicate the bond shared between the Leeds United players with a similar sense of unity at international level. A hard core of players, which included Ray Treacy, Paddy Mulligan, Don Givens and Mick Martin, soon emerged.

Giles was himself still regarded as Ireland's most talented footballer, and for less experienced players – many of whom undoubtedly feared letting down a man who

does not suffer fools gladly – he was an inspirational figure. His fundamental soccer philosophy was based on the importance of possession. Giles liked his teams to play with patience and skill, preferring a sideways or backwards pass to a hopeful punt forward. This, however, was not an approach which always met with appreciation from the Republic of Ireland's notoriously impatient fans, many of whom were keen to see the ball launched upfield at the earliest opportunity.

The Giles era got off to a flying start with a 1-0 win against a Poland team that had arrived at Dalymount

Park just four days after qualifying for the World Cup with a draw against England at Wembley. Victory against the Poles, however, was followed by seven months of inactivity, which eventually came to an end with a three-match tour of South America in May 1974. A 2-1 defeat against Brazil in Rio was followed by a 2-0 reverse at the hands of Uruguay and a 2-1 victory versus Chile. Ireland may have won just onematch, but they had been competitive in all three fixtures and when the European Championship qualifiers got underway the following autumn, expectation was sky high. The boys in green did not disappoint, and in their opening match, at home to group favourites the USSR, they produced a scintillating display which culminated in Don Givens grabbing all three goals in a 3-0 win. However, a draw away to Turkey in the next match would prove costly. Despite winning both their remaining home games (against Switzerland and Turkey) Ireland finished the campaign as runners-up, just a point behind the USSR. But while they had failed to qualify for the European Championships, aspirations had at least been raised. Where before there would have been resignation, there was now disappointment.

In 1975 Giles had taken over from Don Howe as manager of West Bromwich Albion, and in his first season (1975-76) at The Hawthorns he led the Baggies to promotion from England's old Second Division. Despite the demands of his new position, he would continue as Ireland's player-manager. In November 1976 Giles prepared the boys in green for the qualifying rounds of the 1978 World Cup and an away tie against France.

Under Giles, Ireland had become a force to be reckoned with at home but had continued to show a worrying vulnerability away from Dublin – they had won just twice in eight games on their travels – and the match against France brought a familiar result: a 2-0 defeat. However, the scoreline did not reflect the Republic's accomplished performance, which would probably have earned a draw had it not been for an over-eager linesman who ruled out a Frank Stapleton goal when the score stood at 1-0. The worst was yet to come, though, and after reaping revenge over the French with a 1-0 win at Lansdowne Road, Ireland were the victims of a litany of errors from match officials during a clash with Bulgaria in Sofia. The match ended in a 2-1 reverse for Giles's team and called a halt to any dreams of a trip to the Argentine in 1978.

The qualification programme for the 1980 European Championships brought no better fortune for the Republic of Ireland, and defeats in Belfast and at Wembley did nothing for Giles's popularity. The manager of the national team was now back in Dublin full-time, having taken over as player-boss at Shamrock Rovers in July 1977. Giles had ambitious plans for the Hoops. He wanted to turn the club into European trophy contenders inside seven years and signed up the likes of Ray Treacy, Eamon Dunphy, Eoin Hand and Pierce O'Leary for his full-time experiment. His ambitions were to remain unfulfilled though, and the only major trophy he brought to Milltown was the FAI Cup in 1978.

Giles's return to his home city did, however, bring him under intense media scrutiny, and as a PR man he was found wanting. Giles regarded his job as to look after the players and to prepare them for the business of winning games, not to provide a flow of copy for sports reporters. So, with few allies in the media he was given little opportunity to defend himself when the critics began gunning for him in the late seventies. The press snipers found a veritable cache of ammunition with which to attack the Ireland boss. Giles was challenged for selecting himself – though his experience and tactical brain ensured his contributions remained significant until into his 39th year. He was also perceived as a man who was not only wealthy but also earning a lot of money from his position as Ireland boss. Both claims he refuted. Giles's patient, possession football came under attack too. And by the end of the seventies, the situation had deteriorated to the point where sections of the crowd at Lansdowne Road booed when the name of the player-manager was read out from the teamsheet.

In March 1980, shortly after a disappointingly close 3-2 victory over Cyprus in the opening match of the qualifying campaign for the 1982 World Cup, Giles decided that the time was right to resign. In many ways, he had become a victim of his own success. Giles had taken Ireland tantalisingly close to qualifying for a major tournament for the first time, in 1976, and since then the stakes had been raised to unprecedented heights. Only qualification would now satisfy. But while Giles had been unable to deliver the grail of tournament football, he had achieved much during his seven-year managerial tenure. He had continued to improve the scheduling of matches, had injected much needed confidence and had also introduced many talented newcomers to the green jersey, including David O'Leary, Liam Brady, Frank Stapleton, Mark Lawrenson, Chris Hughton and Tony Grealish.

ALAN KELLY

(April 1980)

Games in charge: 1
Won: 1
Drew: 0
Lost: 0

When John Giles took his leave as Republic of Ireland manager in the spring of 1980 the position passed to his assistant Alan Kelly. The former international goalkeeper would, however, resign from the post himself after just one game in charge. Kelly found it impossible to combine the Ireland job with his role as Preston North End manager, but at least had the pleasure of ending his tenure with a 100 per cent record. His one match in charge of the national team was against Switzerland and finished in a straightforward 2-0 victory for the boys in green.

EOIN HAND

(April 1980-November 1985)

Games in charge: 40
Won: 11
Drew: 9
Lost: 20

After the brief reign of Alan Kelly, responsibility for leading the boys in green fell to Eoin Hand.

The 34-year-old Limerick United boss was initially given the Ireland job on a caretaker basis, but after one match – a 1-0 defeat against Argentina in Dublin – his appointment was made permanent. Hand was the youngest manager of an international team in Europe at the time, and had little experience. However, he had shown great promise in his first season in charge at Limerick, having led the club to the 1979-80 League of Ireland Championship. His efforts had also been recognised by the Irish sports writers who named him their Sports Personality of the Year for 1980.

As a player, Hand had been a steady if unspectacular centre-half and, although he had spent much of his career as a full-time professional with Portsmouth, he had never played in England's top division. As a result, his ability to deal with star players would be questioned throughout his five-and-a-half-year reign. But while Hand could not match the awe-inspiring playing record of John Giles, he was a committed and energetic manager who worked tirelessly and prepared methodically for each match. He would make frequent visits to English First Division games to check on players, and also travelled throughout Europe to assess opponents.

Tactically, Hand was more of a pragmatist than Giles and his teams tended to move the ball forward with greater urgency than those of his predecessor. The first competitive action of Hand's reign came in the qualifying rounds for the 1982 World Cup. Ireland had been drawn in a seemingly impossible group along with Holland, Belgium and France. Not for the first time, they would be frustrated by match officials rather than opponents. Hand's team produced superb performances to beat both Holland and France in Dublin, but two inexplicable refereeing decisions in the home match against Belgium proved decisive and denied the Irish a place at Spain 82. Ireland had a Frank Stapleton goal ruled out for an unknown infringement, before having their misery compounded when the referee allowed a late Belgian goal despite a clear foul on goalkeeper Jim McDonagh. At the end of the qualifying campaign, Hand's team found themselves eliminated from the competition on goal difference.

Hand's managerial reign had got off to an encouraging start, but in the summer of 1982 the honeymoon came to an abrupt end after an ill-conceived tour of South America. The trip was originally planned to commence with a match against Argentina, but with Argentina and

Britain at war over the Falklands, English clubs refused to release their players and after a painfully drawn out stand off, the FAI withdrew from the match. Hand was nevertheless left with a much depleted squad, and Ireland lost all three matches, conceding ten goals and scoring just one. The tour took in a record 7-0 defeat against Brazil, but it was the 2-1 reverse against Trinidad and Tobago which provided the greatest humiliation.

The critics were given further ammunition to launch in Hands' direction when Ireland failed to secure a place at the 1984 European Championships. A disappointing qualifying campaign had seen Ireland lose their first competitive home game for seven years when they lost to Holland at Dalymount Park, and even a record 8-0 win against Malta in the last match could not deflect the brickbats aimed at the manager. Hand was accused of defensive tactics after a 2-0 reverse against Spain and his ability to manage the squad's big name stars was, not for the first time, called into question. He would soon lose the support of the Lansdowne Road crowd and was subjected to a series of stinging attacks from Eamon Dunphy in the *Sunday Tribune*.

In 1983 the FAI Executive Committee met to discuss Hand's future, but despite a proposal to replace him with a new man (widely speculated to be Bob Paisley) he survived to lead Ireland into the qualifying rounds of the 1986 World Cup. The campaign started well enough with a 1-0 win against the USSR in Dublin, but after back-to-back defeats against Norway and Denmark the pressure on the manager began to mount once more. Three friendly matches followed, but a goalless draw against Israel coming after consecutive 2-1 reverses against Italy and England did little to relieve the pressure. Ireland bumbled through their next four World Cup matches, recording three 0-0 draws and a 3-0 win at home to Switzerland. Despite their fitful form, they were still in contention for a place at the finals in Mexico when they prepared for their penultimate qualifier against the USSR in Moscow. It was make or break time and Hand knew it. Ireland put up a dogged fight against the Soviets but lost the game 2-0 and, in the post-match press conference, an emotional Eoin Hand announced his resignation.

JACK CHARLTON

(February 1986-December 1995)

Games in charge: 94
Won: 47
Drew: 30
Lost: 17

'I think the people of Ireland will take to him [Jack Charlton]. . . he has enough personality to satisfy the Irish,' predicted Jimmy Armfield in the matchday programme for Jack Charlton's first game as Republic of Ireland manager in March 1986. Armfield's words were to prove prophetic, for over the next ten years Charlton would become the most revered figure in the history of Irish football. The bullish Yorkshireman not only secured qualification for the finals of major tournaments, he also won over the hearts of the Irish people, who quickly came to adore his straight talking and penchant for curt one-liners. So lionised was Charlton that by the early 1990s he had even become a hero to those who hàd previously shown no interest in soccer. His appointment as successor to Eoin Hand, however, had brought few fanfares. It was the first time that the FAI had turned to a non-Irishman to lead the national team and that alone was reason enough for suspicion. Charlton had also only been given the job after a divided FAI Executive Committee had plumped for him in preference to former Liverpool manager Bob Paisley following a long and drawn-out selection process. Paisley, who had been the most successful club manager in English football history, had many supporters in the Irish press and there were rumblings of disappointment when he was passed over by the decision makers in Merrion Square.

As a player 'Big Jack' had gained a reputation as a tough, uncompromising defender and during a 20-year career, with England and Leeds United, he had assembled an impressive trophy collection, which included a World Cup winner's medal earned as a member of Alf Ramsey's triumphant team of 1966. He had enjoyed reasonable success as a manager too, and had led both Middlesbrough and Sheffield Wednesday to promotion on limited budgets. With the Republic of Ireland, Charlton inherited a squad that contained several players of undoubted talent – Liam Brady, Frank Stapleton, Mark Lawrenson and David O'Leary being the most conspicuous – but which had little balance, and which lacked both cohesion and direction. Charlton, however, possessed an incisive footballing brain and wasted little time in building a formidable team. He immediately added two new players to Ireland's playing resources, drafting in Glasgow-born Ray Houghton and Liverpudlian John Aldridge. The recruitment of 'Anglos' to the green jersey was not a new phenomenon, but Charlton, ever the pragmatist, seemed to actively seek out such players and came under criticism from some quarters as a result.

Charlton soon established his favoured line-up and,

whenever possible he stuck to it. He adopted simple tactics, targeting Ireland's long-standing defensive deficiencies as a key area for attention. Every player was given defensive duties, with midfielders and attackers instructed to squeeze the play and pressurise opponents. When they had the ball, Charlton's players were told to pass it into key areas of the field – primarily the space behind the full-backs. And when they were not in possession, they were expected to work as a team to win it back. The goalkeeper – Packie Bonner – was to kick the ball long at all times, and there was to be no slow, patient build-up play from the back. It was a style of play which, although not appealing to the purists, was applauded by many Irish fans who had been too impatient for the possession football of John Giles's team. And what's more, the Charlton method brought results.

In the summer of 1986, after just two friendly matches in charge, Charlton took his new team to Reykjavik for a triangular tournament with Iceland and Czechoslovakia. Ireland recorded victories in both their matches and won what was reported to be their first trophy in international football. It was a largely insignificant success but it was enough to earn the new manager the backing of the fans, whose faith was rewarded 18 months later when Charlton led the boys in green to their first major tournament finals: the 1988 European Championships. Jack was determined that his team would make an impression at the Euro 88 finals in Germany, and an opening game against Bobby Robson's highly-confident England side provided the perfect opportunity to turn heads. A Ray Houghton goal after just five minutes against England proved the only goal of the game and gave Ireland a celebrated victory on their tournament debut. Charlton's team produced an even more accomplished display in their next match – a 1-1 draw with the Soviet Union – and it was only after Holland, the eventual champions, scored a highly fortuitous winning goal in the final group match that Ireland were eliminated. Jack's boys returned 'home' to Dublin as heroes.

The high jinks continued throughout the remainder of the 1980s, with Charlton masterminding the Republic of Ireland's qualification for the 1990 World Cup finals. Ireland had by now established a reputation as unyielding opponents and they conceded just two goals en route to Italia 90 – both in the defeat against Spain in Seville. Charlton's team would no longer be underestimated, but they were still able to progress to the last eight of the World Cup finals in Italy where they lost 1-0 to the hosts. Ireland had made soccer's big time and the majority of Irish people were in no doubt that Jack Charlton was the man responsible for their country's new-found sporting glory. However, Jack was not without his critics.

Journalist and former international midfielder Eamon Dunphy was the man who most famously attempted to burst the euphoria-filled bubble of the Charlton era. Dunphy, in his role as a television pundit for RTE, challenged the manager's tactics after a disappointing draw against Egypt at Italia 90. He felt that Ireland should have shown more ambition against clearly inferior opponents, and questioned the wisdom of leaving talented players like David O'Leary and Ronnie Whelan out of the team. For his troubles, Dunphy would find himself vilified by supporters and media colleagues. However, though he was in a minority, Dunphy was not alone in his critical views. It was frequently contended that Charlton had been unable to get the best out of some of his most skilful players – Liam Brady being the most obvious casualty of the era – while others felt uncomfortable with the many English-born players now wearing the green jersey. It has also been suggested that the successes of Charlton's reign created a divide between the old and the new fans. The game of football had rapidly been popularised in Ireland – with international matches turning into social events as much as sporting occasions – and the net effect was to alienate many of the long-suffering fans who had followed the boys in green through the fallow years that had gone before. Charlton, however, appeared to pay short shrift to those that doubted him and, although Ireland narrowly missed out on a place at the 1992 European Championships, he led his team to a second consecutive World Cup finals in 1994. Ireland again progressed to the second round, where they were defeated by Holland after two uncharacteristically sloppy defensive errors. The highlight of Ireland's tournament, though, had come in the first match when a spectacular goal from Ray Houghton earned a much lauded win against eventual finalists Italy in New York.

Many pundits predicted that Charlton would stand down after the 1994 World Cup finals, but he was not yet ready to take his leave. Alas, his final qualifying campaign was to end in disappointment when Ireland missed out on a place at Euro 96 after a play-off match against Holland at Anfield. Jack, who had been made a freeman of Dublin in May 1994, pondered his future for eight days, but on 21 December 1995 he announced his resignation. His reign had exceeded all expectations and had taken Ireland to the finals of three major tournaments, not to mention the dizzy heights of sixth place in the Fifa world rankings.

MICK McCARTHY

(January 1996-)

Games in charge: 30 (to 1 June 1999)
Won: 10
Drew: 8
Lost: 12

The job of following Jack Charlton would not be an easy one. Charlton may have taken Irish football to new heights, but his achievements had the potential to become a millstone around the neck of any successor. It would need a man of both status and resolve to take the place of big Jack. The FAI deliberated long and hard before whittling the list of potential candidates down to two names. Mick McCarthy

importance of passing the ball through the team. He had also been something of an innovator and had frequently experimented with different formations, often favouring a system based around a midfield diamond.

But it was personnel rather than tactics that would most concern McCarthy in his early days as Ireland manager. He had inherited a squad which was built around a core of players coming towards the end of their careers. However, finding replacements for thirty-somethings like Paul McGrath, Andy Townsend, Ray Houghton and John Aldridge would not be easy. McCarthy's problems were further compounded when, in his first game in charge, the youthful and prodigiously talented Roy Keane was sent off. Keane's dismissal was the lowlight of a forgettable debut for the new manager who watched his team lose 2-0 to Russia before a full house at Lansdowne Road. Two more defeats followed in quick succession before, in June 1996, the first goals and first 'result' of the McCarthy era arrived in a 2-2 draw against Croatia in Dublin.

The opening eight games of McCarthy's reign were all friendlies, and it was not until the last of them – against Bolivia in New Jersey – that Ireland produced a victory. Results, however, were relatively unimportant. What was of more significance was the progress of the many young players whom McCarthy had blooded during the summer of 1996. Shay Given, Kenny Cunningham, David Connolly, Keith O'Neill, Gary Breen and Ian Harte had all made their debuts during this period, with O'Neill and Harte making particularly impressive starts to their international careers.

The qualifying rounds for the 1998 World Cup provided McCarthy's first taste of competitive action as manager of the national team. Ireland started the campaign well enough, with victories over Liechtenstein away and Macedonia in Dublin, but after a somewhat disappointing goalless draw at home to Iceland, disaster struck with a 3-2 defeat in the return against Macedonia. Any lingering hopes of qualification took a further knock four weeks later with a 1-0 reverse against group favourites Romania in Bucharest. The challenge now was to finish as runners-up and thereby secure a play-off match against another second-placed team. The Irish recovered their form and were unbeaten in their remaining six matches to earn a two-legged head-to-head with Group Seven runners-up Belgium. The first leg, in Dublin, ended in a 1-1 draw but defeat in Brussels meant there would be no trip to France for the boys in green in 1998.

By the start of the Euro 2000 qualifiers in the autumn of 1998, McCarthy had successfully assembled a new-look Republic of Ireland line-up which bore little resemblence to that which he had inherited from Jack Charlton. Robbie Keane was now the focal point for Ireland's short passing game, and while the war in the Balkans would hold up the team's progress during 1999, victories over Croatia and Malta hinted at a bright future in store. Memories of the glorious Charlton era remain clear, but Mick McCarthy may yet bring forth a new wave of success to provide followers of the Republic of Ireland with a welcome dose of amnesia.

and Kevin Moran were the men in the frame. Both had enjoyed successful international careers with Ireland, but McCarthy had the advantage of three years' experience as a club manager with Millwall, and it was he who was eventually given the job.

McCarthy had been Charlton's captain from 1988 to 1992 and his appointment seemed a logical one. The two men shared roots in the North of England and Mick, like Jack, was both fiercely competitive and at times dour. Tactically, however, the pair had little in common. During his time at Millwall, McCarthy had shown himself to be a progressive coach who placed great stock in the

Player Statistics

correct to 31 May 1999

Player	Years	Ap	Sb	Gl	Player	Years	Ap	Sb	Gl
John Aldridge	86-96	58	(11)	19	Jerome Clarke	1978	0	(1)	0
John Anderson	79-88	12	(4)	1	Ollie Conmy	65-69	5	(0)	0
Phil Babb	94-	24	(5)	0	David Connolly	96	13	(4)	7
Eric Barber	65-66	2	(0)	0	Terry Conroy	69-77	25	(2)	2
Jim Beglin	84-86	14	(1)	0	Jimmy Conway	66-77	18	(2)	3
Packie Bonner	81-96	79	(1)	0	Owen Coyle	94	0	(1)	0
Synan Bradish	1978	1	(1)	0	Tommy Coyne	92-97	10	(12)	6
Liam Brady	74-90	70	(2)	9	Kenny Cunningham	96	20	(2)	0
Ged Branagan	97-	1	(0)	0	Liam Daish	92-96	3	(2)	0
Gary Breen	96	16	(3)	3	Gerry Daly	73-86	37	(11)	13
Fran Brennan	1965	1	(0)	0	Maurice Daly	1978	2	(0)	0
Shay Brennan	65-70	18	(1)	0	Ken De Mange	87-88	0	(2)	0
Liam Buckley	1984	1	(1)	0	Eamonn Deacy	1982	3	(1)	0
John Byrne	85-93	12	(11)	4	Rory Delap	88-	0	(3)	0
Pat Byrne	84-86	4	(4)	0	John Dempsey	66-72	19	(0)	1
Tony Byrne	69-73	13	(1)	0	Miah Dennehy	72-77	4	(7)	2
Alan Campbell	1985	2	(1)	0	John Devine	79-84	13	(0)	0
Noel Campbell	71-77	8	(3)	0	Terry Donovan	79-81	1	(1)	0
Noel Cantwell	53-67	36	(0)	14	Damien Duff	98	7	(1)	0
Brian Carey	92-94	2	(1)	0	Jimmy Dunne	1971	1	(0)	0
Steve Carr	99-	2	(0)	0	Pat Dunne	65-66	5	(0)	0
Tommy Carroll	68-73	17	(0)	1	Tony Dunne	62-75	32	(1)	0
Lee Carsley	97-	9	(4)	0	Paddy Dunning	1970	2	(0)	0
Tony Cascarino	85-	39	(43)	19	Eamon Dunphy	65-71	22	(1)	0
Jeff Chandler	1979	1	(1)	0	Peter Eccles	1986	0	(1)	0

Player	Years	Ap	Sb	Gl		Player	Years	Ap	Sb	Gl
Mickey Evans	97-	0	(1)	0		Ron Healey	77-80	1	(1)	0
Eamonn Fagon	1973	0	(1)	0		Steve Heighway	70-81	34	(0)	0
Mick Fairclough	1982	0	(2)	0		Jackie Hennessy	64-68	5	(0)	0
Gareth Farrelly	96-	5	(0)	0		John Herrick	71-73	1	(2)	0
Al Finucane	67-71	10	(1)	0		Jimmy Holmes	71-81	29	(1)	1
Kevin Fitzpatrick	1969	1	(0)	0		Ray Houghton	86-97	71	(2)	6
Curtis Fleming	96	4	(6)	0		Gary Howlett	1984	0	(1)	0
Theo Foley	64-67	9	(0)	0		Chris Hughton	79-91	49	(4)	1
Johnny Fullam	60-69	10	(1)	1		Charlie Hurley	57-69	40	(0)	2
Charlie Gallagher	1967	2	(0)	0		Denis Irwin	90	49	(2)	4
Tony Galvin	82-89	27	(2)	1		Graham Kavanagh	98-	0	(3)	1
Mick Gannon	1971	1	(0)	0		Robbie Keane	98-	6	(2)	2
Bobby Gilbert	1966	1	(0)	0		Roy Keane	91-	41	(1)	5
John Giles	59-79	59	(0)	5		Mick Kearin	1971	1	(0)	0
Shay Given	96-	23	(0)	0		Mick Kearns	70-79	16	(2)	0
Don Givens	69-81	51	(5)	19		Alan Kelly	56-73	47	(0)	0
Jon Goodman	97-	2	(2)	0		Alan Kelly Jnr.	93	17	(3)	0
Tony Grealish	76-85	44	(1)	8		David Kelly	87-97	15	(11)	9
Eamonn Gregg	78-79	6	(2)	0		Gary Kelly	94-	25	(3)	1
Ashley Grimes	78-88	16	(2)	1		Mark Kelly	88-90	3	(1)	0
Alfie Hale	62-73	10	(4)	2		Jeff Kenna	95-	19	(7)	0
Eoin Hand	69-75	19	(1)	2		Mark Kennedy	95-	13	(7)	1
Joe Haverty	56-66	32	(0)	3		Mick Kennedy	1986	1	(1)	0
Ian Harte	96-	16	(3)	2		John Keogh	1966	0	(1)	0
Austin Hayes	1979	1	(0)	0		Alan Kernaghan	92-96	18	(4)	1

Player statistics

Player	Years	Ap	Sb	Gl
Kevin Kilbane	97-	2	(2)	0
Joe Kinnear	67-75	24	(2)	0
Mark Kinsella	1988	8	(0)	0
David Langan	78-87	24	(2)	0
Mick Lawlor	70-73	4	(1)	0
Mark Lawrenson	77-87	38	(1)	5
Mick Leech	69-72	7	(1)	2
Jason McAteer	94-	24	(9)	1
Mick McCarthy	84-92	55	(2)	2
Tommy McConville	71-73	6	(0)	0
Jacko McDonagh	83-84	0	(3)	0
Seamus McDonagh	81-85	25	(0)	0
Andy McEvoy	61-67	17	(0)	6
Paul McGee	78-80	10	(5)	4
Eddie McGoldrick	92-95	10	(5)	0
Mick McGrath	58-67	22	0	0
Paul McGrath	85-97	78	(5)	8
Tony Macken	1977	1	(0)	0
Alan McLoughlin	90-	22	(17)	2
Terry Mancini	73-74	5	(0)	1
Mick Martin	71-83	52	(0)	4
Alan Maybury	98-	2	(0)	0
Mick Meagan	61-69	17	(0)	0
Mike Milligan	1992	0	(1)	0
Jackie Mooney	64-65	2	(0)	1

Player	Years	Ap	Sb	Gl
Alan Moore	96-	4	(4)	0
Kevin Moran	80-94	68	(3)	6
Chris Morris	87-93	31	(4)	0
Cathal Muckian	1978	1	(0)	0
Paddy Mulligan	69-79	48	(2)	1
Barry Murphy	1986	1	(0)	0
Jerry Murphy	79-80	3	(0)	0
Billy Newman	1969	1	(0)	0
Fran O'Brien	79-80	2	(1)	0
Liam O'Brien	86-96	9	(7)	0
Ray O'Brien	76-80	4	(1)	0
Brendan O'Callaghan	79-82	5	(1)	0
Kevin O'Callaghan	81-87	11	(10)	1
Tony O'Connell	66-70	1	(1)	0
Turlough O'Connor	67-73	3	(5)	1
Sean O'Driscoll	1982	2	(1)	0
Kelham O'Hanlon	1987	1	(0)	0
Eamonn O'Keeffe	81-85	4	(1)	1
David O'Leary	76-93	64	(4)	1
Pierce O'Leary	79-80	6	(1)	0
Frank O'Neill	61-71	18	(2)	1
Keith O'Neill	96-	6	(6)	4
Kieran O'Reagan	83-85	3	(1)	0
Gerry Peyton	77-92	30	(3)	0
Terry Phelan	91-	34	(4)	0

Player	Years	Ap	Sb	Gl
Niall Quinn	86-	53	(15)	16
Damien Richardson	71-79	1	(2)	0
Michael Robinson	80-86	23	(1)	4
Paddy Roche	71-75	8	(0)	0
Gerry Ryan	78-84	9	(9)	1
Dave Savage	96-	2	(3)	0
Pat Scully	1988	0	(1)	0
Kevin Sheedy	83-93	39	(7)	9
John Sheridan	88-95	27	(7)	5
Bernie Slaven	90-93	4	(3)	1
Mick Smyth	1968	0	(1)	0
Frank Stapleton	76-90	68	(3)	20
Steve Staunton	88-	74	(0)	5
Freddie Strahan	64-66	5	(0)	0
Noel Synnott	1978	3	(0)	0
Peter Thomas	73-74	2	(0)	0
Andy Townsend	89-97	65	(5)	7
Ray Treacy	66-79	35	(7)	5
Liam Tuohy	55-65	8	(0)	4
Gary Waddock	80-90	18	(3)	3
Johnny Walsh	1982	1	(0)	0
Micky Walsh	76-84	11	(10)	3
Mike Walsh	1982	4	(0)	0
Joe Waters	76-79	1	(1)	1
Ronnie Whelan	81-95	40	(13)	3

CAPS WON 50 AND OVER

Player	Caps	Player	Caps
Paul McGrath	**83**	David O'Leary	68
Tony Cascarino	82	Niall Quinn	68
Packie Bonner	80	John Giles	59
Steve Staunton	74	Mick McCarthy	57
Ray Houghton	73	Don Givens	56
Liam Brady	72	Chris Hughton	53
Frank Stapleton	71	Ronnie Whelan	53
Kevin Moran	71	Mick Martin	52
Andy Townsend	70	Denis Irwin	51
John Aldridge	69	Paddy Mulligan	50

LEADING GOALSCORERS

Pos	Player	Goals	Apps	(Sb)
1.	**Frank Stapleton**	**20**	**68**	**(3)**
2.	Don Givens	19	51	(5)
	John Aldridge	19	58	(11)
	Tony Cascarino	19	39	(43)
5.	Niall Quinn	16	53	(15)
6.	Noel Cantwell	14	36	(0)
7.	Gerry Daly	13	37	(11)
8.	David Kelly	9	15	(11)
	Liam Brady	9	70	(2)
10.	Tony Grealish	8	44	(1)
	Paul McGrath	8	78	(5)

MAJOR TOURNAMENTS
SQUADS

European Championships 1988

1. Packie Bonner	6. Ronnie Whelan	11. Tony Galvin	16. Gerry Peyton
2. Chris Morris	7. Paul McGrath	12. Tony Cascarino	17. John Byrne
3. Chris Hughton	8. Ray Houghton	13. Liam O'Brien	18. John Sheridan
4. Mick McCarthy	9. John Aldridge	14. David Kelly	19. John Anderson
5. Kevin Moran	10. Frank Stapleton	15. Kevin Sheedy	20. Niall Quinn

World Cup 1990

1. Packie Bonner	7. Paul McGrath	13. Andy Townsend	19. David Kelly
2. Chris Morris	8. Ray Houghton	14. Chris Hughton	20. John Byrne
3. Steve Staunton	9. John Aldridge	15. Bernie Slaven	21. Alan McLoughlin
4. Mick McCarthy	10. Tony Cascarino	16. John Sheridan	22. Gerry Peyton
5. Kevin Moran	11. Kevin Sheedy	17. Niall Quinn	
6. Ronnie Whelan	12. David O'Leary	18. Frank Stapleton	

World Cup 1994

1. Packie Bonner
2. Denis Irwin
3. Terry Phelan
4. Kevin Moran
5. Paul McGrath
6. Roy Keane

7. Andy Townsend
8. Ray Houghton
9. John Aldridge
10. John Sheridan
11. Steve Staunton
12. Gary Kelly

13. Alan Kernaghan
14. Phil Babb
15. Tommy Coyne
16. Tony Cascarino
17. Eddie McGoldrick
18. Ronnie Whelan

19. Alan McLoughlin
20. David Kelly
21. Jason McAteer
22. Alan Kelly

Picture credits

Acknowledgements in Source Order

Cover: Colorsport: top left, top right, bottom left, bottom right, bottom centre, top centre
Back Cover: Allsport top right; Colorsport top left, bottom left, bottom right

Action Images 50 bottom
Agence France Presse 8-9
Allsport: 1, 62, 73, 88, 95, 126 centre left, 139 right, 140 top, 140 centre left below, 127 left, 98, 105, 119, 69, 107 bottom, 158-159, 141 centre left above, 6-7, 124, 137, 142 top, 142 bottom, 143, 139 centre, 108, 131 bottom, 134, 141 Top, 126 bottom/Inpho: 3, 66, 86, 100, 106 bottom, 126 centre /Billy Stickland 72, 81, 103, 127 right, 139 left, 140 centre, 141 bottom, 157, 141 centre left below
Alpha/Sport & General: 18
Colorsport: 13, 14, 23, 32 bottom, 35, 38 top, 39, 43, 44, 49, 51 top, 51 bottom, 53, 54, 55 left, 55 right, 55 centre, 56, 58, 61, 70 top, 70 bottom, 71, 75 centre left below, 76, 77 left, 77 right, 77 centre, 78 top, 79, 84, 85, 90, 91 left, 91 right, 91 centre, 96, 101, 106 centre, 106 centre left below, 107 top, 110, 114, 115, 118 top, 120, 126 Top, 127 centre, 129, 130, 131 top, 135, 138, 140 centre left above, 150, 150-151, 152-153, 158 Top, 158 bottom /Olympia
Empics: /Peter Robinson, endpapers, 20
Hulton Getty Picture Collection/Allsport Historical Collection 11, 31
/Evening Standard 19, 22, 30, 32 Top, 33, /Topical Press 4
Independent Newspapers Ltd. 26, 50 centre left below
Inpho 50 centre left above, 51 centre right above, 51 centre right below, 65, 74 Top, 74 centre left above, 75 bottom, 78 bottom, 82, 106 centre left above, 112, 117, 118 bottom, 123, 126 centre left below, 128, 132, 136, 140 bottom, 141 Centre, 145, 147, 148-149
Press Association News Ltd. 16, 74 Centre
Popperfoto 50 Top, 74 Bottom, 75 Top, 75 centre left above
Unknown 38 Bottom, 60, 74 centre left below
United Press International 36-37

Bibliography

The Book of Irish Goalscorers, Sean Ryan and Stephen Burke (Irish Soccer Co-op, Dublin, 1987) *The Boys in Green*, Sean Ryan (Mainstream Publishing, Edinburgh, 1997) *Jack Charlton's American World Cup Diary*, Jack Charlton with Peter Byrne (BCA, London, 1994) *Jack Charlton The Autobiography*, Jack Charlton with Peter Byrne (Corgi Press, London, 1997) *The Complete Who's Who of Irish International Football 1945-96*, Stephen McGarrigle (Mainstream Publishing, Edinburgh, 1996) *Football Association of Ireland - 75 Years*, Peter Byrne (Sportsworld Publications, Dublin, 1996) *The Garrison Game - The State of Irish Football*, Dave Hannigan (Mainstream Publishing, Edinburgh, 1998) *The International Line-ups and Statistics Series - Eire 1926-1996*, Gerry Desmond (Soccer Books Publishing Ltd, Lincolnshire,1996) *Ireland - The Quest for the World Cup*, Clive Leatherdale (Two Heads Publishing in association with Desert Island Books, West Sussex, 1994) *Irish Football Handbook 1994-95*, Dave Galvin and Gerry Desmond (Red Card Publications, Cork, 1994) *Con Martin's Soccer Annual*. Various editions. *Only A Game*, Eamon Dunphy (Viking, London, 1976) *Playfair Football Who's Who 1999* (Jack Rollin. Headline, London, 1998) *Simply Red and Green*, John Scally (Mainstream Publishing, Edinburgh, 1998) *The Team That Jack Built*, Paul Rowan (Mainstream Publishing, Edinburgh, 1995)